The Order of Economic Liberalization

The Johns Hopkins Studies in Development
Vernon W. Ruttan and T. Paul Schultz, Consulting Editors

THE

ORDER OF

ECONOMIC LIBERALIZATION

Financial Control in the Transition

to a Market Economy

SECOND EDITION

Ronald I. McKinnon

The Johns Hopkins University Press

Baltimore and London

For Edward S. Shaw

© 1991, 1993 The Johns Hopkins University Press
All rights reserved
Printed in the United States of America on acid-free paper

The Johns Hopkins University Press
2715 N. Charles Street
Baltimore, Maryland 21218-4319
The Johns Hopkins Press Ltd., London

Library of Congress Cataloging-in-Publication Data

McKinnon, Ronald I.

    The order of economic liberalization : financial control in the
transition to a market economy / Ronald I. McKinnon.—2nd ed.
       p.   cm. —(Johns Hopkins studies in development)
    Includes bibliographical references and index.
    ISBN 0-8018-4742-7 (alk. paper).—ISBN 0-8018-4743-5 (pbk. :
alk. paper)
    1. Monetary policy—Europe, Eastern. 2. Monetary policy—
Developing countries. 3. Free enterprise—Europe, Eastern.
4. Free enterprise—Developing countries. 5. Europe, Eastern—
Economic policy. 6. Developing countries—Economic policy.
I. Title. II. Series.
HG930.7.M35   1993
332.4'947—dc20   93-21886
                                              CIP

A catalog record for this book is available from the British Library.

CONTENTS

PREFACE

When Anders Richter, Vernon Ruttan, and Paul Schultz asked me to contribute to their influential series Johns Hopkins Studies in Development, the initial idea was to consolidate the essays and articles in the area of finance and foreign trade liberalization that I had written since the publication of *Money and Capital in Economic Development* in 1973. In the course of opening up repressed domestic capital markets in less developed countries (LDCs), what sobering lessons had we learned about the problems of sustaining financial control over the price level and over the exchange rate? After all, my earlier book, and one by my Stanford colleague Edward Shaw, *Financial Deepening in Economic Development* (also written in 1973), identified and labeled what we called "financial repression." To supplant government control over the flow of credit and the allocation of scarce capital in poor countries, this terminology is now commonplace in making the case for a liberalized capital market where borrowing and lending take place at susbstantial, positive real rates of interest.

But this initial, fairly limited concept of the book was overtaken by the rapid pace of events in the socialist economies of Eastern Europe and in East Asia. The remarkable ideological change in previously contrally planned economies toward adopting market mechanisms still staggers the minds of virtually everyone whose professional life began before 1985. At that time, Mikhail Gorbachev announced the need for perestroika, that is, economic restructuring, in the former Soviet Union (FSU). But Gorbachev himself had been strongly influenced by the earlier agricultural successes in China when, beginning in 1979, giant rural communes were broken up in favor of largely market-based small-farmer leaseholds—the so-called household responsibility system. By 1986, Vietnam and Laos had embarked on their "new economic mechanisms," similar to China's earlier experience. By the dismantling of the Berlin Wall in 1990, all the smaller economies of Eastern Europe had begun some form of economic liberalization.

Whence the need to redirect this book in the process of producing the first edition in 1991. Starting from a web of government-mandated controls on outputs and prices, what are the main technical economic issues in defining an optimum order of liberalization from a socialist to a market economy? The first ten chapters, based on essays written over the past twelve years, distill the experiences of previously less-developed countries whose governments were highly interventionist, in their struggles to open their domestic capital markets and liberalize their foreign trade.

Chapters 11 and 12, which were written expressly for the first edition, applies this distillation to the transition problems facing socialist economies in Eastern Europe and Asia. The resulting focus is more on securing financial control and macroeconomic stability in a transition that could last a decade or so, and rather less on redefining property rights (itself an extremely important issue) or on some crash program to rapidly privatize state-owned industrial assets and the banking system.

Despite the remarkable reversal in ideology, not only have socialist economies experienced difficulties in effecting a satisfactory transition, but they have followed different paths. Asian socialist economies, particularly China, have taken a more gradualist approach to policy reforms. Hence the need for two new chapters to address these differences. In this expanded edition, Chapter 13, "Financial Growth and Macroeconomic Stability in China, 1978–1992: Implications for Russia and Eastern Europe," and Chapter 14, "Gradual versus Rapid Liberalization in Socialist Foreign Trade: Concluding Notes on Alternative Models," constitute the substantial and necessary addition. Although the Chinese still protect their old state-owned industries in various ways, they have managed to establish remarkably high growth in liberalized sectors within industry and agriculture. Into the 1990s, however, these Asian successes are tempered by the precariousness of their macroeconomic stability in the face of sharply declining government revenues.

Perhaps more by political necessity than by economic design, most of the countries of Eastern Europe and the FSU have followed a "big-bang" approach to economic liberalization—led by Poland's big bang in January 1990. Rapid price decontrol and the cessation of centrally planned input allocations were accompanied by a sudden opening to freer trade with the hard-currency industrial economies. Trade with other socialist economies, under the Council for Mutual Economic Assistance (disbanded at the beginning of 1991), collapsed. But economic liberalization in Eastern Europe, impacted by the crumbling of traditional trade patterns, has been associated with initial sharp falls in output and often explosive inflation. In particular, Russia's precipitate decontrol of prices and input allocations in its old state-owned heavy industry in January 1992 seems to have had disastrous economic and political consequences—with futher sharp falls in real output and near hyperinflation as of this writing, in April 1993.

Those readers primarily concerned with the current travails of the socialist economies in transition might well want to start with the overall order of liberalization given in Chapter 1, and then move on quickly to the detailed analyses of "representative" socialist economies in chapters 11, 12, and 13 before ending with the concluding notes on alternative models for liberalizing foreign trade. For particular technical problems such as establishing bank reserve requirements or setting the exchange rate in inflationary circumstances, however, they can then cast back to the lessons gleaned from the LDC experiences in earlier chapters.

But students of economic development might well follow the chapters in sequence. The earlier chapters build on, but do not supplant, the analytical framework laid out back in 1973 in *Money and Capital,* which is still best read first. Since 1973, however, much has been learned, both positively, in terms of the handsome rewards to developing economies that do liberalize successfully, and negatively, from those that got the order of liberalization wrong. Indeed, liberalizing a highly repressed economy has been likened to walking through a minefield: your next step might be your last.

On the other hand, the gains from persistently pursuing a liberalization cum free trade strategy despite financial setbacks along the way can be enormous. In Chile's liberalization, begun in 1973, misplaced foreign exchange, wage, and domestic bank-regulatory policies in the late 1970s led to a financial crash in the early 1980s, as documented in Chapters 4 and 6. This crash and sharp fall in output threatened to undermine the country's underlying commitment to economic openness. Nevertheless, Chile did not regress by turning inward and instead maintained its basic free trade stance. In the 1990s, Chile's very high growth rates in domestic commerce and foreign trade are now reminiscent of Asian tigers like Korea and Taiwan, whose financial policies also frequent the following pages.

Of all the socialist economies, China since 1979 has the longest running, and only now quite well documented, experience with economic liberalization. Building on its agricultural successes in the early 1980s, China's light-industry nonstate sector boomed from the mid-'80s to now, with rapidly growing exports becoming the engine of growth by the late 1980s. As price controls were systematically but gradually dismantled after 1979, China's macroeconomy remained remarkably stable, if only by Eastern European standards, with low price inflation and rapid financial deepening.

Yet, China started with the same Stalinist-type financial system—with a very soft-money circuit for enterprises and a distinct hard-money circuit for households—characteristic of all the formerly centrally planned economies in Europe or Asia. Because of this, the Chinese government also experienced a sharp decline in public revenue as liberalization proceeded that was, and still is, qualitatively similar to that experienced by the other socialist economies. Thus, how China managed to maintain financial control in its transition to a market economy, and whether that control is sustainable, is a valuable lesson for other liberalizing socialist economies seeking to avoid financial calamities.

The breakup of the former Soviet Union, in part because of these calamities, posed an editorial problem for this expanded edition. Chapter 11, "Stabilizing the Ruble," is largely an examination and critique of the fiscal, monetary,

and foreign trade policies followed by the former Soviet Union up through
1990. Despite the breakup, I decided to leave Chapter 11 unchanged. This
critique remains useful in showing the nature of the old Stalinist-type financial
system, where the liberalization attempts of the Soviets were going on the
rocks, how the Soviet economy could have been "ideally" and more gradually
liberalized, and as a historical backdrop for analyzing how the Russian big-
bang reforms went even further off the rails in 1992. What happened in the
Russian part of the Soviet Union is picked up in the new Chapter 13, which
concludes by briefly analyzing the Russian big-bang reforms of January 1992
and the wild inflation that followed into early 1993.

ACKNOWLEDGMENTS

The first part of Chapter 2 and Chapter 3 adapt and extend "Financial Liberalization in Retrospect: Interest Rate Policies in LDCs," in Gustav Ranis and T. Paul Schultz, eds., *The State of Development Economics* (New York: Basil Blackwell, 1988), 386–415. Chapter 4 is adapted from "Financial Repression and Economic Development," Chung-Hua Series of Lectures by Invited Eminent Economists, no. 8, 1984, Institute of Economics, Academia Sinica, Nankang, Taiwan. Chapters 5 and 9 are adapted from Ronald I. McKinnon and Donald Mathieson, "How to Manage a Repressed Economy," Essays in International Finance No. 145, December 1981. Copyright © 1981. Reprinted by permission of the International Finance Section of Princeton University. I would like to thank Philip Brock for his enormous analytical and empirical contributions to Chapter 5; many of these insights are contained in his "Government Deficits and the Composition of Inflationary Finance," Center for Research and Economic Growth, Stanford University, memo no. 254, 1982, and "Inflationary Finance in an Open Economy," *Journal of Monetary Economics* (July 1984): 37–54. Chapter 6 is adapted from "Financial Liberalization and Economic Development," International Center for Economic Growth, Occasional Papers, no. 6, Panama City, 1988. Chapter 7 is adapted from "Macroeconomic Instability and Moral Hazard in Banking in a Liberalizing Economy," in P. Brock et al., eds., *Latin American Debt Adjustment* (New York: Praeger, 1989), 99–111. Chapter 8 is adapted from "Foreign Trade Regimes and Economic Development: A Review Article," *Journal of International Economics* 9 (August 1979): 429–52. Chapter 10 is adapted from "The International Capital Market and Economic Liberalization in LDCs," *The Developing Economies* 22, no. 4 (December 1984). Chapter 11 is a much extended and revised version of "Stabilizing the Ruble" appearing in *Communist Economies* 2 (June 1990): 131–42. I would like to thank John Hussman and David Robinson for contributing ideas to and improving the exposition of Chapter 12. Michael Bernstam, Qingyi Qian, and Christine Wong provided invaluable inside information on Russia and China without which the new Chapters 13 and 14 would not have been possible.

In writing this book, I have been enormously helped by the enthusiasm and analytical insights of more than one generation of Stanford students working on dissertations in development finance and in international trade. In particular, Raylynn Oliver helped put the book together and prepare the index. Through Stanford's Center for Economic Policy Research, Dr. Ralph Landau extended invaluable financial support and encouragement—although the final product may not yet be exactly what he intended.

I dedicate the book to my early mentor Edward S. Shaw, professor emeritus at Stanford University, for stimulating my lasting interest in development finance and how capital markets can be organized. The prolific and insightful research of Professor Maxwell Fry of the University of Birmingham (England), as exemplified by his Johns Hopkins study *Money, Interest, and Banking in Economic Development* (1988), has also contributed enormously to development finance and to the ideas in this volume.

Finally, Henry Tom and Therese Boyd, of the Johns Hopkins University Press, and Pamela Bruton and Margaret McKinnon deserve much thanks for being such supportive editors during the book's change in direction and long gestation.

CHAPTER ONE

Introduction

The Order of

Economic Liberalization

From the end of World War II into the 1960s, the formative period of what we now call "development economics," intense debate centered on why some countries grew rich while others languished. Because scars from the Great Depression were still fresh, the traditional nineteenth-century liberal approach based on free trade in domestic and foreign markets was somewhat discredited. Instead, influential economists tended to emphasize problems of market failure and the need for informed official intervention—with import tariffs or domestic subventions—to overcome economic or technical backwardness. Also, in the 1950s and 1960s, the centrally planned economies of Eastern Europe apparently grew exceedingly fast, with the former Soviet Union (FSU) in particular showing impressive overall technical achievements.

Thus, governments in less-developed countries (LDCs) throughout Latin America, Africa, and parts of Asia were emboldened to intervene quite massively in their domestic economies. Protectionism in foreign trade, price controls and subsidies in domestic trade, and exclusive franchises for parastatals (state-owned enterprises) proliferated in all branches of industry. Instead of an open capital market, detailed controls over the flow of money and credit ensured that the repressed financial markets passively served the governments' own ends. Indeed, in the centrally planned socialist economies, the banking system was completely passive: credits at zero or disequilibrium low rates of interest were provided automatically if necessary to ensure plan fulfillment.

However, in the mid-1980s, an astonishing change occurred in this once-dominant ideology of economic development. In the marketplace for ideas in the late 1970s, few could have predicted that the principle of decentralized economic liberalism would by the 1990s triumph so completely over that of centralized planning and control.

Nowhere is this change in economic thinking, although not necessarily in economic practice, more remarkable than in the centrally planned socialist economies themselves. In the early 1980s, the agrarian reforms in the People's

Republic of China, where most of the fertile land was leased for long periods to peasant families, enjoyed great initial success: farm output almost doubled. After 1985, the concept of perestroika—the Soviet version of economic liberalism—was introduced. But the Soviets failed to maintain adequate financial control (for reasons to be considered in Ch. 11), leading to economic failure that hastened the end of the Soviet Union itself. How bad things had become under central planning was then more or less fully revealed to the outside world.

> The Soviet Union, China, and Eastern Europe have given us the clearest possible proof that capitalism organizes the material affairs of humankind more satisfactorily than socialism: that however inequitably or irresponsibly the marketplace may distribute goods, it does so better than the queues of the planned economy; however, mindless the culture of commercialism, it is more attractive than state moralism; and however deceptive the ideology of business civilization, it is more believable than a socialist one. (Heilbroner 1989, 98).

This doctrinal change has carried over to the Third World. Progress in the more obviously (world) market-oriented economies—a short list of South Korea, Taiwan, Hong Kong, and Singapore, to which Chile, Thailand, and Malaysia might now be added—compares favorably with the economic malaise gripping the Indian subcontinent and much of Latin America, as well as Africa, where detailed state intervention has been the norm. Shorn of any ideological underpinning or general economic rationale for continuing down the interventionist road, most Third World governments have lost confidence in the efficacy of their long-standing policies favoring state ownership or control of the means of production in industry and agriculture. Only appeals to raw populism, such as to support food subsidies, or to the power of special interests, to maintain foreign trade restrictions or credit subsidies, keep many of these interventionist regimes in place.

THE PROBLEM OF FINANCIAL CONTROL

Paradoxically, however, all is not well in the liberal camp. Despite this great ideological shift toward market liberalism in the 1980s and into the 1990s, relatively few previously highly centralized economies have been able to effect a satisfactory transition. Although the pervasive external indebtedness—the highly publicized "international debt problem"—is a conveniently plausible explanation of economic decline in Latin America and perhaps Africa, it obscures a more fundamental domestic financial conundrum. These economies have not been able to put sufficient *internal* fiscal and monetary controls in place to support a dismantling of their interventionist policies.

The general case favoring financial liberalization has been called into question by a series of bank panics and collapses in the Southern Cone of Latin America (Diaz-Alejandro 1985). In the late 1970s and early 1980s, Argentina, Chile, and Uruguay all made serious efforts to end wild inflation while deregulating and privatizing their commercial banks. Interest rates on both bank deposits and loans were completely freed, with the latter often increasing to unexpectedly high levels in real terms. That these attempted financial liberalizations led to an undue buildup of foreign indebtedness and government reintervention to prop up failing domestic banks and industrial enterprises, is well documented in a series of revealing studies edited by Vittorio Corbo and Jaime de Melo (1985). In the later 1980s, nonliberal, or "heterodox," stabilization plans, variously called austral or cruzado plans, based on state reinterventions to freeze the general price level and brake inflationary expectations generally failed to secure financial equilibrium in Argentina, Brazil, and Peru. In the early 1990s, the success of new stabilization programs in Mexico and Argentina still hangs in the balance. (Chile is the one Latin American country that has succeeded in finally establishing a more liberal economic environment in which exports and domestic production are flourishing while inflationary pressures remain reasonably well contained.)

None of the (previously) socialist economies of Eastern Europe have established sufficient financial equilibrium to support the desired marketization of their economies. Indeed, many smaller Eastern European economies that have been struggling to create "social market economies" for more than a decade are threatened with severe internal inflations and falling output. The republics from the FSU are in more severe financial disarray.

In the People's Republic of China, the initial great success with agrarian reforms and the subsequent apparent success with establishing special free-trade enclaves have been associated with severe fiscal decline: the inability of the central government to collect taxes. Nevertheless, the gradualist Asian approach to economic liberalization, as pursued in China, Vietnam, and Laos, seems to be faring much better than the big-bang approach in Eastern Europe and the FSU.

How to secure financial equilibrium and price-level stability within such liberalizing economies as these is the main focus of this book. How can one succinctly characterize this otherwise tricky and arcane financial problem? Before direct central government controls are fully dismantled, the monetary-financial-fiscal system has to be converted from the *passive* mode that had simply accommodated the planning mechanism into an *active* constraining influence on the ability of decentralized enterprises, households, and even local governments to bid for scarce resources. Implementing such financial and fiscal restraint at the microeconomic level then permits the aggregate domestic price level to be stabilized by a suitable choice of monetary policy—without resorting to direct controls over the prices of individual commodities.

What evidence do we have from developing countries that real economic growth is higher when the monetary system is stable and financial markets are open? Chapter 2 reviews the extensive evidence on the financial determinants of economic growth since the end of World War II. Generally, those countries that succeeded in stabilizing their price levels and real exchange rates, while maintaining moderately positive real yields on bank deposits in an open capital market, show a much higher productivity of physical capital than those whose financial systems remained "repressed."

THE OPTIMUM ORDER OF ECONOMIC LIBERALIZATION

In securing this noninflationary financial equilibrium, however, there are definite limits on the relative speeds of liberalization in commodity and capital markets and on how fast interventionist policies or planning controls over domestic and foreign trade can be withdrawn (McKinnon 1973, 1982; Edwards 1984). How fiscal, monetary, and foreign exchange policies are *sequenced* is of critical importance. Governments cannot, and perhaps should not, undertake all liberalizing measures simultaneously. Instead, there is an "optimal" order of economic liberalization, which may vary for different liberalizing economies depending on their initial conditions, as described in the various country studies contained in Chapters 3 to 14, but whose common characteristics are the unifying theme of this book. Let us, therefore, begin with a brief overview of the optimum sequencing of financial policies in the transition from centralized controls repressing domestic and foreign trade to a full-fledged market economy. Consider the domestic side first.

Often before price inflation can feasibly be phased out, and before the capital market is opened for free borrowing and lending, the first and most obvious need is to balance the central government's finances. Fiscal control should precede financial liberalization. Direct government spending is best limited to some small share of gross national product (GNP), which could increase modestly as per capita income rises. Equally important, successful liberalizing governments must levy broadly based, but low-rate, taxes on both enterprises and households. The sine qua non of successful reform governments is an internal revenue service capable of collecting taxes in a decentralized market setting (McKinnon 1973, ch. 10). After giving up direct ownership or control of most business activity, the liberalizing government must quickly develop a regularized tax system for retrieving the revenue lost from giving up ownership of the means of production—a stumbling block that most socialist economies have so far failed to avoid, as discussed in Chapters 11 and 13. Only with a broad tax base can the government raise sufficient revenue to avoid inflation without resorting to arbitrary ex post seizures of enterprise profits or personal property, which result in the adverse incentive effects that currently bedevil the socialist economies (Litwack 1991; McKinnon 1990).

Put the matter another way. Starting from a "classical" socialist economy where all the means of production—industrial and agricultural property—are government-owned, the surpluses of these state enterprises constitute effective tax revenue to the government. In the optimum order of liberalization, therefore, the pace at which these assets can be safely privatized is severely constrained by the fiscal system. Until a full-fledged internal revenue service for collecting taxes from the private sector can be put in place, many industrial assets and most natural resources best remain government-owned as revenue sources for the public treasury. Otherwise, privatization or price decontrol could themselves create deficits in the public finances.

In both LDCs and transitional socialist economies, *indirect* (off-budget) government spending, usually outside the control of any parliament or legislature, is increasingly commonplace. In order to better protect the central bank from being forced into the excessive issue of domestic base money, these off-budget government subsidies should either be folded into the regular (balanced) budget or be phased out. Central banks often incur large net losses in supplying foreign exchange, domestic credit, or deposit insurance too cheaply to domestic farms, households, urban enterprises, or commercial banks (Blejer and Chu 1988). In the former Yugoslavia, for example, a formal constitutional provision required that its central government's budget be balanced, as it had been more or less in practice before the breakup; nevertheless, inflation in the 1980s ran out of control because of large losses in forward foreign exchange contracting by the central bank (covered by the issue of domestic money) and the proclivity of regional governments to force regional banks to supply cheap credit to loss-making regional enterprises.

In the 1990s, strict budget balance has become more necessary than it was in the 1960s, when the Keynesian advocacy of "moderate" deficit financing by governments was, unfortunately, all too common. Why this modern need for tighter fiscal discipline? Because of the much less favorable expectations on the part of the government's potential creditors, either foreign or domestic.

Both the liberalizing socialist economies and the deficit-prone less-developed countries (LDCs) of Latin America and Africa have used up any credibility that some of them may once have had to finance fiscal deficits domestically in a noninflationary manner, that is, without issuing money. The socialist economies do not have significant domestic capital markets for marketing government bonds directly to the nonbank public. Thus, public sector deficits tend to be directly monetized by the socialist banking system, although China is an important, if temporary, exception (Ch. 13). The inflation-prone governments of Latin America now find they cannot issue nonmonetary debt internally at anything but exorbitant real rates of interest.

One of the most striking financial developments of the late 1980s was the extent to which the governments of Mexico, Argentina, and Brazil went into debt *domestically* (Parker 1989). Because of the cumulative effect of very high interest rates (over 30 percent real was not unusual) on their existing domestic liabilities, government debt-to-GNP ratios have been building up in an unsustainable fashion even though most of these countries are not paying much on their debts to the international banks. In many LDCs, people now anticipate that the government will default on its own domestic bonds—as in March 1990 with the Brazilian government's freeze of 80 percent of its own outstanding liabilities in the hands of Brazilian firms and households. Except for a few mature industrial economies with an established record of reasonable price-level stability, expectations have become so adverse regarding the future fiscal performance of governments like Brazil's that noninflationary domestic deficit finance has become almost infeasible, and certainly less desirable than what economists generally believed less than three decades ago.

Second in the order of liberalization is the opening of the domestic capital market so that depositors receive, and borrowers pay, substantial real (inflation-adjusted) interest rates. But unrestricted borrowing and lending among decentralized enterprises and households can only proceed satisfactorily once the price level is stabilized and fiscal deficits are eliminated. The banking system, that is, money-issuing depository institutions, should be freed from onerous reserve requirements and official guidance in setting "standard" interest rates on deposits and loans only *after* tight fiscal controls are in place, so that the government no longer has to rely on the inflation tax or undue reserve taxes on depositors to generate revenue (see Chs. 3–5).

To minimize the probability of bank panics and financial breakdowns, where risk premiums in real interest rates rise to exorbitant levels that impair the creditworthiness of virtually any borrower, the pace of deregulation of banks and other financial institutions in liberalizing economies must be carefully geared to the government's success in achieving overall macroeconomic stability (see Chs. 6 and 7). Without price-level stability, unpredictable volatility in real interest rates or exchange rates makes unrestricted domestic borrowing and lending by deposit-taking banks—which must always be regulated to ensure the safety of the payments mechanism—simply too risky. Because of the moral hazard associated with "private" monetary intermediaries, whose deposit base remains insured (implicitly or explicitly) by the government, as with the savings and loan crisis in the United States, the decentralization of the banking system through private ownership or control of the commercial banks might well come near the end of the reform process.

Starting off with a highly centralized but "passive" state-owned banking system, the socialist economies must move vigorously at the outset of liberalization to harden the system of money and credit. They must make interest rates positive in real terms to both borrowers *and* depositors, force repayment by chronically indebted enterprises, and strictly limit the flow of new credit until the price level is stabilized. If the financial circumstances are sufficiently chaotic, with inflationary pressure or great moral hazard in bank lending such that past loans are not being repaid, then I argue in Chapter 11 that newly liberalized enterprises do *without* credit from the organized banking system, following the Chinese example (Ch. 13). Until financial conditions are stabilized, decentralized firms in industry and agriculture best rely mainly on *self-finance,* on borrowing from nonmonetary financial sources, and by broadening equity participation in the enterprise itself.

Even if bank credit must be severely curtailed at the outset of the liberalization, important reforms in the payments mechanism, the deposit side of the banks' balance sheet need not wait. The monetary authorities should move quickly to unify the monetary circulations of both households and liberalized enterprises so that the resulting domestic money becomes attractive to hold and fully convertible for *internal* transacting (whose meaning and rationale are discussed more fully in Ch. 11). If newly unblocked enterprise deposits with positive real yields replace the excess inventories that most enterprises now use as a monetary store of value, the abysmally low productivity of capital characteristic of many socialist economies could rapidly improve.

However, the authorities should move cautiously, perhaps waiting for some years before establishing independent commercial banks that are only indirectly regulated or controlled by the central bank. Indeed, the bad (uncollectable) loans of the existing state banks may require a major recapitalization of both banks and enterprises before privatization—or even decentralization—can safely take place.In the 1980s, China, Hungary, the FSU, and Poland undertook premature decentralizations of their banking systems; the consequent loss of control over the flow of credit contributed to upsurges in inflationary pressure that seriously undermined their efforts to decontrol prices and liberalize quantitative restrictions in commodity markets.

Although the flow of credit, for private or public purposes, from monetary intermediaries best remains circumscribed for many years, private capital markets not based on deposit-taking (money-issuing) banks can operate relatively freely at the outset of the liberalization. Indeed, the government should move quickly to establish a framework of commercial law in which private debt contracts are adjudicated and, if necessary, enforced by the state for all tax-paying citizens, corporate or household. Then ordinary commercial credits, urban markets in commercial bills, rural credit cooperatives, and other forms of short-term money lending could begin even before monetary stability was achieved. However, as long as the future price level is uncertain, thus leaving the economy without any standard of deferred payment, the natural (unsubsidized) development of longer-term bond or equities markets is virtually impossible, even with contractual enforcement mechanisms in place.

After the (successful) liberalization of domestic trade and finance, there is an appropriate pace for the liberalization of the foreign exchanges. In the balance of international payments, transacting on current account is best liberalized much faster than international capital flows (as analyzed in considerable detail in Chs. 8–10).

Freeing foreign commodity trade should proceed in parallel with the decontrol of (disequilibrium) prices in the domestic trade of goods and services. But the *unification* of the exchange rate for all current-account transacting—so that every importer and exporter deals with the same effective price of foreign exchange—should precede the elimination of centralized controls over who can export or who can import. In the FSU, for example, the centralized state trading company was dismantled in 1989 and hundreds of individual enterprises were authorized to negotiate their own foreign trade contracts *before* (1) domestic commodity prices were rationalized and decontrolled, (2) enterprise budget constraints were hardened by suitable fiscal and monetary reforms, and (3) the system of multiple exchange rates—involving literally hundreds of different rates for different commodities—was unified. In such a chaotic situation with literally hundreds of different exchange rates and where the price of foreign exchange may be ten times as expensive for some purposes as for others, no market mechanism can ensure that such decentralized foreign trade is efficient. Clearly, in decentralizing the buying and selling of foreign exchange, the Soviet authorities did not get the order of liberalization right (see Chs. 11 and 12).

After January 1992, Russia more or less unified the exchange rate but allowed capital flight and much too deep an exchange depreciation (Ch. 13): this was a major factor contributing to the inflationary explosion that followed. More subtle is the proper specification of commercial policy in the course of a trade liberalization. In moving to unrestricted convertibility on current account (at a unified exchange rate), the optimum initial restraints on trade depend heavily on the preexisting system of protection. Before liberalization, most LDCs have both tariff and quota protection formally written into generally available legal codes—with the quota restrictions being more significant.

But quotas and other direct administrative controls on importing and exporting generally distort the economy much more than do "equivalent" tariffs (Chapter 8). Besides raising much needed revenue, pure tariffs don't discriminate among various classes of would-be importers or exporters. In their classic joint study of protectionism in LDCs, Anne Krueger (1978) and Jagdish Bhagwati (1978) define trade "liberalization" as the replacement of quantitative restrictions (QRs) with moderate import tariffs or export subsidies. If variance in the (now unified) real exchange rate is limited, such "tarification" of QRs could be the optimal first step in an eventual move to free trade—as in the case of Chile from 1974 to 1979 described in Chapter 6.

In a traditional centrally planned economy, on the other hand, protection for domestic manufacturing is almost entirely *implicit* and is not codified. Informal quota restrictions on both importing and exporting proliferate. Domestic users of energy and other material inputs are heavily subsidized by keeping the effective domestic prices of these primary inputs below those prevailing in world markets. For finished goods, exchange controls and the apparatus of state trading in socialist economies provide virtually absolute protection from competing foreign manufactures. Imports that would potentially compete with domestic manufactures are simply not authorized, although no formal quota restrictions or tariffs appear in any legal codes.

Nevertheless, the tariff "equivalents" of these informal quota restrictions follow a common pattern (Chapter 12). Like formal trade restraints often found in LDCs, the implicit structure of tariff equivalents in socialist economies "cascades" downward from very high levels protecting domestic finished consumer goods, to lower levels for manufactured intermediate products, to negative protection for domestic producers of industrial raw materials and energy.

These cascaded implicit tariffs raise effective protection for domestic finished goods to the point where most manufacturing exhibits negative (or very low) value added at world market prices. A precipitate move to free trade could, therefore, provoke the widespread collapse of domestic manufacturing—no matter how the exchange rate is set, and no matter that some of this industry might eventually be viable at world market prices. The precipitate industrial declines in East Germany, Poland, and Russia in their sudden openings to free trade in the early 1990s suggest that a more deliberate approach is warranted.

In one optimum order of liberalizing foreign trade (Chapter 12), the socialist economy might begin by converting its implicit quota restrictions into explicit tariffs. Once formally codified, the highest tariffs in the cascade can then be reduced toward zero over a preannounced five- to ten-year adjustment period. After this well-defined commercial policy is in place, free currency convertibility for exporting or importing on current account can be maintained.

An alternative gradualist approach for trade liberalization begins by opening a few tax-exempt "special economic zones" with free access to international markets while only slowly expanding rights to retain foreign exchange by exporters in other areas. This is the Chinese model discussed in Chapter 14. But even this gradualist approach has the disadvantage of impairing the government's revenue position as foreign trade grows relative to the rest of the economy.

However, even these rationalizations of foreign trade policy need not warrant extending full foreign exchange convertibility to capital-account transactions in either LDCs or socialist economies. Before allowing enterprises (or households) to borrow freely from, or deposit in, international capital markets, the national capital market should be fully liberalized, which in turn depends on the stabilization of the domestic price level and the elimination of substantial reserve taxes on domestic banks (monetary intermediaries). As long as domestic banks remain restricted and heavily taxed, it is pointless—indeed destructive—to allow foreign banks or other foreign financial institutions to operate freely in domestic financial markets. Even more destabilizing is to allow "hard" foreign currencies to circulate in parallel with the still "soft" domestic one. (But joint ventures with foreign industrial enterprises can still be an efficient way to absorb foreign technologies.)

Only when domestic borrowing and lending take place freely at equilibrium (unrestricted) rates of interest and the domestic rate of inflation is curbed so that ongoing depreciation in the exchange rate is unnecessary, are the arbitrage conditions right for allowing free international capital mobility. Otherwise, the premature elimination of exchange controls on foreign capital flows could lead to unwarranted capital flight or an unwarranted buildup of foreign indebtedness or both (as discussed further in Chs. 5, 9, and 10). Free foreign exchange convertibility on capital account is usually the *last* stage in the optimal order of economic liberalization, as we shall see.

In subsequent chapters, examples from a variety of LDCs and transitional socialist economies are drawn to illustrate important facets of the financial problems that affect the optimum order of liberalization. However, the experiences of the (now) advanced capitalist countries are not neglected. Japan, after 1949, exemplified a poor country embarking on rapid real economic growth while keeping suitable financial constraints in place. But whether the Japanese government was "liberal" or "interventionist" in the flow of credit and in the setting of interest rates remains controversial. In Chapter 3, Japanese financial policy and the similarly successful experience of Taiwan a decade or so later are reviewed in order to establish historical benchmarks of countries that did get their order of liberalization more or less "right."

First, however, Chapter 2 reviews the evidence from a broader cross-section of countries on the nexus between financial liberalization and real economic growth.

CHAPTER TWO

Financial Repression and

the Productivity of Capital:

Empirical Findings

on Interest Rates

and Exchange Rates

If governments tax or otherwise distort their domestic capital markets, the economy is said to be financially "repressed."[1] Usury restrictions on interest rates, heavy reserve requirements on bank deposits, and compulsory credit allocations interact with ongoing price inflation to reduce the attractiveness of holding claims on the domestic banking system. In such a repressed financial system, real deposit rates of interest on monetary assets are often negative and are difficult to predict when inflation is high and unstable. Foreign exchange rates also become highly uncertain. Thus, the demand for domestic money— broadly defined to include savings and term deposits as well as checking accounts and currency—falls as a proportion of Gross National Product (GNP).

But these monetary assets naturally dominate the financial portfolios of small savers in less-developed countries (LDCs). Thus, back in 1973, Edward Shaw and I hypothesized that repressing the monetary system fragments the domestic capital market, with highly adverse consequences for the quality and quantity of real capital accumulation:

1. The flow of loanable funds through the organized banking system is reduced, forcing potential borrowers to rely more on self-finance.

2. Interest rates on the truncated flow of bank lending vary arbitrarily from one class of favored or disfavored borrower to another.

3. The process of self-finance within enterprises and households is itself impaired. If the real yield on deposits, as well as on coin and currency, is negative, firms cannot easily accumulate liquid assets in preparation for making discrete investments. Socially costly inflation hedges look more attractive as a means of internal finance.

4. Significant financial deepening outside the repressed banking system

---

1. Terminology introduced by Edward Shaw (1973) and McKinnon (1973). Further discussion of optimal financial management in a repressed economy is found in Fry (1982) and, more completely, in Fry (1988).

becomes impossible when firms are dangerously illiquid and/or inflation is high and unstable. Robust open markets in stocks and bonds and intermediation by trust and insurance companies require monetary stability.

5. Inflows of foreign financial capital may be unproductive when the domestic capital market is in disarray and foreign exchange rates are unpredictable.

Remedying financial repression is implicit in its definition. We suggested keeping positive and more uniformly high real rates of interest within comparable categories of bank deposits and loans by eliminating onerous reserve requirements, interest ceilings, and mandated allocations of cheap credit on the one hand, while stabilizing the price level through appropriate macroeconomic measures on the other. Then, domestic savers and investors would better "see" the true scarcity price of capital and thus reduce the great dispersion in the profitability of investing in different sectors of the economy.

Similarly, by stabilizing the domestic price level while keeping real interest rates "close to" market-clearing levels, financial flows through the foreign exchanges would be less volatile, with fewer fluctuations in the nominal (and real) exchange rate. Then producers of internationally tradable goods, both exportables and import substitutes, could more safely undertake longer term and more productive investments—with less need to hold excess inventories and other hedges against domestic price-level or exchange-rate risk.

In the 1990s, these strictures for liberalizing and stabilizing the financial system seem now like mere truisms to most economists—although not always to politicians. Today, both the World Bank and the International Monetary Fund (IMF) stress the importance of stabilizing the domestic price level and increasing the flow of domestic loanable funds at interest rates near market-clearing levels. From the perspective of the postwar period, those countries with substantially positive real interest rates and high real financial growth, such as Japan, Taiwan, South Korea, and Singapore (as shown in more detail below), are regarded as leading success stories.

This current emphasis on the advantages of financial liberalization is quite remarkable. Well into the 1970s, many development economists still favored the generation of "forced" saving through inflation or through shifts in the internal distribution of income by such means as turning the internal terms of trade against agriculture in order to transfer an economic "surplus" to the industrial sector. Credit subsidies, at below market rates of interest, were once widely promoted as a means of stimulating socially desirable investments. Unless so manipulated or repressed, the financial sector was not then viewed as a leading force in the development process. Now, however, there is widespread agreement that flows of saving and investment should be voluntary and significantly decentralized in an open capital market at close to equilibrium interest rates.

But there are important caveats to financial liberalization. As discussed in

Chapter 1 and developed further in Chapters 5 and 6, the optimal order of liberalization may require major fiscal reforms—increases in tax revenues and cuts in properly consolidated government expenditures—*before* the inflation tax and other repressive financial policies may be safely phased out. Even then, in immature bank-based capital markets, upper limits exist on the extent to which interest rates can be raised without incurring undue adverse risk selection among industrial and agricultural borrowers and undue moral hazard in the banks themselves, as discussed in Chapters 3 and 7. And, without proper bank supervision, these limits could well be breached during some major attempt to disinflate, as we shall see in Chapter 6.

Given the difficulties involved in securing an open capital market and a stable price level, what systematic evidence has become available from the IMF, World Bank, and elsewhere since the publication of *Money and Capital in Economic Development* (McKinnon 1973) to assure policymakers that the effort is well worth making?

In this chapter, I begin by reviewing how financial liberalization and significantly positive real rates of interest lead to rapid financial deepening, as measured by the ratio of bank deposits, currency, and other financial assets to GNP. Then by examining the cross-country evidence from a variety of LDCs, the link between these domestic financial variables and real economic performance—higher output growth and the more efficient use of physical capital—is assessed. Finally, I consider how exchange-rate variability per se is linked to output and productivity growth in LDCs—both during the Bretton Woods period of the 1950s and 1960s, when exchange rates among the industrial countries were relatively fixed, and then after the fixed-rate dollar standard broke down.

FINANCIAL DEEPENING, REAL INTEREST RATES, AND ECONOMIC GROWTH

What lessons have been learned about financial repression in the longer run—say over a decade or more? Countries that have sustained higher real rates of interest and more stable prices have generally had more robust real financial growth. Data on private holdings of "broad" money throw light on these issues. Table 2.1 presents ratios of the broad money supply (M3)—coin and currency, savings deposits, and shorter-term time deposits in banks or other quasi-monetary institutions (such as postal savings)—to GNP. One noticeable characteristic is that even the slower-growing Asian countries tend to be more financially developed than typically more inflationary Latin American countries. However, both groups of slowly or erratically growing economies have fairly low levels of domestically held financial assets, with the ratio of M3 to GNP averaging about 0.227.

In contrast, Table 2.2 shows financial development in the rapid-growth economies—West Germany, Japan, South Korea, Taiwan and Singapore—

TABLE 2.1

Bank Loanable Funds in Typical Semi-industrial LDCs

(Ratio of M3 to GNP)

	1960	1965	1970	1975	1980	1985	Mean 1960–85
Argentina	0.245	0.209	0.267	0.168	0.234	0.152	0.213
Brazil	0.148	0.156	0.205	0.164	0.175	0.179	0.171
Chile	0.123	0.130	0.183	0.099	0.208	0.263	0.168
Colombia	0.191	0.204	0.235	—	0.222	0.290	0.228
Mean ratio of M3 to GNP for four Latin American countries							0.195
India	0.283	0.262	0.264	0.295	0.382	0.412	0.316
Philippines	0.186	0.214	0.235	0.186	0.219	0.204	0.207
Sri Lanka	0.284	0.330	0.275	0.255	0.317	0.371	0.305
Turkey	0.202	0.223	0.237	0.222	0.136	0.228	0.208
Mean ratio of M3 to GNP for four Asian countries							0.259

Source: IMF, *International Financial Statistics,* various issues.

Note: Following the *International Financial Statistics,* M3 is defined as money (line 34) + quasi-money (line 35) + deposits outside commercial banks (line 45). M3 is a stock tabulated as of June 30 for each calendar year, whereas GNP is the flow of output for that year.

TABLE 2.2

Bank Loanable Funds in Rapidly Growing Economies

(Ratio of M3 to GNP)

	1955	1960	1965	1970	1975	1980	1985
West Germany[a]	0.331	0.294	0.448	0.583	0.727	0.913	1.019
Japan	0.554[b]	0.737[b]	0.701[b]	0.863	1.026	1.390	1.599
South Korea	0.069	0.114	0.102	0.325	0.323	0.337	0.396
Taiwan	0.115	0.166	0.331	0.462	0.588	0.750	1.264
Singapore	—	—	0.542[b]	0.701	0.668	0.826	0.788

[a] As well as deposits and currency, the West German series includes bank bonds sold directly to the public.

[b] The bias is downward because deposit information on specialized credit institutions was not collected.

Source: IMF, *International Financial Statistics,* various issues.

Note: See note to Table 2.1.

from 1955 to 1985. *A high or rising M3/GNP ratio indicates a large real flow of domestic loanable funds for new investments.* Because capital markets in these economies were dominated by banks, ratios of M3 to GNP encompass the main domestic flow of loanable funds in the system. By 1985, Japan, Taiwan, West Germany, and Singapore had M3/GNP ratios of 0.75 or much more despite all having started with much less financial depth back in 1955. Only South Korea had a much lower ratio of M3 to GNP: only about 0.32 from 1970 to 1980. During this decade when its domestic financial growth was negligible, South Korea borrowed heavily abroad, unlike the other four countries. Subsequently in the early 1980s, when South Korea's domestic financial growth resumed, led by higher real deposit rates with lower price inflation, its foreign borrowing was scaled back, with its foreign debt to GNP

TABLE 2.3
Selected Developing Countries Grouped According to Interest Rates on Bank
Deposits: Growth of Real Financial Assets and Real GDP, 1971–1980
(Compound Growth Rates, Percentage per Year)

	Financial Assets[a]	GDP
1. Countries with Positive Real Interest Rates		
Malaysia	13.8	8.0
South Korea	11.1	8.6
Sri Lanka	10.1	4.7
Nepal	9.6	2.0
Singapore	7.6	9.1
Philippines	5.6	6.2
2. Countries with Moderately Negative Real Interest Rates		
Pakistan[b]	9.9	5.4
Thailand	8.5	6.9
Morocco	8.2	5.5
Colombia	5.5	5.8
Greece	5.4	4.7
South Africa	4.3	3.7
Kenya	3.6	5.7
Burma	3.5	4.3
Portugal	1.8	4.7
Zambia	−1.1	0.8
3. Countries with Strongly Negative Real Interest Rates		
Peru	3.2	3.4
Turkey	2.2	5.1
Jamaica	−1.9	−0.7
Zaire	−6.8	0.1
Ghana	−7.6	−0.1

[a]Measured as the sum of monetary and quasi-monetary deposits with the banking sector, corrected for changes in the consumer price index.
[b]The period covered is 1974–80.
Source: IMF, 1983.

ratio falling sharply. (See a fuller discussion of the recent South Korean experience in Ch. 6.) The other high-growth countries shown in Table 2.2 are now net international creditors.

Although a higher rate of financial growth and rising M3/GNP ratios are positively correlated with higher growth in real gross domestic product (GDP), Patrick's (1966) problem remains unresolved: what is the cause and what is the effect? Is finance a leading sector in economic development, or does it simply follow growth in real output, which is generated elsewhere? Perhaps individuals whose incomes grow quickly want financial assets simply as a kind of consumer good (i.e., financial growth is an incidental outcome of the growth process).

To disentangle these issues, Table 2.3 presents data from an IMF study on interest-rate policies in developing countries, where A. Lanyi and R. Saracoglu were the principal investigators. The availability of pure data and membership

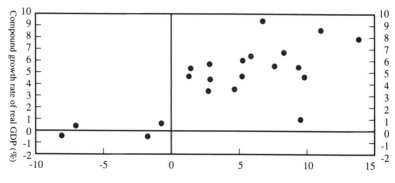

Compound growth rate of real financial assets[a] (%)

[a]As defined in Table 2.3.

FIGURE 2.1. Growth of Real GDP and Real Financial Assets for Selected Developing Countries, 1971–80. (*Source:* IMF 1983.)

in the IMF were the criteria for selecting the twenty-one countries. For any one country over time, the real deposit rate of interest can vary a great deal, from positive to negative or vice versa. For the period 1971–80, the IMF calculated an average real interest rate for each country on a fairly common asset, usually a thirty-day deposit deflated by the rate of change in its consumer price index (CPI). Countries were then classified according to whether their average real deposit rate over that period was positive, moderately negative, or highly negative: groups 1, 2, and 3, respectively. Because most of these countries have fragmented interest-rate structures, a representative deposit rate of interest is not easy to select. Nevertheless, from the "average" experience of the twenty-one countries over the ten-year period, the IMF managed to devise the three-way classification shown in Table 2.3 and Figures 2.1 and 2.2. Real financial growth (which is not the same as measured personal saving) is shown in Figure 2.1 to be positively correlated with real GDP growth.

Similarly, the left-hand panel of Figure 2.2 also shows that those countries that maintain positive real rates of interest have higher growth in real financial assets, as might be expected. More important, the right-hand panel of Figure 2.2 shows a significant positive correlation between real deposit rates of interest and real growth in GDP. In pioneering earlier work using pooled cross-section and time-series data from 1961 to 1972 for seven Asian economies, Maxwell Fry (1978) obtained a similarly strong positive correlation when he regressed real output growth on real deposit rates of interest.

More recently, Fry (1988, 151) replicated the IMF's cross-country regression technique but added Taiwan (not an IMF member) to group 1 of Table 2.3. Using the scaled variable SR for the real deposit rate over the three groups in Table 2.3 and defining DYY to be the real rate of growth in GDP, Fry reestimated the IMF's cross-section study for 1971–80 (now with twenty-two countries) to get the following equation:

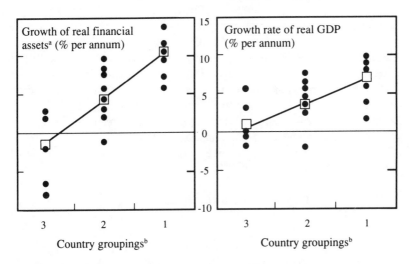

[a]As defined in Table 2.3.
[b]See Table 2.3 for specifications of these groupings.

FIGURE 2.2. Selected Developing Countries Grouped According to Interest-Rate Policies: Growth of Real Financial Assets and Real GDP, 1971–80. (*Source:* IMF 1983.)

$$(2.1) \qquad DYY = 4.451 + 2.592\,SR \qquad (RsqAdj = 0.426).$$
$$\qquad\qquad (9.474) \quad (4.074)$$

Despite the errors in measurement from the crudely averaged data, the positive correlation between higher real output growth and higher real deposit rates in (2.1) is striking (t-statistics are in parentheses). Because of the ordinal nature of the right-hand side variable, however, the regression coefficient of SR in equation (2.1) is not a point estimate of the impact of raising real interest rates on real economic growth.

In a more comprehensive study for the World Bank, Alan Gelb (1989) analyzed the relationship between average three- to six-month deposit rates (deflated by the CPI rate of inflation) and average real GDP growth. From financial data first assembled by Hanson and Neal (1987), Gelb analyzed a broader set of thirty-four LDCs over the longer time period, 1965–85. Because of the sharp fall in productivity growth throughout the world economy after 1973, Gelb split his sample into two subperiods: 1965–73 and 1974–85. As with the earlier IMF study, Gelb first classified countries qualitatively according to whether their real deposit rates of interest were positive, moderately negative, or strongly negative for each subperiod. Then he tabulated average growth in real GDP and indicators of financial performance in each of the three interest-rate categories. The results were published in the World Bank's *World Development Report, 1989* and are reproduced here as Table 2.4. For the subperiod 1974–85, average output growth was 5.6 percent for countries with positive real interest rates, 3.8 percent for those with moderately negative real interest rates, and only 1.9 percent for those with strongly negative real interest rates—results that strongly corroborate the earlier IMF study.

However, Gelb's (1989) work goes further in incorporating the other monetary and investment-saving variables (shown in Table 2.4) and in using his point estimates for interest-rate effects to undertake further quantitative analysis. From this continuous (cardinal) measure of the real deposit rate of interest RR, Gelb also found a strong positive correlation with output growth over the 1965–85 period:

$$(2.2) \qquad DYY = c + 0.256\,RR \qquad (RsqAdj = 0.489).$$
$$(5.72)$$

With the breakdown of the Bretton Woods system of fixed exchange rates after 1973, measured average growth in real GDP fell from 6 percent per year to about 4 percent per year in the thirty-four countries. Hence, Gelb introduced a dummy variable, SHIFT, which has the value 0 for 1965–73 and 1 from 1974–85, and then calculated countrywide averages for RR and DYY for each of the two subperiods (seventy-eight observations in all). He then reran the regression pooled over the two subperiods to get

$$(2.3) \qquad DYY = c + 0.197\,RR - 0.018\,SHIFT \qquad (RsqAdj = 0.464).$$
$$(5.96) \qquad (-3.47)$$

Beyond what can be explained by a decline in real interest rates (Table 2.4), the SHIFT variable indicates a marked decline in output growth after 1973—a subject to which we shall return when exchange-rate performance is considered. But interest-rate policy remains very important. If we literally interpret equations (2.2) and (2.3), for every 1 percent increase in the real deposit rate, output growth increases by 0.2–0.25 percent. Gelb's single-equation point estimates of the apparent payoff to improved financial policy (despite the caveats discussed below on reverse causation) are impressive. Nevertheless, earlier point estimates by Maxwell Fry (1988, 152) were higher. From several pooled time-series and cross-country studies for Asian economies for the 1960s and 1970s, Fry found that "a one percentage point increase in the real deposit rate of interest towards its competitive free-market equilibrium level is associated with a rise in the rate of economic growth of about one half a percentage point." Because bank earnings are not tapped to subsidize favored borrowers (including the government), so that real rates of interest to depositors are correspondingly higher, nonrepressive financial policies appear to promote higher economic growth.

However, care must be taken in deciding which variables are exogenous

TABLE 2.4

Growth Rates and Other Economic Indicators for Country Groups with Positive, Moderately Negative, and Strongly Negative Real Interest Rates

Indicator	1965–73			1974–85		
		Negative			Negative	
	Positive	Moderately	Strongly	Positive	Moderately	Strongly
Real interest rate	3.7	−1.7	−13.7	3.0	−2.4	−13.0
GDP growth rate	7.3	5.5	4.6	5.6	3.8	1.9
M3/GDP	28.9	27.0	29.1	40.3	34.0	30.5
Investment/GDP	21.4	19.7	21.4	26.9	23.2	23.0
Change in GDP/investment	36.7	31.1	21.7	22.7	17.3	6.2
Change in real M3/real saving	18.7	12.7	6.4	16.6	8.2	−0.9
Inflation rate	22.2	7.1	40.2	20.8	23.9	50.3
Volatility of inflation	17.1	5.3	27.2	12.2	9.1	23.5

Note: Real interest rates were calculated from nominal rates according to the following formula: $[(1 + r)/(1 + p) - 1] \times 100$, where r is the deposit rate and p is the inflation rate. Inflation is the percentage change in the CPI. M3 is currency plus the sum of nonbank deposits of the public at all identified deposit-taking institutions. Real saving is gross domestic savings deflated by the average annual CPI rate. Volatility of inflation is the absolute deviation of the inflation rate from its level the year before.

Source: World Bank, *World Development Report, 1989*, 31. This classification covers thirty-four developing countries in Africa, Asia, and Latin America and thus is more inclusive than the data set of Table 2.3.

and which endogenous. Positive correlations between growth in financial assets and growth in GDP do not show which way the causality operates. But for the purposes of portfolio choice by individual investors, a case can be made for treating the real rate of interest on depository claims on banks as exogenous. Governments usually intervene to set ceilings on nominal rates of interest on bank deposits, and at the same time they determine the aggregate rate of price inflation; the real deposit rate of interest is, therefore, more or less determined by public policy. Nevertheless, this assumption that the real deposit rate is an exogenous indicator of financial policy remains to be considered in the context of a structural model of how financial processes work themselves out.

THE PRODUCTIVITY OF CAPITAL AND THE SAVING-INVESTMENT RATE

What are the channels by which increased financial deepening, price-level stability, and positive real interest rates contribute to higher output growth? Back in 1973 when writing *Money and Capital*, I was rather agnostic regarding the relative importance of higher social saving (as a share of GDP) versus the improved productivity of capital. As financial assets become more attractive, does the release of financial repression have its major impact on growth through the increased share of investment (saving) in GDP or through the improved "quality" of investment?

For each of the thirty-four countries in his panel, Alan Gelb (1989) derives estimates of both the incremental output-capital ratio, IOCR, and the ratio of investment (domestic plus foreign saving) to GDP, denoted by IGDP, that are summarized in Table 2.4. After he partitioned the sample interval, the average IOCR for the thirty-four countries fell sharply from 0.32 in the earlier period (1965–73) to just 0.14 in the recent one (1974–85)—a rather spectacular fall in investment efficiency that could be linked to the higher inflation as well as the greater volatility in exchange rates in the later period. On the other hand, the IGDP rose slightly from 0.21 to 0.24—perhaps in part from the large absorption of foreign capital (borrowing from the international banks) in the late 1970s and early 1980s.

Over the whole 1965–85 period (using his pooled observations from the two subperiods), however, Gelb found that the varying investment efficiency *across* countries was strongly and positively correlated with the average real deposit rate:

$$(2.4) \qquad \text{IOCR} = c + 0.989 \, \text{RR} - 0.139 \, \text{SHIFT} \qquad (\text{RsqAdj} = 0.563).$$
$$\qquad\qquad\qquad (5.90) \qquad (-5.39)$$

Gelb found the regression (2.4) to be very robust, as did Fry (1988). Adding more explanatory variables to the right-hand side seemed, if anything, to strengthen the positive effect of higher interest rates on the productivity of new investment. In contrast, Gelb found (along with Fry) that the effect of the real interest rate on measured social saving—domestic and foreign—explained much less of the variance:

$$(2.5) \qquad \text{IGDP} = c + 0.248 \, \text{RR} + 0.042 \, \text{SHIFT} \qquad (\text{RsqAdj} = 0.090).$$
$$\qquad\qquad\qquad (2.21) \qquad (2.43)$$

The statistical significance of (2.5) tended to fade when Gelb added more explanatory variables on the right-hand side; the coefficient of RR becomes smaller and less significant in explaining aggregate saving as a share of GNP.

In assessing the effect of higher interest rates *across countries*, how important is the "efficiency effect" relative to the "investment (saving) effect" in explaining the increase in the real rate of growth? Before pursuing Gelb's statistical analysis further, let us consider the problem of making cross-country comparisons conceptually in the context of the traditional Harrod-Domar one-sector growth model. The total stock of capital K is the only input and has average productivity σ such that output Y is determined by

$$(2.6) \qquad\qquad\qquad Y = \sigma K.$$

Equation (2.6) is also a valid representation of the productivity of capital in the presence of unlimited supplies of labor if the real wage is fixed (Kapur

1986, ch. 1). Then any increase in K is implicitly associated with proportional increases in the supply of labor. We can now represent the *change* in output growth, $\dot{Y}$, across countries as

$$(2.7) \qquad\qquad \dot{Y} = \sigma\dot{K} + K\dot{\sigma}, \qquad \text{where } \dot{K} = I = S.$$

Equation (2.7) partitions the sources of growth into that associated with new investment for a given σ *and* increases in σ for a given capital stock. The impact of new investment per se on output growth is captured by the first term on the right-hand side. However, the second term, the increased output from a given capital stock, could be important, as when a higher M3/GNP ratio (greater financial deepening) led to a higher average productivity of existing capital. However, most analyses—either theoretical or empirical—proceed as if $\dot{\sigma} = 0$ and presume that new investment with productivity σ is the only source of increased output. For example, the familiar Harrod-Domar growth model simply assumes that the second term on the right-hand side of equation (2.7) is 0; then, dividing through by Y, we get

$$(2.8) \quad \dot{Y}/Y = \mathrm{DYY} = \sigma(I/Y) = \sigma(\mathrm{IGDP}) = \sigma s, \qquad \text{where } s = S/Y = \mathrm{IGDP}.$$

The rate of growth for a single country is simply the propensity to save times the average (marginal) productivity of capital. In typical cross-country studies of investment productivity based on comparing incremental output/capital ratios (IOCRs), a similar simplification is used. In order to calculate the IOCRs empirically, investigators (implicitly) assume that the right-hand term in (2.7) is 0 by attributing all the observed differences in output growth across countries to differing levels of investment. By construction with available data, $\mathrm{IOCR} = (\mathrm{DYY})/(\mathrm{IGDP}) = \sigma$. Thus any empirical analysis (such as Alan Gelb's) that uses this constructed definition of IOCR may well miss important financial or technological changes that lead to output growth from improvements in the existing capital stock, even when there is no new investment. With that caveat in mind, let us reproduce Alan Gelb's partitioning of the sources of output growth from increases in the real deposit rate of interest. Differentiate (2.8) with respect to RR to get

$$(2.9) \qquad \frac{d(\mathrm{DYY})}{d(\mathrm{RR})} = \frac{d(\mathrm{IOCR})}{d(\mathrm{RR})}\,\underline{\mathrm{IGDP}} + \frac{d(\underline{\mathrm{IGDP}})}{d(\mathrm{RR})}\,\underline{\mathrm{IOCR}},$$

where the underlined variables are cross-country averages.

For explaining output growth rates across countries, Gelb then assessed the relative importance of the two terms on the right-hand side of (2.9): the efficiency effect, measured by weighted changes in IOCR, versus the investment effect, measured by weighted cross-country differences in investment as a share of GDP. Gelb used his point estimates for the coefficients of RR in the pooled regression equations (2.3), (2.4), and (2.5) to measure $d(DYY)/d(RR)$, $d(IOCR)/d(RR)$, and $d(IGDP)/d(RR)$, respectively. He then weighted the last two with IGDP and IOCR and found that the efficiency effect was almost four times as important as the investment effect in explaining differences in real GDP growth across his sample of thirty-four countries. *Higher real deposit rates of interest had their major impact through increased investment efficiency (as measured by IOCRs) rather than through increased investment or aggregate saving as a share of GDP.*

That aggregate saving, as measured in the GNP accounts, does not respond strongly to higher real interest rates is now well established; and cross-country statistical studies linking inflation rates to aggregate saving have also been quite ambiguous (Leff and Sato 1980; Gonzales Arrieta 1988; Deaton 1990). This ambiguity is puzzling: shouldn't saving be discouraged as inflation erodes the real values of financial assets?

In an inflationary economy, real rates of interest on financial assets are usually negative and thus less attractive to savers. Because of the inflation itself, however, the private sector is forced to abstain from current consumption, that is, to "save." Individuals must keep adding to their nominal money balances in order to prevent their real balances from declining. But this inflation "tax" extracted by the government is classified in the GNP accounts as if it was private saving. However, real personal financial assets are not accumulating, and the flow of loanable funds to the private sector may be quite low, even though the flow of private "saving," as measured in the GNP accounts, might be quite high. Because this forced saving effect offsets the negative substitution effect of inflation on accumulating liquid financial assets, systematic relationships between the flow of social saving and real rates of interest or between aggregate saving and inflation are weak or ambiguous.

From cross-country studies such as those by Gelb and Fry, however, the positive correlation between real interest rates and real growth seems strong and unambiguous. Apparently the quality, if not the quantity, of investment improves significantly when financial intermediation is robust.

THE QUALITY OF INVESTMENT: DOMESTIC FINANCE

How best can one characterize this quality effect? What are the financial mechanisms whereby monetary stabilization coupled with positive real interest rates can so markedly increase the productivity of a country's stock of physical capital? Over his whole sample period from 1965 to 1985, Gelb found that the high-growth half of the countries sampled grew fully 3 percentage points per year faster than the low-growth half. One reason is the greater "financialization" of the domestic economy, and the second is the stabilization of the foreign exchanges. Let us discuss each in turn.

Unfortunately, there is no single domestic financial indicator of the success of a monetary stabilization program. The empirical analyses reviewed above relied heavily on the real deposit rate of interest—perhaps too much so—as the sole indicator of financial efficiency. But simply stabilizing the price level per se (apart from raising real interest rates) serves to limit financial risk and lengthen the term structure of borrowing and lending. And, apart from price-level and interest-rate policies, the M3/GDP ratio might also be increased by building bank branches in rural areas or taking other steps to increase the convenience and liquidity of holding-bank deposits.

In fact, one could define domestic "financialization" either *marginally*, associated with the extent new investment appears to be intermediated by the banking system, or *intramarginally*, by simply considering cross-country variation in the M3/GDP ratio. The former is important when considering the payoff to new net investment; whereas the latter could also be important for the efficiency of the existing capital stock. For example, in looking at the country's stock of working capital, inventories need not be accumulating (investment is zero) but the efficiency with which that stock is deployed may depend positively on the size of M3/GDP—the extent to which cash balances substitute for "nonproductive" inflation hedges like excess commodity inventories.

Consider first the investment margin: the extent to which new investment appears to be intermediated by the banking system. Alan Gelb defined the ratio of financial saving to total saving (RFSTS) as the real increase in M3/real gross saving.

Illustrative numbers for RFSTS in Gelb's sample of thirty-four countries appear in Table 2.4. "Averaged over the entire period, it ranges in value from 0.45 (for the most rapidly monetizing economy) to −0.18 (for a rapidly demonetizing economy)" (Gelb 1989, 24). and Gelb finds that RFSTS does respond to real interest rates:

$$(2.10) \qquad \text{RFSTS} = c + 0.817\,\text{RR} \qquad (\text{RsqAdj} = 0.259).$$
$$(4.90)$$

However, no other explanatory variables for RFSTS were significant when included on the right-hand side of (2.10). Somewhat surprisingly, the rate of price inflation itself did not explain any of the variance in RFSTS as long as RR was in the estimating equation.

But Gelb did find that output growth seemed to respond to RFSTS:

$$(2.11) \qquad \begin{aligned} \text{DYY} = \\ 0.113\,\text{RFSTS} + 0.058\,\text{TSGD} - 0.019\,\text{SHIFT} \quad (\text{RsqAdj} = 0.430), \\ (2.17) \qquad\quad (2.026) \qquad\quad\; (-3.46) \end{aligned}$$

where TSGD is defined as total saving as a share of GDP. Combining the coefficient of RR in equation (2.10) with that of RFSTS in equation (2.11)

and substituting into the right-hand side of the following chain rule, Gelb
estimates that

(2.12)
$$\frac{d(\text{DYY})}{d(\text{RR})} = \frac{d(\text{DYY})}{d(\text{RFSTS})}\frac{d(\text{RFSTS})}{d(\text{RR})} = 0.08$$

The estimate 0.08 is about 40 percent of the effect of real deposit rate on
output growth contained in the direct regression equation (2.3). Only a portion
of the interest-rate effect on growth appears to go through the marginal financialization ratio RFSTS: the extent to which new investment is intermediated
by banks. Indeed, interest rates seem to explain relatively little of the variance
in RFSTS in equation (2.10)—perhaps due to the difficulty of coming up with
an all-purpose statistical measure of the degree of financial development.
Thus Gelb, in his otherwise excellent analysis, is probably *not* warranted in
suggesting that the remaining 60 percent of the interaction is reverse causation:
from real growth to real interest rates. Nevertheless, there remains a substantial
mystery as to the best method of determining how interest rates operate through
the financial system to influence real growth.

For example, the impact of the real deposit rate of interest on the intramarginal variable measuring financial depth, M3/GDP, was minor:

(2.13)
$$\begin{aligned}
\text{M3/GDP} = c &+ 0.251\ \text{RR} + 0.0002\ \text{GNPPE} \\
&\quad (1.13) \qquad (5.92) \\
&- 0.141\ \text{INF} + 0.099\ \text{SHIFT} \qquad (\text{RsqAdj} = 0.416), \\
&\quad (-3.36) \qquad (3.31)
\end{aligned}$$

where GNPPE is GDP per head. Thus M3/GDP naturally tends to be high in
high-income countries. In addition, equation (2.13) shows that the rate of
price inflation (INF) itself, if not the real deposit rate of interest, has a major
impact on financial depth. When the price level is stable, there are substantial
incentives to hold more coin and currency and non-interest-bearing demand
deposits. And financial depth, as measured by M3/GDP, has a positive effect
on growth beyond that explained by the interest rate:

(2.14)
$$\begin{aligned}
\text{DYY} = c +& \\
0.180\ \text{RR} &+ 0.034\ \text{M3/GDP} - 0.021\ \text{SHIFT} \qquad (\text{RsqAdj} = 0.486), \\
(5.22) \qquad &(2.13) \qquad\qquad (-3.91)
\end{aligned}$$

In summary, Gelb's equation (2.14) neatly captures the benefits of monetary
stabilization operating through domestic financial variables. *To increase eco-*
nomic growth, raising real deposit rates by reducing inflation is more effective,
percentage point by percentage point, than simply raising nominal interest
rates to offset ongoing inflation. (In any event, there are limits to which

nominal interest rates can safely be increased in an inflationary and thus riskier environment, as shown in Chapters 6 and 7.) Suppose for a given structure of (regulated) nominal deposit rates, the authorities succeeded in reducing price inflation through fiscal or other financial measures. Then equation (2.14) suggests that both the increase in RR and the increase in M3/GDP should, in the long run, induce substantially higher growth in real GDP.

This greater domestic financialization operates mainly to increase the quality of the capital stock—both by raising the incremental output/capital ratio *and* by increasing the productivity with which the existing capital stock is deployed. The former effect might be (loosely) associated with new investment meeting a more stringent market test when firms borrow from banks at a positive real interest rate. Higher deposit rates of interest increase the flow of bank funds available for new investment, even as lower-productivity investments are foreclosed if lending rates of interest are also increased from "repressed" levels where loans had been tightly rationed. However, real loan rates could—in some circumstances discussed in Chapter 4 and 5—actually fall when inflation or bank reserve requirements are reduced. Nevertheless, the flow of loanable funds intermediated by banks would still increase.

But increased and more efficient bank lending to industry and agriculture is not the only favorable impact from a less-repressive financial policy. In most LDCs, there exists a large fringe of smaller firms, farms, or investing house-holds (small artisans) without access to credit from the formal banking sector. The costs of servicing such small-scale loans are just too high per dollar lent. Even larger firms may (correctly) be rationed out of the market for bank loans if they appear to be too risky without adequate collateral (see Ch. 7). And state-owned enterprises in centrally planned economies in transition may well fall into this "too-risky" category (as discussed in Ch. 11). In providing real liquidity to these would-be investors who must rely on *self-finance*, the deposit side of the banks' balance sheet becomes more important than the loan side.

By making real deposit rates on all forms of money somewhat higher, that is, by reducing the rate of price inflation, firms in industry and agriculture are deterred from undertaking very low yield internal investments or from holding nonproductive inflation hedges. Instead, all firms can hold cash balances, as measured by the M3/GNP ratio in equation (2.14). Most important, smaller or riskier firms can more easily undertake discrete or large-scale self-financed investments in the future even if they cannot borrow from the banks. Because they can build up their cash balance position without being penalized by inflation, many will eventually undertake more productive internal investments simply by drawing down (spending) their previously accumulated savings balances when a good investment opportunity presents itself.

In effect, the holding of various forms of stable valued money—from coin and currency, to demand deposits, to saving and time deposits with attractive yields—is *complementary* with investment in more productive physical capital. For the very poorest economies where bank lending on commercial terms may not be feasible, and where directed credit subsidies are almost always undesirable, Thornton and Poudyal (1990) provide new empirical evidence from Nepal linking price stability to increased self-financed investments.

But wealthier economies sometimes suffer from severe moral hazard in bank lending. In many reform socialist economies, for example, the authorities might do best at the outset of the liberalization process to impose the constraint of self-finance for some months or years—as argued in Chapter 11. In financially chaotic circumstances, cutting firms off from bank credit may be the only feasible method to secure control over the price level while improving the very low productivity of capital in socialist enterprises. Despite its anti-Keynesian tenor, this complementarity between making money more attractive to hold while making physical capital more productive, both marginally and intramarginally, was a major theme of *Money and Capital* back in 1973.

THE QUALITY OF INVESTMENT: THE FOREIGN EXCHANGES

Besides reducing domestic financial depth and the flow of loanable funds for new investment, repressive domestic financial policies can also reduce the quality of investment by inducing instability in the foreign exchanges. In Gelb's sample of thirty-four countries, average annual growth rates fell by about 2 percentage points from 1965–73 to 1974–85 (Gelb 1989, 15). But how much of this economic decline was due to

1. increased exchange-rate variability per se, in part prompted by the general breakdown in the commitment to fixed exchange rates after 1973;

2. more severe terms-of-trade shocks from, say, increases in the relative price of oil;

3. greater domestic financial repression—higher inflation and lower deposit rates of interest—of the kind analyzed above?

Important though it may be, factor 3 does not seem to be the whole story. Average real deposit rates fell from −2 percent in 1965–73 to about −5 percent in 1974–85 (Gelb 1989, 15), even as M3/GNP ratios drifted slightly upward (Table 2.4). But this substantial drop of three percentage points in the real deposit rate explains less than half the fall in the average growth rate—even if we rule out reverse causation from growth rates to interest rates and accept the coefficient of RR of 0.18 in equation (2.14) at face value. When both RR and M3/GDP are included as explanatory variables in equation (2.14), the coefficient of the SHIFT parameter remains negative and statistically significant. Clearly, the remarkable downward shift in average productivity from 1965–73 to 1974–85 remains to be fully explained.

The important empirical work of Sebastian Edwards (1988 and 1989) throws light on this problem. Edwards collected extensive exchange-rate, trade, and price-level data for a sample of twenty-three Asian, Latin American, and African LDCs over the 1965–85 period. Unfortunately his sample data do not precisely match those of Gelb or Fry, nor was he interested in purely domestic financial variables such as interest rates or M3/GDP ratios. Instead, Edwards focuses on the behavior of "real" exchange rates under alternative definitions.

First, for each of his twenty-three LDCs, Edwards defines the *bilateral* real exchange rate against the dollar as

$$(2.15) \qquad\qquad \text{BRER} = \frac{EP^*}{P},$$

where E is domestic currency/dollars, P is the domestic CPI, and P^* is the American wholesale price index (WPI). If he had used the WPI for each country, fluctuations in BRER would correspond to deviations from purchasing-power parity. However, Edwards wants to define the "real exchange rate" as the relative price of tradable to nontradable goods, where the foreign WPI is a proxy for domestic tradables and the domestic CPI is a proxy for the price of nontradables. Clearly, these are crude proxies; and fluctuations in BRER as defined in equation (2.15) are similar whether one uses the domestic WPI or CPI.

Second, because the U.S. dollar began to fluctuate sharply against other major currencies after 1973, Edwards also defines each LDC's real exchange rate on a multilateral trade-weighted basis as the "real effective exchange rate":

$$(2.16) \qquad\qquad \text{REER} = \frac{\Sigma \alpha_i E_i P^*_i}{P} \qquad (i = 1, 2, \ldots, k),$$

where k is the number of partner countries over which the summation proceeds, α_i is the trade weight assigned to each, and E_i is an index nominal exchange rate between the country in question and its ith trading partner.

Clearly, under either definition of the real exchange rate, the potential for variation in the real exchange rate increases when inflation in P, the domestic level and denominator of (2.15) and (2.16), is high and unstable. The difficulties of trying to index the real exchange rate in order to keep it fairly constant in inflationary circumstances are discussed in Chapters 6, 9, and 10. The real exchange rate varies enormously in many LDCs—often by over 100 percent (Edwards 1989). Investment risk in both exportable and import substitution industries is correspondingly increased. Time horizons for investments in fixed capital shorten, and firms might well begin to hold excess inventories as a hedge against, or in anticipation of, exchange-rate changes.

After 1973, Edwards' sample of twenty-three LDCs shows a substantial increase in the degree of real exchange-rate variability as well as a fall in the productivity of capital. Thus Edwards (1988) partitions his data (although slightly differently from Gelb) into a 1965–71 and a 1978–85 interval. He uses the variability in the real exchange rate—along with the ratio of investment to GDP and variability in the terms of trade—as explanatory variables for growth in real output. For the more recent post–Bretton Woods period (1978–85), Edwards establishes a strong, negative relationship between average rate of growth of real GDP and real exchange-rate variability:

$$
\begin{array}{l}
\text{DYY} = \\
(2.17) \quad \underset{(1.036)}{1.898} \; - \; \underset{(-3.044)}{0.185 \; \text{VBRER}} \; + \; \underset{(3.261)}{0.194 \; \text{IGDP}} \; - \; \underset{(-0.895)}{0.043 \; \text{VTOT}} \quad (\text{Rsq} - 0.579),
\end{array}
$$

$$
\begin{array}{l}
\text{DYY} = \\
(2.18) \quad \underset{(1.120)}{2.244} \; - \; \underset{(-2.593)}{0.279 \; \text{VREER}} \; + \; \underset{(2.500)}{0.157 \; \text{IGDP}} \; - \; \underset{(-0.300)}{0.016 \; \text{VTOT}} \quad (\text{Rsq} = 0.532),
\end{array}
$$

where DYY is the average growth of real GDP, VREER and VBRER are the variability of the effective and bilateral real exchange rates, IGDP is the investment ratio, VTOT is the variability of terms of trade, and t-statistics are again in parentheses. "Variability" is calculated as the coefficient of variation of the real exchange rate and the terms of trade, respectively. The coefficients of the VBRER and VREER variables are negative and statistically significant. That of the real effective exchange rate in equation (2.18) is somewhat higher. Indeed, one would expect this more general multilateral measure of exchange-rate turbulence to be more important for real growth in LDCs after the Bretton Woods Agreement broke down, and the U.S. dollar began to float with respect to other major currencies such as marks and yen.

In the earlier, 1965–71 period, however, Edwards finds that this inverse relationship between exchange-rate variability and growth is much weaker:

$$
\begin{array}{l}
\text{DYY} = \\
(2.19) \quad \underset{(0.600)}{1.716} \; - \; \underset{(-0.747)}{0.091 \; \text{VBRER}} \; + \; \underset{(2.436)}{0.303 \; \text{IGDP}} \; - \; \underset{(-0.457)}{0.068 \; \text{VTOT}} \quad (\text{Rsq} = 0.306),
\end{array}
$$

$$
\begin{array}{l}
\text{DYY} = \\
(2.20) \quad \underset{(0.519)}{1.460 \; \text{P}} \; - \; \underset{(-0.681)}{0.086 \; \text{VREER}} \; + \; \underset{(2.428)}{0.310 \; \text{IGDP}} \; - \; \underset{(-0.383)}{0.056 \; \text{VTOT}} \quad (\text{Rsq} = 0.302).
\end{array}
$$

Although negative, the coefficients of the VBRER and VREER in equations (2.19) and (2.20) are no longer statistically significant. The lesser variability in exchange rates during 1965–71 could bias the regression coefficients of these imperfect proxies for exchange-rate variability toward zero. Then too, exchange-rate changes in LDCs under the Bretton Woods regime could have been more predictable and thus less damaging to economic growth.

Two other economically significant features of Edwards's empirical results stand out in the above equations.

First, variability in the LDCs' terms of trade, VTOT, did not systematically affect growth in either period. True, a sustained fall in the price of a key primary export can be very damaging in an individual LDC whose export mix is otherwise undiversified. But, compared with variance in the real exchange rate, fluctuations in the terms of trade (including the import price of oil) do not seem to strongly reduce growth. This distinction is important. The terms of trade are outside the control of the typical "small" LDC in question; whereas fluctuations in the real exchange rate are very much influenced—although perhaps not wholly determined—by its domestic financial policy, as we shall see in succeeding chapters.

Second, Edwards's independently constructed data for twenty-three countries show a sharp drop in the productivity of investment after 1973 similar to that found by Gelb. For example, in explaining output growth, the regression coefficient of IGDP drops from 0.310 in 1965–71 (equation [2.20]) to just 0.157 in 1978–85 (equation [2.18]). This spectacular drop in the average efficiency of investment, not quite the same as the incremental output/capital ratio used by Gelb, could in large measure be explained by indicators of increased *domestic* financial repression in the 1978–85 period, which Edwards does not consider. For example, in his thirty-four countries, Gelb found that the average real deposit rate of interest fell by 3 percentage points after 1973, thus helping to explain Edwards's findings of lower investment efficiency.

Similarly, including Edwards's calculations of the variability in the real exchange rate as an additional right-hand variable in Gelb's equations could further enhance the extent to which Gelb succeeded in "explaining" real output growth *and* variations in the quality (efficiency) of investment. The residual importance of, and need for, Gelb's SHIFT parameter across the two apparently dissimilar periods could be correspondingly reduced. If foreign exchange and domestic financial variables are used together, this more general empirical analysis could generate still more insight into how a loss of monetary control reduces economic growth in poor countries. But that remains an exercise for another time.[2]

2. There is a further problem in interpreting more recent interest-rate data from LDCs. Before 1985, the real deposit rate was, on average, inversely or negatively related to the degree of financial "repression." When governments imposed the inflation tax or tapped the banking system for officially designated finance, this tended to reduce the real yield to depositors so that the inflation tax was not associated with build-up of internal government debt. Whence the strength of Gelb's (1989) and Fry's (1988) regressions showing the strong positive relationship between the real deposit rate and economic growth.

In the late 1980s into the 1990s, there developed a new trend in Latin America—and perhaps elsewhere—where governments continued to tap the banking system for most of the available finance, but were now forced to pay a positive, and very high, real yield on outstanding debt to the banks (who passed it on to depositors) or to the nonbank public. In

CONCLUDING REMARKS

Even without this more general empirical model at hand, however, the importance of domestic price-level stability per se for increasing the productivity of
capital—both marginally and intramarginally—seems abundantly clear. Stable
prices permit greater domestic financial deepening and higher real deposit
rates while limiting risk (as will be shown in Ch. 3); and the liberalizing
government's task of stabilizing its real exchange rate is greatly simplified.
However, without any agreement among the advanced industrial countries to
maintain a common monetary standard, that is, to maintain stable exchange
parities among themselves, the authorities in other countries will continue to
experience more difficulty in stabilizing their real exchange rates and their
domestic price levels.

   This rather quick, some might say unduly econometric, overview of the
main cross-country empirical findings on how financial instability influences
the productivity of capital does not itself provide an immediate policy menu
for what needs to be done in any one country. In succeeding chapters, such
menus will be proposed within the specific institutional and historical contexts
of individual developing countries, socialist economies in transition, and even
more mature industrial economies. Getting the order of liberalization right in
each case is critically important.

   My purpose here has been to marshal the evidence from highly aggregated
cross-country studies to show that achieving financial liberalization, while
retaining monetary control, has a real payoff, even when the international
monetary system remains in some disarray. Stabilizing the domestic price
level without resorting to direct price controls and keeping deposit (and thus
lending) rates of interest sustainably positive in real terms while limiting
variance in the real exchange rate are crucial for successful economic development.

---

effect, the public could no longer be coerced into holding much in the way of depreciating
monetary assets. The result was a massive build-up of internal government debt within
LDCs, such as Argentina and Brazil, that crowded out productive investment (Parker 1989).
In these countries, very high real interest rates on deposits or internal government debt
have become directly or positively related to the degree of financial repression—and thus
negatively related to real economic growth.
   Hence, if the more recent and earlier data were to be pooled in the same simple regression
format, the economic implications would be difficult to intepret.

CHAPTER THREE

High Real Interest Rates:

Japan and Taiwan

versus

Chile

The broad cross-country studies reviewed in Chapter 2 establish the presumption that higher and positive real deposit rates of interest increase the quality of real capital formation and economic growth. Nevertheless, the particular combination of nominal interest and inflation rates that determines the real yield to depositors can make a big difference to economic performance.

If the price level is stable, higher real deposit rates of interest can be sustained with minimal risk. Indeed, robust real financial growth may be possible even when the government is intervening to set ceilings on deposit and loan rates of interest in the monetary system. On the other hand, when price inflation is high and unpredictable, having to offset it with high nominal interest rates can be very risky—particularly when interest rates are completely decontrolled and bank supervision is lax.

But these principles, and other important aspects of banking policy, are best seen in the context of individual country examples. In this chapter, we draw on the early postwar financial experience of Japan when per capita income was still low and compare it with the experiences of Taiwan and Chile a decade or more later.

FINANCIAL POLICY IN JAPAN, 1950–1970

Does the postwar Japanese experience support the case for financial liberalization with substantially positive real rates of interest? Starting with a very low per capita income after World War II, the Japanese economy grew very rapidly from the early 1950s to the early 1970s. Indeed, the Japanese now rather nostalgically refer simply to their "era of rapid economic growth." Moreover, Japan's high and rising ratio of money supply (M3) to gross national product (GNP) during this period (see Table 2.2) demonstrates robust real financial growth.

But, paradoxically, this era was and still is widely considered to be one of financial repression (using our more recent terminology). It was conventional wisdom that Japan was following a "low interest rate" policy in order to provide cheap bank credits, directed by government officials, to support officially sanctioned industrial investments. Interest ceilings in the form of standard loan and deposit rates were observed by all significant banks, and open market sales of corporate bonds and other debt instruments were limited and monitored by government officials. In the documents of the Bank of Japan and the Ministry of Finance, numerous references to administrative guidance could be construed as allocating the flow of most bank loans to officially preferred uses.

However, in his paper "The 'Low Interest Rate Policy' and Economic Growth in Postwar Japan," Akiyoshi Horiuchi (1984) provides a convincing alternative view that the Japanese financial system had not been significantly repressed after all. For the era of rapid economic growth, Horiuchi shows that officially controlled real interest rates in Japan were relatively high by international standards. Moreover, he argues that variability in the free interbank call money rate and in large compensating balances required of business borrowers meant that the effective loan rates charged Japanese industry fairly accurately reflected the true scarcity price of capital in the economy.

Tables 3.1, 3.2, and 3.3 simply reproduce Horiuchi's data comparing Japanese interest rates with those in the United States, United Kingdom, and West Germany. One can easily see that nominal interest rates on both the deposit and loan sides were generally higher in Japan from the early 1950s through 1972. And remember that the yen/dollar exchange rate was fixed from 1950 to 1970, so that nominal interest rates can be directly compared.

But whether "real" interest rates were higher depends strongly on which index is used to measure Japanese price inflation, that is, the opportunity cost of holding yen-dominated financial assets. If one uses the relatively rapidly increasing consumer price index (CPI) to deflate nominal interest rates, Table 3.1 shows that Japanese real interest rates were not so high and, on occasion, were even negative. However, if one uses the slowly growing wholesale price index (WPI) as the relevant deflator, Table 3.1 shows that Japanese real interest rates were relatively high: 4 to 5 percent on deposits and 6 to 7 percent on loans. And attractive real deposit rates are consistent with the enormous growth in the size of the Japanese banking system in the 1950s and 1960s. By 1970, when Japanese per capita income was still very low by American standards, M3 had grown to 86 percent of the Japanese GNP (Table 2.2), whereas U.S. M3/GNP was less than 70 percent.

Elsewhere (McKinnon 1973, 96–97; McKinnon, 1979b, 234–36), I have argued that the WPI, which represents claims on a wide range of (tradable) goods, is the better deflator. The CPI depends heavily on movements in the prices of domestically produced services that cannot be held directly in asset portfolios. In inflationary circumstances, the relevant alternative to holding yen-dominated financial assets is a portfolio of tangible goods (not intangible

TABLE 3.1
Official Discount Rates, Deposit Rates, and Money Market Rates
(Annual Average Percentage)

	1953–57	1958–62	1963–67	1968–72	1973–77	1978–82
Japan						
Discount rate	6.9	7.1	5.9	5.4	7.1	5.6
Call money rate	8.7	9.6	7.4	7.0	8.6	7.1
Deposit rate[a]	5.1	5.3	5.0	5.0	6.0	5.2
WPI rate of change	1.1	−1.0	1.4	1.3	11.4	5.1
CPI rate of change	3.1	3.6	5.6	5.9	13.1	4.6
United States						
Discount rate	2.4	3.1	4.2	5.2	6.5	11.0
Treasury bill rate	2.1	2.7	4.0	5.4	6.2	10.7
Deposit rate[b]	2.6	3.2	5.0	5.0	5.5	5.7
WPI rate of change	1.0	0.3	1.1	3.6	10.4	9.1
CPI rate of change	1.2	1.5	2.0	4.6	7.7	9.8
United Kingdom						
Discount rate	4.7	4.7	6.4	7.2	11.4	14.5[c]
Treasury bill rate	3.5	4.4	5.2	6.6	9.9	12.2
Deposit rate[d]	2.8	2.7	4.4	4.9	8.2	11.2
WPI rate of change	1.7	1.4	2.3	5.8	17.9	11.4
CPI rate of change	2.9	2.2	3.3	6.6	16.3	12.0
West Germany						
Discount rate	3.8	3.4	3.6	4.7	4.6	5.8
Call money rate	3.7	4.0	3.8	5.3	6.3	7.7
Deposit rate[e]	3.5	2.9	3.1	5.4	6.0	6.8
WPI rate of change	−0.5	0.5	0.9	2.6	6.2	5.4
CPI rate of change	0.9	2.0	2.7	3.5	5.7	5.8

[a]The interest rate on six-month deposits.

[b]The interest rate in time deposits less than U.S. $100,000 (maximum). From 1953 to 1967, the maximum rate on deposits of more than one year.

[c]1978–80. The Bank of England stopped announcing the minimum lending rate, that is, the discount rate.

[d]The interest rate on deposit accounts repayable at seven days' notice (maximum).

[e]The interest rate on three-month deposits (maximum).

Source: Horiuchi 1984.

services) or foreign exchange assets, which are a claim on foreign goods.[1] In Tables 3.2 and 3.3, Horiuchi recognizes this by using just the WPI to show that in the 1950s and 1960s, real loan rates in Japan were higher than in the United States and the United Kingdom and comparable to those prevailing in West Germany—another high-growth country.

Horiuchi goes on to show that the Japanese government was far less successful than is commonly believed in influencing the domestic flow of capital. The relatively small flow of government-directed cheap credit was largely allocated to "sunset," or declining, industries. Internationally competitive firms had no

1. From the well-known Scandinavian model of inflation, we can expect the CPI to increase rapidly when productivity growth is relatively high in tradables industries so that the relative cost of nontradable services increases continually through time—as was true in the case of Japan.

TABLE 3.2
International Comparison of Prime Rate
(Annual Average Percentage)

	Japan[a]		United States[b]		United Kingdom[c]		West Germany[d]	
1953–57	7.8	(1.1)	3.7	(1.0)	5.2	(1.7)	8.4	(−0.5)
1958–62	7.4	(−1.0)	4.5	(0.3)	5.2	(1.4)	7.9	(0.5)
1963–67	6.2	(1.4)	5.2	(1.1)	6.9	(2.3)	8.1	(0.9)
1968–72	5.7	(1.3)	6.7	(3.6)	7.7	(5.8)	9.5	(2.6)
1973–77	6.9	(11.4)	8.4	(10.4)	12.4	(17.9)	10.4	(6.2)
1978–82	6.0	(5.1)	15.2	(9.1)	14.6	(11.4)	11.3	(5.4)

Note: The numbers in parentheses are rates of changes in the WPI.
[a]Discount rate of commercial bills eligible for rediscount by the Bank of Japan (more than 3 million yen).
[b]The prime rate.
[c]The interest rate on overdrafts for the prime corporations.
[d]The maximum level of interest rate on overdrafts (until 1966). The interest rate on overdrafts of /DM 1 million or less (from 1967).
Source: Horiuchi 1984.

TABLE 3.3
Interest Rates on Bank Loans in Japan
(Annual Average Percentage)

	Loan Rates Covered by Formal Control: All Banks	Loan Rates Not Covered by Formal Control: All Banks	Rate of Change in WPI
1953–57	8.2	9.5	1.1
1958–62	7.6	8.9	1.0
1963–67	7.1	8.5	1.4
1968–72	6.9	8.2	1.3
1973–77	7.7	8.8	11.4
1978–82	6.6	7.9	6.1

Note: Ceilings were imposed on interest rates of short-term (less than a year) bank loans by the Temporary Interest Rate Adjustment Law (1947). Within the legal ceilings, the short-term loan rates were determined by a de facto cartel among the private banks. Though interest rates on other loans were exempted from the control, they also were determined by a type of cartel. The Japanese authorities can influence the decision making of these cartels.
Source: Horiuchi 1984.

trouble bidding for funds at close to the market rate of interest. In summary, in the era of Japan's rapid economic growth, the Japanese financial system was not significantly repressed.

But neither did the Japanese authorities fully liberalize their banking system by removing ceilings on deposit rates of interest, by allowing the standard loan rate charged to nonbanks to be unrestricted, or by allowing banks to borrow freely abroad. Nor did the central bank in any way abandon its close monitoring of what the commercial and savings banks were doing in terms of the safety of their asset portfolios. Because of fiscal surpluses and the absence of a significant market in government bonds, the Bank of Japan in the 1950s and into the 1960s was deeply involved in discounting a fairly large proportion of the commercial banks' portfolio of private loans—the famous "overloan" situation (Suzuki 1980). Overloan meant that the Japanese government, through the discount window of the Bank of Japan, lent back more to the private sector than it collected in the form of seigniorage—new issues of currency plus the buildup of commercial bank deposits with the central bank. Besides reflecting a high level of saving in the government sector, overloan greatly facilitated the central bank's monitoring of the quality and safety of loans to the private sector, even as the overall supply of loanable funds was increased.

From the late 1970s to the present time, the Japanese have greatly liberalized what their commercial banks can do in both foreign and domestic financial markets. Moreover, the Japanese government no longer runs fiscal surpluses, and the Bank of Japan now increases the monetary base through open-market purchases of government bonds. Thus the overloan situation has long since disappeared. But in assessing the quite different Latin American experiences below, what does the earlier Japanese experience in the 1950s and 1960s suggest for the correct order of financial liberalization?

1. The government did *not* tap the monetary system as a source of finance for itself. Quite the contrary, monetary seigniorage was funneled back through the banking system to increase the flow of bank lending to the private sector.

2. Monetary stabilization with a constant domestic price level, aided by a commitment to a stable nominal exchange rate, was the principal mode by which high real interest rates and high real financial growth were secured. The Japanese government was not put into a situation of having to permit (decide on) high nominal interest rates in order to offset high and variable domestic inflation.

3. Only after substantial financial deepening in the nonbank parts of the capital market (growth in primary securities trading and increased intermediation by finance and insurance companies, pension funds, and so on) did the authorities substantially loosen (or begin thinking about loosening) their restrictions on the actions of the commercial banks and other depository intermediaries whose deposits were implicitly or explicitly insured by the government.

4. The domestic banking system was never put in the situation of being the principal financial intermediary for significant amounts of net capital flows from abroad—with the attendant direct or indirect exchange risks. The limited foreign capital coming into Japan was in the form of direct investment, or more commonly, it took the form of company-to-company licensing agreements.

HIGH REAL INTEREST RATES IN TAIWAN

Through its price-level and interest-rate policies since 1960, Taiwan has promoted real financial growth more consistently than any other developing country. Beginning a decade later than Japan, Taiwan established a monetary

TABLE 3.4

Interest Rates and Inflation Rates in Taiwan (Percentages)

End of Year	At Banks			Curb-Market Unsecured Loan	Consumer Price Inflation
	Savings Deposit[a]	Unsecured Loan	Export Loan		
Average					
1956–62	17.0	20.9	11.2	41.1	8.4
1963–73	10.1	14.1	7.7	25.4	3.4
1974	13.5	15.5	9.0	29.3	47.5
1975	12.0	14.0	7.0	26.4	5.2
1976	10.7	12.7	7.0	27.6	2.5
1977	9.5	11.5	6.5	25.6	7.0
1978	9.5	11.5	6.5	27.2	5.8
1979	12.5	15.2	10.5	30.1	9.8
1980	12.5	16.2	10.5	31.3	19.0
1981	13.0	15.2	11.0	30.1	16.3
1982	9.0	10.7	8.2	27.7	3.3
1983	8.5	10.2	8.0	26.8	1.8
1984	8.0	10.0	7.7	29.9	1.7

[a]One-year savings deposits.

Sources: Cheng 1986; Central Bank of China (Taiwan, China), *Financial Statistics Monthly,* various issues; Council for Economic Planning and Development (Taiwan, China), *Taiwan Statistics Data Book, 1984,* June 1984.

policy that succeeded in eliminating domestic sources of inflationary pressure by 1960. From 1963 to 1973, Taiwan's dollar exchange rate was fixed, with consumer price inflation averaging about 3.4 percent per year (Table 3.4), and the wholesale price index was virtually stable. Subsequently, episodes of major inflation in 1974 and again in 1980–81—with irregular inflation in between—were mainly due to unsettled conditions in the international economy, in part associated with the two oil shocks.

Then, from 1982 to 1987, the CPI remained unchanged, while the WPI actually fell about 10 percent as Taiwan's currency appreciated somewhat against the U.S. dollar.[2] Hence, in the minds of Taiwanese savers, the threat of domestic inflation became negligible. Even though international inflation might hit the economy quite hard on occasion, as in 1974 and 1980–81, foreign exchange assets would not be much of a refuge in comparison to New Taiwan dollars.

To complement this remarkable control over the domestic price level, Taiwan has run with nominal interest rates which were and are high relative to Japan and other industrial countries. Table 3.4 shows that interest rates on a one-year savings deposit were kept at about 10 percent in the 1960s, when prices were stable, and then raised somewhat in the more inflationary 1970s, to be lowered again beginning in 1982, when the domestic WPI began to fall.

2. For the more recent data, see the Central Bank of China, *Financial Statistics* (compiled in accordance with the *International Financial Statistics* format), May 1988.

The incentives for Taiwanese savers to build up their claims on the domestic banking system were well maintained. Indeed, by 1985, Table 2.2 shows that Taiwan's M3/GNP was 126 percent, which was over six times that of the "typical" Latin American country shown in Table 2.1. The flow of private loanable funds to support domestic, and now foreign, investment has become enormous.

To support these high yields to depositors, standard loan rates were also kept high—about 2 to 3 percentage points higher than the standard interest rate on a one-year savings deposit—and were anywhere between 10 and 14 percent per year in normal noninflationary times. Although some financial repression existed in the form of preferential interest rates for exporters (Table 3.4), these rates were generally kept positive and substantial in real terms; nor was this commitment to finance exporters sufficient to undermine the central bank's control over the monetary base, unlike the Korean experience, to be discussed below.

In addition, a vigorous curb market remained an important marginal source of finance to those Taiwanese firms (or households) that might be arbitrarily denied bank credit. Competition among banks was limited if only because they were state-owned, and this, in effect, provided implicit deposit insurance. To further limit banks from undertaking unduly risky lending and vying for deposits, the government imposed standard (albeit high) ceilings on deposit and loan rates of interest. This created a large fringe of unsatisfied borrowers who could then bid for finance at interest rates of 25 percent or more (Table 3.4) in the curb market without impairing the safety of the monetary system.

But even in curb-market lending, the robustness of the monetary system remained important. The principal financial instrument, the promissory note from borrower to lender, was the postdated check. If the check on the state-owned bank bounced, the government could jail the borrower. In addition, the overall stability of the price level made such contractual arrangements more attractive to both borrowers and lenders at longer terms to maturity than in similar curb-market transactions in other developing countries.

Only in the early 1980s did the development of more conventional money market instruments—such as commercial bills, bankers' acceptances, or negotiable certificates of deposit—become significant. In order to bid for funds in competition with these money market instruments with variable interest rates, the commercial banks were progressively decontrolled and decentralized (Kohsaka 1987). In the longer term, financing by insurance and trust companies and new stock issues rose to more than marginal importance. Thus, only after almost two decades of remarkable financial deepening with price-level stability, did Taiwan finally loosen up its tight controls on what its banks could do.

To ensure the correct order of financial liberalization, how best might the Taiwanese financial system mature further? Further deregulation of the commercial banks is not only welcome but virtually unavoidable, although their risk-taking activities should remain limited in order to preserve the safety of the monetary system. However, the relative importance of the commercial banks and other institutions with publicly insured deposits should diminish. New higher yield and uninsured money market instruments in the "organized" capital market should gradually replace the curb market on the one hand (if tax laws are properly enforced) and the use of fixed-rate demand and savings deposits on the other. Longer-term bonds and mortgages should become more commonplace—along with new equity issues for riskier activities—if the government maintains a stable price level into the indefinite future.

PREMATURE FINANCIAL DECONTROL IN CHILE

Although measured and carefully delimited financial liberalizations have worked well in the cases of Japan and Taiwan, more sweeping attempts at financial decontrol have sometimes come to grief, as in Turkey, Sri Lanka, and the Southern Cone of Latin America in the 1970s and 1980s. It is worthwhile tracing one such experience.

In the late 1970s, all three countries in the Southern Cone—Argentina, Chile, and Uruguay—had substantially deregulated their banking systems before bringing inflation under control and achieving significant financial deepening. Indeed, all three countries suffered from substantial macroeconomic instability at the time that interest ceilings on bank deposits and loans were removed and banks were allowed to compete freely in the capital market.

Only Chile, however, had sufficient fiscal control to make price stabilization and financial liberalization a fully credible objective of public policy. Thus the Chilean experience with bank supervision from 1976 to 1982 is a somewhat clearer example of how uncontrolled interest rates might work when inflation is still very high and difficult to predict.

Price inflation started off at over 170 percent per year in 1976 before falling to less than 10 percent in 1981 and then rising again. Table 3.5 summarizes some extensive Chilean financial data provided by Rolf Luders (1985) on the extraordinary pattern of deposit and loan rates, both nominal and real, after most commercial banks had been returned to the private sector in 1976 and official interest ceilings had been removed. Two characteristics stand out.

The first is the very high real interest rate, calculated ex post on the basis of experienced inflation rather than on ex ante expectations of it. For example, in 1978 the "real" lending rate on peso loans was 42.2 percent on an annualized basis, although lending was typically much less than a year in duration. The net annualized spread between peso deposits and loans was about 10.7 percentage points, after taking out the effects of reserve requirements. To achieve these real yields, the nominal peso loan rate was 85.3 percent, albeit less than a quarter of what it had been in the more inflationary year of 1976.

TABLE 3.5
Interest Rates on Thirty-Day Bank Deposits and Loans in Chile
(Percentage per Annum)

	1976	1977	1978	1979	1980	1981	1982
Peso deposits							
Nominal	197.9	93.7	62.8	45.1	37.4	40.8	47.8
Real[a]	8.6	18.5	24.9	4.4	4.8	24.8	22.4
Peso loans							
Nominal	350.7	156.4	85.3	62.0	47.0	51.9	63.1
Real[a]	64.3	56.8	42.2	16.6	11.9	38.7	35.1
Gross spread	57.2	33.7	14.5	12.1	7.1	12.3	10.7
Net spread[b]	8.1	17.4	10.7	7.4	5.2	6.3	9.5
Interest differential[c]							
Peso/dollar deposits	2.9	7.9	0.0	8.7	14.0	19.5	−1.2
Peso/dollar loans[a]	48.9	36.4	8.6	14.1	17.1	24.3	5.6
Dollar deposits							
Nominal	8.9	8.9	11.1	13.5	15.1	17.8	14.6
Real[d]	−18.1	7.9	4.6	−5.8	12.3	7.6	40.0
Dollar loans							
Nominal	13.9	13.9	16.1	20.7	19.9	22.2	18.3
Real[d]	−14.3	12.9	9.3	0.1	−8.6	11.6	44.5
Change in consumer prices	174.3	63.5	30.3	38.9	31.2	9.5	20.7

Source: Luders 1985. Data taken from Central Bank of Chile, Sintesis Monetaria y Financiera.

[a]All real peso interest rates are calculated monthly, based on monthly changes in the Chilean CPI in pesos, before being annualized.

[b]Net spread after effects of compulsory non-interest-bearing reserve requirements against peso deposits are taken out.

[c]To calculate interest differential, nominal interest rates in dollars are first adjusted upward by the (experienced) rate of exchange devaluation.

[d]The real interest rate in dollars is

$$\frac{(1 + \text{nominal rate}) \ (1 + \text{devaluation rate})}{1 + \text{peso inflation rate}} - 1.$$

The second striking characteristic of Table 3.5 is the large spread between the apparent interest costs of borrowing in pesos compared with borrowing from domestic banks in dollars, which, after the deregulation of the mid-1970s, accounted for almost half of total bank loans (Luders 1985). Adjusted downward for the experienced rate of peso devaluation, this spread was as high as 48.9 percentage points in 1976 and then fell to a still high 8.6 percentage points in 1978 before increasing to 24.3 percentage points in 1981. It then fell sharply with the "surprise" devaluations in 1982. Indeed, often the "real" cost (adjusted for the domestic rate of price inflation less the rate of exchange devaluation) of borrowing in dollars was negative, even though real borrowing costs in pesos remained very high.

At the time, virtually everyone thought this difference was due to imperfections in financial arbitrage because of the remaining restrictions on foreign capital inflows. Indeed, this belief prompted the authorities to loosen capital restrictions even further in 1980—thus worsening the overborrowing syndrome. Corbo (1985) and Edwards and Edwards (1987) analyzed the unsustainable real appreciation of the Chilean peso, associated with the buildup of external debt in 1977–81, which led to a sharp decline in the profitability of the tradable goods sector.

Sadder but wiser, we now understand that these incredibly high interest rates on peso loans in large part represented the breakdown of proper financial supervision over the Chilean banking system. Neither officials in the commercial banks themselves nor government regulatory authorities adequately monitored the creditworthiness of a broad spectrum of industrial and agricultural borrowers: "The internal source of difficulty in Chile was a proliferation of bad loans within the banking system. The rolling over of these loans, capitalising interest along the way, created what I call a 'false' demand for credit, which, when added to the demand that would normally be viable, allowed real interest rates to reach unprecedented (and, to many, incredible) levels" (Harberger 1985, 237).

This form of Ponzi game, however, had a peculiarly international flavor in that Chilean financial intermediaries, not only banks, incurred exchange risk as they extended bad loans. James Tybout (1986) and others have shown that the large economic groups, the so-called Grupos, used their control over domestic banks together with their overseas contracts to get dollar credits at relatively low interest rates to relend at the extremely high interest rates denominated in pesos to borrowers of dubious creditworthiness.

Because banks were officially restricted from directly assuming foreign exchange exposure, they simply made dollar loans to the Grupos' industrial companies, which then did most of the ongoing lending in pesos. Thus, by assuming the foreign exchange risk themselves, these Grupos continued to show increases in their nonoperating earnings in 1980 and 1981, well after their operating earnings had soured because of the exchange overvaluation and continued high interest rates. Some were recording unrealized capital gains, from some very dubious assets, as earnings on their books.

Of course, many Chilean firms need not have known at the time that they were engaged in a Ponzi game. Many probably suffered from excessive optimism regarding future asset values and rates of return—hopes that were ultimately dashed by the real exchange rate overvaluation and downturn in the international economy in 1981–82 that led to massive losses by firms across the export- and import-competing sectors. The resulting series of defaults on outstanding bank credits—including those to the large Grupos—forced bankruptcy on virtually all of Chile's financial intermediaries.

In 1982–83, the Chilean banks were all renationalized in order to protect the positions of domestic depositors and foreign creditors, even though the government had not previously committed itself to deposit insurance. In a similar set of bankruptcies in Argentina, official deposit insurance had been explicitly in place. Nevertheless, the outcome in the two countries was the same. The special position of the banks—as the custodians of the nation's money supply—effectively meant that the depositors and the banks could behave ex ante as if their deposits would be insured in the event some major financial breakdown occurred.

REPRESENTATIVE INTEREST RATES FOR SUSTAINING FINANCIAL GROWTH

What are the lessons to be learned from the rather cautious approach to bank regulations in Japan and Taiwan in comparison to the Southern Cone experiences with complete decontrol? Obviously, stability in the domestic price level is a necessary condition for achieving high real financial growth without undue risk of some major financial panic and collapse.

When general macroeconomic and price-level instability is pronounced, the use of extremely high nominal rates of interest to offset anticipated inflation and to balance the supply and demand for loanable funds in the capital market becomes necessary to limit the lack of intermediation from the banking system. But high price inflation is always unpredictable inflation. Thus, as inflation and nominal interest rates increase, the real interest rate realized ex post facto becomes increasingly uncertain. This increase in risk can then induce greater adverse risk selection (in the sense of Stiglitz and Weiss 1981) of borrowers from the banks as less-reliable loan applicants come forward. Similarly, potential moral hazard in the deposit-taking commercial banks—whose monetary liabilities are implicitly or explicitly insured by the government—becomes more acute. The uncomfortable interaction between adverse risk selection and moral hazard will be analyzed in more detail in Chapter 7.

Here it suffices to note that when such macroeconomic instability is pronounced, deposit-taking commercial banks have to be particularly tightly monitored and regulated—likely with lower real deposit and loan rates (albeit still positive) in comparison to situations when the price level is stable. Some degree of "financial repression" coupled with credit rationing may be warranted. Indeed, in the 1950s, when Taiwan had high and variable inflation that was more or less successfully offset by high and variable nominal interest rates, the commercial banks were state-owned and did not compete much among themselves.

Suppose, however, that the domestic price level (as measured by the WPI) is successfully stabilized, as it was in Japan after 1951 and in Taiwan after 1960. In similar liberalizing but capital-short economies, what are representative real deposit and loan rates for which governments should aim in order to sustain high real financial growth while limiting undue risk taking by domestic banks? On a representative intermediate-term deposit, the standard interest rate (nominal and real) in both countries was about 5–9 percent, and the corresponding loan rates varied between 7 and 14 percent, with Japan at the lower, and Taiwan at the higher, end of these scales. However, the effective Japanese loan rate may well have been substantially higher, closer to 10 percent, once compensating balances that borrowers commonly held with the lending banks are taken into account. Such rules of thumb for nominal interest rates seem applicable to other liberalizing economies whose price levels are stable and whose governments need not tap their own banking systems for cheap finance.

CHAPTER FOUR

Instruments

of

Financial Repression

U sing credit subsidies to promote the immediate goals of the development plan is a seductive idea for less-developed countries (LDCs). The minister of finance is usually hard-pressed to raise revenue to directly subsidize this or that production activity by outright grants. Tariffs and other restrictions on foreign trade to protect such industries have been effectively criticized on grounds of economic inefficiency. Moreover, in LDCs the central bank is often under the direct control of the minister of finance or other important economics ministers in the cabinet. Thus selective credit subsidies to favored borrowers on an industry-by-industry or firm-by-firm basis are easy to administer, as we shall see below for Nicaragua from the 1980s to the present.

This mode of intervention, quite typical of the semi-industrial LDCs, is well illustrated by the case of Colombia in the early 1970s, which has changed little down to the early 1990s. Figure 4.1 provides an oversimplified sketch of the flow of funds from savers to investors in the Colombian banking system. The flow depicted is typical of that found in most other developing countries. Three characteristics stand out: high reserve requirements, specialized credit agencies, and interest ceilings on deposits and loans.

1. High reserve requirements: In Colombia in 1972 (with the situation being qualitatively much the same in the early 1990s), the commercial banks kept 31 percent of their deposits as non-interest-bearing reserves with the central bank, and another 26 percent of their loan portfolio was directly specified by the central authorities. Similarly, the savings banks kept 25 percent of their deposits in non-interest-bearing reserves, whereas another 44 percent of their deposits had to be placed in low-yield (6 percent) housing bonds. This Colombian pattern of high "reserve" requirements is typical of the other Latin American countries, as shown in Table 5.1 (in the following chapter), but is not typical of the advanced industrial economies, where reserve requirements were closer to 6 or 7 percent of the deposit base of the commercial banks in the 1970s (and are even less today).

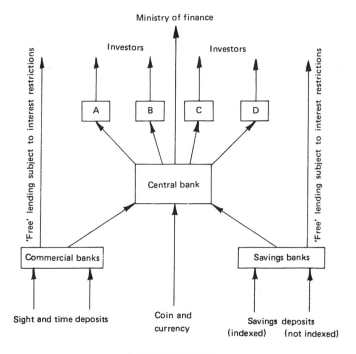

PRIMARY SAVERS

Note: A, B, C, D, and so on are specialized credit agencies (banks) that get cheap finance from the central bank. A could be the export promotion fund; B, the agricultural bank; C, the central mortgage bank; and D, the industrial development bank.

FIGURE 4.1. Bank Intermediation in a Typical Semi-industrial LDC

2. Specialized credit agencies: With this very substantial resource flow at its disposal, the central bank channels cheap credit to various specialized banking agencies (A, B, C, etc., in Fig. 4.1), which in turn lend at low disequilibrium rates of interest for export promotion, credit for small farmers, industrial projects the government wishes to subsidize, and so forth. Because the government has very detailed credit allocations in mind that can vary on a week-to-week basis, these agencies decentralize the potentially huge administrative burden. Central-bank credits can also flow directly to the ministry of finance (shown in Fig. 4.1) to cover deficits in the government's own budget.

3. Interest ceilings on deposits and loans: In Colombia, the standard commercial lending rate of interest on the "free" part of the bank's portfolio normally had a 14–16 percent official ceiling, with interest ceilings on loans as high as 22 percent if banks obtained funds by selling certificates of deposit to firms and households. On the other hand, the specialized credit agencies (A, B, C, D, etc., in Fig. 4.1) were required to lend for predesignated uses with interest rates starting as low as 2–4 percent.

For the holders of monetary assets, the nominal yield on sight (demand) deposits was kept at zero, and savings deposits for small depositors carried a low, 5–8 percent interest coupon. A few firms and households could buy certificates of deposit at much higher nominal rates of interest if they met the extremely large minimum deposit requirements.

Between 1970 and 1973 in Colombia, the annual rate of inflation in the wholesale price index (WPI) was of the order of 18 percent. Thus in terms of maintaining the capital value of their savings, those households receiving an 8 percent nominal yield would be getting minus 10 percent as the "real" yield. Those savers holding sight deposits or non-interest-bearing coin and currency would be receiving minus 18 percent as their "real" yield. Moreover, recipients of credit from the subsidized special agencies would receive an unrequited gift insofar as the rate of inflation exceeded their low nominal borrowing costs.

In a repressed and therefore small financial system, where the money supply (M3) was only 23 percent of gross national product (GNP) in Colombia in the 1970s (Table 2.1), the paradoxical proliferation of specialized credit agencies is worth further examination. As of 1972, Colombia had seven of these specialized credit institutions directly under the control of the central bank. In addition, many industrial financieras (finance companies) and specially designated institutions for buying home mortgages were authorized to borrow from deposit-collecting banks at less-than-market rates of interest. Chile in the late 1960s had many similar institutions, but the government also owned a large "commercial" bank, Banco del Estado, that had unlimited discount privileges with the central bank in order to finance politically designated credits in agriculture, industry, or housing. Every country, as with the farm credit loan program in the United States, tends to evolve a somewhat different institutional format for directing the flow of cheap credits to officially designated preferred users.

Besides being expensive to administer, this elaborate institutional structure, within which many agencies have predetermined discount privileges with the central bank, can make control over the monetary base next to impossible. At the margin, however, there is continual pressure on the government to create even more such agencies. With so many already in existence, why should this pressure exist?

Because of the diversion of their resources to the central bank, commercial bankers are prevented from making an adequate capital market for channeling funds into socially profitable investments. There is always a large queue of "worthy" unsatisfied borrowers. Moreover, with the interest rate restrictions, the system is very rigid in the sense that newcomers with potentially productive investment opportunities cannot bid funds away from the existing (subsidized) users. Thus, serious new gaps in the provision of credit continually develop, from the leasing of industrial equipment to fertilizer distribution. Politically sensitive authorities respond by commissioning additional specialized credit agencies to satisfy these new needs. But these new agencies drain even more resources from the regulated commercial banks and savings institutions either by borrowing from them directly or by having automatic rediscount privileges with the central bank (see Fig. 4.1). Repression in the rest of the financial system is thereby worsened even as monetary control is further undermined.

Nevertheless, at the margin and taking the existing repressed financial system as given, the social cost of creating one more special credit agency may be worthwhile if the perceived gap to be filled is sufficiently important at the microeconomic level. Because there is no open organized capital market for "worthy" borrowers, the government may be forced to open up new specially designated credit lines when new claimants come forward. Thus does financial repression feed on itself.

ECONOMIC PARALYSIS FROM DIRECTED CREDIT SUBSIDIES: NICARAGUA IN THE 1980s AND EARLY 1990s

Beyond displacing projects yielding potentially higher returns, and encouraging the bureaucratic proliferation of various credit-gathering agencies, are there further economic consequences from directing subsidized credits to particular uses and users?

Extreme cases can sometimes be instructive. From 1980 into 1991, farm credit in Nicaragua was essentially given away by not requiring effective repayment of direct or indirect bank debts. Commercial banks were nationalized and state trading companies were set up to purchase agricultural crops and sell inputs to farmers. These institutions then provided credit for the production, storage, and marketing of all the significant crops: coffee, cotton, cattle, beans, rice, and so on. Because continuing near hyperinflation sharply reduced the real purchasing power of the cordoba from one week to the next, loans fixed in terms of cordobas at one point in time (with a modest nominal interest rate) became virtually costless in real terms when repaid in nominal cordobas some months later. In addition, even nominal agricultural debts were forgiven outright in April 1990. In late 1990, subsequent attempts to index agricultural loans to the U.S. dollar (to offset the continuing devaluation of the cordoba) led to outright nonrepayment. Unsurprisingly, moral hazard in bank lending had become so pronounced that farmers treat(ed) credit as a welfare payment rather than as a commercial transaction.

But more is involved than a simple, albeit massive, transfer payment (financed by the continuing inflation tax) to Nicaraguan farmers. There will always be excess demand for credit if it doesn't have to be repaid—or if real lending rates of interest are negative. Thus the Nicaraguan government had to develop narrow bureaucratic guidelines to establish credit eligibility for each crop: acreage planted, purchases of intermediate inputs, estimates of final output, and so on. Farmers can only collect the subsidy if they stay within these guidelines, stick with their traditional crop, and produce with prescribed dependence on domestic and foreign inputs for which specific credits are given.

Some crops, say cotton, may look quite unprofitable if output prices are directly compared to (unsubsidized) input prices. Nevertheless, many farmers still decide to produce cotton because it is the surest way of qualifying for their "gift of credit." In addition, they may grossly overuse pesticides and fertilizer inputs because the credit subsidies are tied to the purchase of these inputs. Much agricultural land in cotton in Nicaragua appears to have been contaminated by the overuse of herbicides tied to credit subsidies.

Aside from distortions in particular crops, however, there is a general paralysis in embarking on new crops or methods of production. Before planting, farmers don't want to change what crop they produce and how they produce it for fear of losing their eligibility for the free gift of credit. Once a crop cycle begins, actual planting or harvesting is seriously impeded if credit is not made available as expected, so tremendous pressure is imposed on the government to actually provide the credit even though it is highly inflationary. Lacking any substantial deposit base of their own because of the continuing high inflation, the nationalized commercial banks simply discount their agricultural loans (borrow from) the Nicaraguan central bank—thus accounting for much of the excessive issue of base money. (Besides this "unofficial" fiscal deficit from financing credit subsidies through the banking system to agriculture, the official deficit appearing in the formal government accounts was an equally important drain on the central bank from the 1980s into the 1990s.)

As a capital market, the current system is a complete failure. Credit subsidies to much of the agricultural sector and some of the industrial sector keep many inefficient firms and farms in business. Even the development of potentially efficient enterprises is seriously hampered because all farms distort the nature of their operations in order to qualify for credit subsidies. Moreover, these credit subsidies are treated as claims on consumption rather than as a basis for real capital formation. Despite massive farm credit subsidies for the last decade, there has been no lasting real investment. In the early 1990s, most observers of the Nicaraguan economic scene complain about the decapitalization and run down of the country's agricultural infrastructure. This is consistent with the sharp decline in Nicaraguan real GNP over the past decade, and with exports falling to less than one-quarter of the level they had reached in the 1970s.[1]

1. A number of other distortions imposed on the Nicaraguan economy in the 1980s also contributed to this economic decline. But this is not the place to provide a complete analysis of Nicaragua's current economic predicament, nor its historical origins. Suffice it to note

CENTRAL BANK FINANCING OF GOVERNMENT DEFICITS

Last but not least in contributing to financial repression, the state of the government's regular budget and its need for debt finance should also be considered. Having no recourse to organized open markets in primary securities, the government may also impose heavy "reserve" requirements against deposits in commercial and savings banks to force these institutions to buy low-interest government bonds in a noninflationary manner. (The optimal "reserve tax" for minimizing inflation is discussed in Ch. 5.)

If reserve requirements are already high, the failure of the government in an LDC to cover further expenditures by taxation often means that government bonds must be sold to the central bank and directly monetized. That is, government bonds can no longer be forcibly "placed" with the commercial banks or other deposit-taking intermediaries by yet higher reserve requirements. The resulting price inflation reduces real rates of interest perceived by potential depositors (savers). Realized private financial saving falls, contracting the flow of loanable funds and reducing productive investment and possibly employment.

INFLATION AND THE RESERVE REQUIREMENTS OF COMMERCIAL BANKS: A PARTIAL-EQUILIBRIUM ANALYSIS

Before analyzing how to get out of this syndrome of financial repression if and when a fiscal improvement makes that possible, let us first analyze how higher price inflation coupled with high reserve requirements interact to determine relative deposit and loan rates of interest in commercial banks. Suppose initially that usury restrictions are absent so that interest rates are free to adjust in some kind of competitive equilibrium. Suppose further that the overall rate of price inflation—actual and expected—is exogenously determined so that interest-rate adjustment in the commercial banking system can be analyzed in partial equilibrium. (Reverse causation—from interest rates and reserve requirements to the rate of inflation—is considered in Ch. 5.) I will show that the relationship between the real lending rate of interest and the nominal rate of inflation is strong and positive and that the relationship between inflation and the real deposit rate of interest is negative.

Let π be the actual and expected rate of price inflation, that is $\dot{P}/P$, where P is the relevant general price index (such as the WPI, as discussed in Ch. 3) that depositors and borrowers use in determining their real returns. Let i_d be the average nominal deposit rate of interest offered by the banking system across all classes of deposits (including checking accounts) at all maturities.

---

that the program of directed credit subsidies in agriculture was a major factor in the decline— and that subsidized farm credit is commonplace in much of the developing world.

Similarly, let i_l be the representative nominal loan rate charged to all classes of borrowers. Then the "real" deposit rate, r_d, and the real loan rate, r_l, are

(4.1) $$r_d = i_d - \pi, \quad \text{and} \quad r_l = i_l - \pi.$$

Consider the consequences of high and uniform reserve requirements against all deposits that siphon potential loanable funds out of the commercial loan market. An (average) reserve requirement of k percent, where $0 < k < 1$, is imposed on all deposits, D, such that private loans, L, are only $(1 - k)$ percent of the deposit base:

(4.2) $$L = (1 - k)D.$$

Suppose this reserve requirement is non-interest-bearing so that k percent of commercial bank assets earn no return. Even with no official interest ceilings or other usury restrictions, the reserve requirement forces the commercial banks to substantially reduce deposit rates of interest and raise loan rates, thus contracting the flow of loanable funds. Somewhat surprisingly, the amount of contraction depends heavily on the rate of price inflation even when nominal rates of interest can be freely adjusted to take inflation into account!

To see this in sharpest relief, assume further that the deposit-taking banks operate with zero profits: current earnings from loans are fully paid out to depositors.[2] This zero-profit condition is reflected in equation (4.3), where the nominal interest rate paid out to depositors is just $(1 - k)$ of that received from borrowers per dollars (peso) lent:

(4.3) $$i_l = \frac{i_d}{1 - k}.$$

To recast this zero-profit condition in terms of real interest rates, subtract π from each side of equation (4.3) and substitute $(r_d + \pi)$ for i_d to get

(4.4) $$r_l = \frac{r_d}{1 - k} + \frac{\pi k}{1 - k}.$$

Equation (4.4) indicates that the amount by which the real loan rate exceeds the real deposit rate is an increasing function of k, π, and r_d. In particular, for

2. These assumptions that commercial banks break even, and that their loans not exceed their deposit base less required reserves, are much more constraining than those under which the Nicaraguan banks operated as discussed above. In Nicaragua, the nationalized commercial banks were not limited by their deposit base, which hardly existed because of the hyperinflation; instead, the commercial banks simply discounted all their agricultural loans with the central bank.

TABLE 4.1

Rates of Interest with a 50 Percent Reserve Requirement on Commercial Banks

On Deposits			On Loans	
i_d	r_d		i_l	r_l
		10 Percent Expected Inflation		
+0	−10	....	+10	0
+10	0	....	+20	+10
+15	+5	....	+30	+20
+20	+10	....	+40	+30
		20 Percent Expected Inflation		
0	−20	....	0	−20
+5	−15	....	+10	−10
+10	−10	....	+20	0
+15	−5	....	+30	+10
+20	0	....	+40	+20
+25	+5	....	+50	+30

Note: The quantities i_d and i_l are nominal rates of interest, and r_d and r_l are real rates that are calculated by subtracting the expected rate of inflation from the respective nominal rates of interest. The calculations assume the banks are making zero profits.

a given real deposit rate, r_d, and reserve requirement, k, the second term on the right-hand side of equation (4.4) shows that the *real* loan rate must increase with the rate of inflation.

Putting it another way, if nominal interest rates on deposits are always scaled upward to reflect π, then the wedge between deposit and loan rates of interest will increase with π. As inflation increases, banks are forced to pay a higher nominal interest rate on deposits in order to maintain their real deposit base. Because of the non-interest-bearing reserve requirement, however, the loan rate must increase even more for the banks to continue to break even. Thus, when these nominal interest rates are free to adjust, inflation increases the wedge between deposit and lending rates of interest. To see this wedge effect algebraically, subtract the real deposit rate from both sides of equation (4.4) to get

$$(4.5) \qquad r_l - r_d = \frac{r_d k}{1 - k} + \frac{\pi k}{1 - k} = i_l - i_d.$$

For any given r_d, the wedge between deposit and loan rates increases with k and with π. And the effect is multiplicative. The higher the reserve tax k, the greater the effect of inflation in increasing the wedge between deposit and loan rates.

This fundamental nexus among reserve requirements, nominal and real interest rates, and the rate of price inflation is illustrated in Table 4.1, from which the following example is drawn. Suppose that $k = 0.5$ and $\pi = 0.10$ (10 percent per year); then, if the real deposit rate is 5 percent, the real loan rate must be 20 percent. When inflation increases to 20 percent, however, the *real* loan rate must increase to 30 percent if the real deposit rate of 5 percent is to be maintained and the commercial banks are still constrained to break even.

The moral of our story is clear. The burden of a given reserve requirement k on the flow of loanable funds depends directly on the rate of price inflation even when no other interest restrictions exist. If k is high and inflation is high, the gap between deposit and loan rates must be enormous, reflecting the proportionately greater seigniorage that is being extracted from the banking system. The high non-interest-bearing reserves of the commercial banks are essentially the base on which the inflation tax is levied, and the system of intermediation by commercial banks in LDCs is very sensitive to the rate of inflation that the authorities select.

A rather extreme example of this point is provided by the Chilean attempts to liberalize their banking system during the mid-1970s, as shown in Table 3.5 and discussed earlier in Chapter 3 and in McKinnon (1977). In 1976, conventional usury restrictions on time deposits and loans were completely abolished, but high reserve requirements were retained on the deposit banks and financieras, and price inflation continued out of control at over 100 percent per annum. Although the banking system was reasonably competitive, the spread between real deposit and lending rates in pesos was 4 percentage points per month for most of 1976. Because real deposit rates of interest were less than 1 percent per month, the real bank lending rate of interest was of the order of 60–70 percent per annum—a level so high that it astonished all outside observers! Needless to say, the real flow of *productive* bank loans made during this period was a mere trickle; and severe adverse risk selection at the high interest rates greatly increased the proportion of noncreditworthy borrowers, as described in Chapter 3.

Finally, one should say a word about the other class of distortions—direct ceilings or usury restrictions on deposit and/or loan rates of interest—and how they interact with reserve requirements when inflation is present. One example should suffice.

Suppose that a 50 percent reserve requirement in the presence of 10 percent inflation—and no formal interest ceilings—led to a 5 percent real deposit rate (15 percent nominal) and a 20 percent real loan rate, as in the third row of Table 4.1. Now impose a ceiling on nominal deposit rates of interest of just 10 percent so that the real deposit rate falls to zero. With banks regulated to just break even, the second row in Table 4.1 shows that the real loan rate falls to 10 percent so that the wedge is reduced by 10 percentage points. But the opportunity cost of using such interest ceilings to limit the wedge and real loan rates in the presence of high reserve requirements is to drive the real deposit rate below market-clearing levels and create a shortage of loanable funds: an excess demand for loans. The real size of the banking system then shrinks.

Suppose we now allow banks to earn positive profits—and to hold free reserves against possible defaults. This would add another 3 or more percentage points to the wedge between deposit and loan rates. Then real deposit rates can feasibly be kept only in the 5–9 percent range and real loan rates in the 10–14 percent range (inclusive of compensatory balances), suggested in Chapter 3 for sustaining high real financial growth without undue adverse risk selection, if both (non-interest-bearing) reserve requirements and price inflation are reduced to very modest levels.

DILEMMAS IN FINANCIAL POLICY IN THE LIBERALIZING ECONOMY

A rather acute choice between best and second-best policies faces government authorities eager to eliminate financial repression and promote rapid growth in the flow of loanable funds in the semi-industrial LDCs. If one takes the general character of the repressed financial system (including high and variable inflation) as given, then various second-best microeconomic policies, as were implicit in the above analysis, suggest themselves. New credit agencies, perhaps with special discount privileges, may be necessary to cover obvious credit gaps not being served by the regular banking system. The authorities may have to work with independently wealthy private capitalists or foreign firms in promoting new projects. A certain tolerance for possible extralegal activities in the inevitable black market for loans might seem wise. A variety of other ad hoc decisions by the planning authorities to divert funds from the rather constipated financial system to support this or that enterprise may have some chance of improving resource allocation when considered one at a time. But savers in the deposit banks would be left with low or negative real yields.

The best policy, however, would be to stabilize the price level and eliminate reserve "taxes" on the commercial banks. In the order of liberalization, this of course is likely to entail a prior massive improvement in fiscal policy, including the phasing out of all credit subsidies. The banks would still be carefully regulated toward safety—with modest required prudential reserves of say 5 percent of deposits and a carefully monitored loan portfolio. As long as the domestic capital market was immature with uncertain credit standards among potential bank borrowers, however, the government could still set standard rates of 8–9 percent on intermediate-term deposits and 10–14 percent on loans, as Taiwan did. The M3/GNP ratio would rise as depositors, rather than the government, received the higher yield earned on bank loans. The real credit flow through the banking system would increase in the mode of the rapidly growing economies portrayed in Table 2.2.

At the microeconomic or institutional level, however, success with this optimal policy requires the government to move on a broad front in the *opposite* direction from the second-best strategy. Instead of commissioning more special credit agencies and new banks, the authorities must be prepared to withdraw the hundreds of subventions, interest regulations, and special credit facilities or foreign exchange allotments that already influence the microeconomic allocation of investment resources in the economy. Old government bureaucracies for funneling credit or foreign exchange to industry or agriculture would have to be dismantled. In particular, government ministers would have to give up their seats on the board of the central bank and allow discount policy and foreign exchange policy, along with fledgling open-market operations, to be run by a largely independent board whose mandate was to stabilize the domestic price level while remaining largely "neutral" regarding the ordinary flow of credit in the domestic capital market. Of course, the newly restructured central bank would remain a classic lender of last resort in avoiding systemwide financial panics.

An important element in such a successful reform is to have the commercial banks and related institutions—with newly reduced reserve requirements— move aggressively to provide high-interest loans to well-diversified segments of industry and agriculture whose special credit lines and other interest subsidies have been phased out. But these deposit-collecting banks may have little experience in aggressively seeking out borrowers who can pay high real yields on their loans, yields that accurately reflect high social productivity of the investments they are undertaking. Indeed, the whole process of seeking out small and innovative entrepreneurs in industry and agriculture outside the urban enclaves may be quite foreign to the banking system's previous experience— particularly in the socialist economies analyzed in Chapters 11 and 12. Then, in the initial stages of the transition to a more open capital market, reliance on nonbank sources of finance and on self-finance might well be preferred (Ch. 11).

In the transition to a more competitive banking system, another rather acute short-run problem may arise. As interest rates on deposits and loans increase and *new* unencumbered commercial banks are allowed to begin operations, the older commercial banks may face a serious bankruptcy threat. "Old" loans will bear rates of interest that had been artificially depressed (Mathieson 1979) and the term to maturity of the banks' loan portfolios is typically longer than that of their deposits. New entrants would have an artificial competitive advantage in not having such a burden of old low-yield loans. However, the liberalizing monetary authority can take offsetting administrative action: until they mature, old low-yield loans can be assumed by the state, or they can be used for credit against the (declining) reserve requirements of the bank that owns them. In effect, the "old" commercial banks may have to be completely recapitalized. In the initial stages of liberalization, therefore, licensing a host of new domestic or foreign banks to enter the newly opened domestic capital market could be a mistake.

Small borrowers pose particular difficulties as credit applicants. Their real borrowing rates need be of the order of 18–24 percent or even higher in order for the banks to cover their administrative costs and still pay depositors an attractive return that properly reflects the opportunity costs of scarce capital in the economy (Donald 1976, 32). Indeed, large commercial banks may be the wrong institutions for small-scale loans, and an informal credit market that includes rural credit cooperatives, the factoring of ordinary trade credits, and traditional moneylending could well remain important for many years, as in the Taiwanese example discussed in Chapter 3. Nevertheless, by having commercial banks provide attractively liquid and high-yield *deposits* to farmers and small urban enterprises, including households, their self-financed investment activities can become much more productive right at the outset of the liberalization process.

CHAPTER FIVE

The Inflation Tax,

Monetary Control

and Reserve Requirements

on Commercial Banks

In the previous chapter examining the instruments of financial repression, the rate of price inflation was simply taken as given. It interacted with interest ceilings or reserve requirements to reduce real deposit rates of interest and to slow real financial growth. In this chapter, the rate of inflation is an endogenous variable that the authorities at the central bank do their best to minimize given the fiscal needs of the rest of government.

We consider the problem of macroeconomic control when an uncovered fiscal deficit exists that makes some financial repression inevitable. Government expenditures, including credit subsidies, exceed revenues. Because a significant open market in primary securities does not exist, the government cannot sell treasury bonds or bills directly to the public. Instead, the government extracts seigniorage—implicit tax revenue from the financial system—by the issue of base money. Reserve requirements on the banks and inflation interact to tax the holders of money and near monies—and to tax borrowers from the domestic banks through higher real loan rates.

Conventional models of the inflation tax and the extraction of noninflationary seigniorage, such as Friedman's (1971) seminal analysis, assume a single homogeneous demand function for non-interest-bearing base money—whether it be coin and currency or official reserves held by the banking system. The flow of loanable funds through the commercial banking system is not explicitly considered in Friedman's analysis. In contrast, here I distinguish two forms of the demand for base money: for currency held by households (and firms) and for commercial (and savings) bank reserves held with the central bank.

In less-developed countries (LDCs) with repressed financial systems, official reserve requirements are relatively important in comparison to direct holdings of coin and currency by the nonbank public. Table 5.1 indicates that official reserve requirements against deposits typically averaged over 30 percent in Latin America. But as our analysis of Colombia in Chapter 4 made clear, this

TABLE 5.1
Effective Reserve Ratios on Bank Deposits

	1971	1972	1973	1974	1975	1976	1977	1978	1979	1980
United States	7.8	6.7	6.6	6.6	6.7	5.3	5.2	5.4	5.2	4.6
West Germany	10.3	12.5	12.3	11.8	10.2	10.8	10.2	10.5	10.5	8.7
United Kingdom	5.3	6.1	9.6	7.2	6.9	8.4	6.6	5.4	5.4	2.8
Chile	52.0	57.1	55.8	37.2	35.9	60.7	54.3	41.3	33.1	28.2
Uruguay	32.5	30.9	34.9	33.2	35.9	34.5	37.2	29.5	15.3	11.9
Mexico	20.7	47.8	50.6	65.8	79.2	31.2	52.5	50.0	50.5	51.4
Colombia	33.1	30.4	32.3	29.7	29.3	31.5	34.3	48.6	52.2	45.2
Brazil	34.4	28.3	30.2	20.4	28.4	32.7	34.7	32.5	36.2	33.4

Sources: Brock 1982 (for 1971–73: IMF, *International Financial Statistics,* September 1978; for 1974–80: ibid., September 1981).

Note: The effective reserve ratio is calculated using the formula $(14 - 14a)/(34 + 35 - 14a)$, where 14, 14a, 34, and 35 refer to *IFS* line numbers of total reserve money, currency held outside banks, money, and quasi-money, respectively. The effective reserve ratio expresses legal reserves as a percentage of total bank deposits (both sight and time deposits).

TABLE 5.2
Currency as a Percentage of the Monetary Base

	1971	1972	1973	1974	1975	1976	1977	1978	1979	1980
United States	60.1	62.7	62.0	64.5	66.0	68.6	68.8	68.0	68.9	71.3
West Germany	51.7	46.4	44.8	49.2	52.6	51.1	52.7	52.6	52.4	57.2
United Kingdom	80.3	75.3	61.4	68.6	71.5	67.8	73.8	77.7	77.0	85.2
Chile	40.9	46.7	30.9	34.8	38.1	32.3	32.0	35.7	38.1	39.3
Uruguay	69.7	66.7	63.2	61.1	50.2	45.6	37.1	38.3	53.0	56.9
Mexico	65.5	46.7	45.6	40.7	37.3	62.3	28.2	28.9	27.9	26.8
Colombia	55.6	56.7	50.1	52.7	55.2	53.9	54.1	46.3	45.0	43.6
Brazil	34.9	38.2	37.1	47.0	40.7	39.7	37.8	38.3	37.0	40.8

Sources: Brock 1982 (for 1971–73: IMF, *International Financial Statistics,* September 1978; for 1974–80: ibid., September 1981).

Note: The figures in the table express the percentage 14a/14, where 14 and 14a refer to *IFS* line numbers for total reserve money and currency held outside banks, respectively.

greatly understates the extent to which the commercial banks in LDCs are forced to make low-interest loans to various public agencies beyond just the reserves they hold with the central bank. Whereas in industrial countries, Table 5.1 shows that official reserve requirements are typically less than 10 percent, and the other forms of forced lending are relatively minor.

As a result, coin and currency constitute a much higher proportion of the monetary base in mature industrial economies. Table 5.2 (Brock 1982) shows that currency as a percentage of the monetary base is typically 70 percent or so in industrial countries, whereas it is closer to 40 percent in Latin America.

Finally, Table 5.3 shows that Latin American LDCs typically extract four to five times as much seigniorage (as a share of gross national product [GNP]) from their monetary systems as do the industrial economies, and more than half of this comes from the required reserve component of the monetary base.

TABLE 5.3
Revenue from the Monetary System in Industrial and Developing Economies:
1972–80
(As a Percentage of GNP)

	Total Revenue	Currency Component	Required Reserve Component
United States	0.46	0.39	0.07
West Germany	0.74	0.43	0.31
United Kingdom	0.85	0.62	0.23
Mexico	4.3	1.2	3.1
Colombia	2.7	1.2	1.5
Brazil	2.3	0.9	1.4

Source: Brock 1984.
Note: Total revenue is (base$_t$ − base$_{t-1}$)/GNP$_t$ ≡ Δbase/GNP; the currency component is Δcurrency/GNP; and the required reserve component is Δrequired reserves/GNP. Figures for the monetary base, currency, required reserves, and GNP are taken from lines 14, 14a, 14-14a, and 99a of *International Financial Statistics*, September 1978 to September 1981. The figures in the table are simple arithmetic averages.

Mexico, Colombia, and Brazil pay below-market interest rates on a proportion of required reserves, thus lowering the inflation tax rate on those reserves. The figures in the table are not corrected for interest payments.

Thus any model of the inflation tax in LDCs must explicitly take into account how reserve requirements are set.

THE MODEL

Consider the financing problem facing the government of a repressed economy. Let Z denote the consolidated government deficit that must be financed by extracting revenue (seigniorage) from the domestic banking system:

$$(5.1) \qquad Z = G - T.$$

The quantity G is our inclusive measure of government expenditures and T is the flow of ordinary taxes collected. Besides ordinary expenditures that appear in most government budgets, G is defined very generally to include the subsidy element in low-cost credits flowing through the central bank to designated users (see Fig. 4.1), as well as other mandated central bank "expenditures" such as losses on forward exchange contracts favoring particular importers or exporters that reduce the monetary seigniorage available to be turned back to the treasury. A full discussion of how to consolidate such central bank expenditures with the government's ordinary budget is included in Blejer and Chu (1988). Here, however, let us simply assume that this tricky and extremely important accounting problem has been resolved so that the technicians at the central bank can accurately estimate what Z will be over the coming year.

The deficit Z is stated in purely nominal terms and will of course vary with the price level. In order to avoid specifying a complete macroeconomic model of domestic income determination and the way in which the public finances are embedded in it, let the government's known need for real finance from the domestic monetary system be given exogenously such that

(5.2) $Z/P = \alpha Y + v,$

where P is a general price deflator, Y is exogenously given real income (GNP) used here as a scale factor, and v is a random stochastic disturbance reflecting some lack of official control over the fiscal system. In principle, α could be treated as a policy parameter. A reduction in α could signal, say, an increase in ordinary tax collections or a decrease in official credit subsidies to preferred borrowers. However, to reflect steady-state financial repression, we assume that α is a positive constant and that v has significant variance with mean zero. In effect, an ongoing and somewhat variable fiscal deficit is predetermined and simply dumped into the laps of the monetary technicians at the central bank; they must design an overall financial policy to make the best of the situation.

What objective function should be imposed on the technicians? To simplify the analytics, suppose that the government instructs the technicians to minimize the rate of expected price inflation in the steady state, subject to the constraint that the fiscal deficit must be financed by the domestic banking system. (Foreign borrowing is omitted from the analysis.) Apart from maintaining the interest-rate subsidies on credits to officially designated borrowers that are part of the government deficit in equation (5.2), the technicians are not otherwise constrained to maintain general interest-rate controls (usury laws) unless they prove useful in reducing the rate of price inflation. Moreover, the technicians remain free to manipulate reserve requirements on all classes of deposits without any direct concern for the "crowding out" of private borrowers. (Somewhat surprisingly, it turns out that no conflict necessarily exists between minimizing inflation and limiting crowding out. To be sure, the fiscal deficit ensures that there will be some crowding out and some inflation. But as long as the monetary technicians allow the banking system to issue term deposits that are subject to reserve requirements but free of interest ceilings, minimizing the inflation rate need not lead to undue crowding out, as will become clearer in what follows.)

In the context of this repressed economy, how can the instruments of financial policy best be manipulated in order to minimize the inflation rate? The government effectively taxes the financial system by establishing non-interest-bearing reserve requirements. (To avoid unnecessary complications, required bank purchases of government bonds at preferential rates of interest are ignored here, although they are not unusual in practice.) Suppose that the technicians decide that demand deposits will not bear interest because they compete directly with currency as a means of payment, and currency is part of non-interest-bearing base money. Official reserve requirements against demand deposits are set at a very high level, close to 100 percent, that is roughly tailored to absorb abnormal bank profits after the costs of servicing checking accounts are deducted. Although somewhat repressive, this "suboptimization" strategy has the advantage of maintaining the margin of substitution between currency and demand deposits in the portfolios of money holders despite possible variability in the rate of price inflation or in rates of interest on other financial assets.

Next, suppose that the technicians allow banks of all classes to issue just one other type of liability, thirty-day term deposits that are unrestricted as to the interest rate that may be paid to depositors. Moreover, the net proceeds from attracting such deposits may be lent out in the free part of the capital market, with no restrictions on the interest rate charged to various borrowers. However, a non-interest-bearing reserve requirement of k percent is imposed on all such thirty-day deposits, whether they are in commercial banks, savings banks, or various classes of nonbank intermediaries such as money market transactions. Thus k becomes the key monetary-control variable for responding to different levels of the fiscal deficit. We ignore the additional financial complexity associated with low-interest savings deposits, which are hardly different from demand deposits under high inflation. We likewise omit deposits maturing in more than thirty days because financing is very short term in an inflationary environment. Simplicity is a virtue both analytically and institutionally, and this two-asset strategy roughly corresponds to Chilean financial policy in the mid-1970s, when inflation was still severe. (A more differentiated structure of officially set interest rates at various terms to maturity is examined by Fry [1981].)

On the central bank's balance sheet, all narrow money usable for making payments to third parties is aggregated into the variable C, and all reserves against term deposits are denoted by R. The accumulated sum of past government deficits, $\Sigma(Z_t)$, is the central bank's only asset in this, as yet, closed economy. (The central bank holds no foreign exchange reserves in this highly simplified example.)

CENTRAL BANK

Government debt	$\Sigma(Z_t)$	Currency and reserves against demand deposits	C
		Reserves against time deposits	R
		Monetary base	M

The real revenue flow accruing to the government from the issue of base money must be

$$(5.3) \qquad Z/P = \dot{M}/P = (\dot{M}/M)(M/P) = \mu(M/P),$$

where $\dot{M}$ is the absolute rate of change in base money, and μ is its proportional rate of change. Equation (5.3) yields the conventional result that real revenue from the banking system is the percentage change in nominal money supply times the real monetary base, whose scale in the steady state roughly depends on the level of real income, Y. We assume initially an exogenously given steady growth in real income, γ, to which there corresponds a steady-state inflation that depends on μ such that

$$(5.4) \qquad\qquad \pi = \mu - \gamma,$$

where π is the rate of price inflation, $\dot{P}/P$. In the steady state where γ is given, minimizing π corresponds to minimizing μ, the percentage rate of issue of base money.

What is unconventional is to partition the demand for base money into two components: currency (plus demand deposits) and the reserves held against interest-bearing term deposits, which are k percent of such term deposits, D. Disaggregation is necessary because the demand for currency is negatively related to the interest rate on term deposits, i_d, whereas the derived demand for reserves held against term deposits is positively related to i_d. (Remember that in a repressed economy there is no open-market interest rate on "bonds," that is the opportunity cost of holding "money" in the conventional sense of Keynesian liquidity-preference analysis.) The demand function for currency is

$$(5.5) \qquad\qquad C/P = f(\underset{-}{\pi}, \underset{-}{i_d})Y.$$

The demand function for term deposits is

$$(5.6) \qquad\qquad D/P = q(\underset{-}{\pi}, \underset{+}{i_d})Y.$$

Together, these yield a demand function for base money:

$$(5.7) \qquad\qquad M/P = kD/P + C/P.$$

Note that the demand for term deposits is not homogeneous of degree 0 in π and i_d. One cannot specify this demand purely in terms of the real deposit rate $r_d = i_d - \pi$, because equal percentage point increases in π and i_d will still attract depositors away from currency, which has no interest rate that can adjust in response.

An additional distinguishing feature of this analysis is the importance of the demand for unsubsidized loans in the free part of the capital market. Based on resources attracted through the issue of term deposits, commercial banks may lend at whatever interest rate, denoted by i_l, they can get. The demand function for real loans is

$$(5.8) \qquad\qquad L/P = h(\underset{+}{\pi}, \underset{-}{i_l}),$$

where L is the nominal quantity of loans. The deposit rate of interest has been left out of the function describing the demand for loans, and the loan rate of interest has been left out of the function describing the demand for deposits, because the qualitative direction of each effect is unclear.

Moreover, as analyzed extensively in Chapter 4, the non-interest-bearing reserve requirement on term deposits drives a wedge between the open-market interest rate on deposits and that on loans. The inflation tax on reserves is shared between depositors, whose yields are driven down, and borrowers, whose costs are driven up. The way in which price inflation interacts with the reserve requirement to make the wedge bigger was described in equation (4.5). How much r_l increases absolutely and r_d falls absolutely depends on the elasticity of demand for loans in equation (5.8) compared with the elasticity of supply of deposits in equation (5.6), assuming that both markets clear.

RESERVE REQUIREMENTS FOR MINIMIZING INFLATION

For alternative inflationary steady states, our constrained macroeconomic optimization procedure may now be reduced to its bare essentials: minimize the inflation rate, π, with respect to k subject to these market-clearing conditions:
Private loanable funds are $(1 - k)$ percent of deposits

$$(5.9) \qquad\qquad L/P = (1 - k)D/P = h(\pi, i_l) = (1 - k)q(\pi, i_d).$$

From equations (5.4) and (5.7), the government deficit is equal to the rate of change in base money:

$$(5.10) \qquad\qquad Z/P = (kq + f)(\pi + \gamma).$$

Competition drives bank profits to zero:

$$(5.11) \qquad\qquad i_l(1 - k) - i_d = 0.$$

This optimization procedure, based on the above three equilibrium conditions, determines the endogenous variables i_l, i_d, and π. Starting from equation (5.10), the exogenously given government deficit Z/P must be financed by issuing currency and reserves against term deposits. As k increases, the relative tax burden is shifted toward the term-deposit part of the market; how much

Price inflation

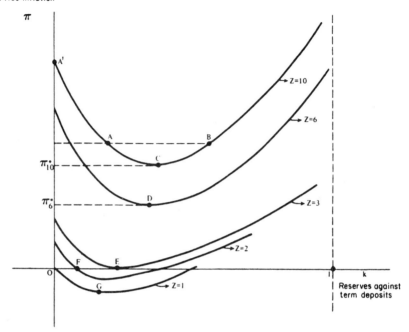

Note: Income growth and the current levels of income and prices are given. Z denotes various levels of the fiscal deficit.

FIGURE 5.1. Inflation, the Fiscal Deficit, and Optimal Required Reserves. (Source: Adapted and simplified from a similar diagram in Brock 1982.)

depends on the elasticity of response of depositors and borrowers. The more inelastic is the demand for term deposits and for real loans with respect to a fall in i_d and a rise in i_l, the greater will be the optimal reserve requirement to minimize the inflation rate, π. Conversely, the more inelastic is the demand for currency, the lower will be the optimal reserve requirement, as more of the inflation tax burden is shifted toward currency holders. According to commonly accepted canons of public finance, one taxes where the inelasticity of demand is most pronounced in order to minimize the erosion of the tax base. Of course, the more inelastic the demand for either financial asset, the lower will be the minimum necessary inflation rate and rate of base-money creation. Similarly, from equation (5.10), the higher the natural real rate of growth and the flow of noninflationary seigniorage in the economy, the lower will be the minimum necessary inflation rate to finance the given fiscal deficit.

A full algebraic development of the macroeconomic optimization problem, where interior solutions are distinguished from corner solutions, is too lengthy and tedious to present here. Instead, Figure 5.1 illustrates the more important ways in which the optimal reserve requirement, the inflation rate, and different levels of the exogenous fiscal deficit are likely to interact. For a given current level of real income and prices, each Z represents a different level of the fiscal deficit. Our only decision variable, the reserve requirement, k, ranges between 0 and 1. If it is set at 0, the government gets no revenue from the term-deposit part of the system. Similarly, if it is set at 1, so that the nominal yield on term deposits falls to zero, everyone will abandon term deposits in favor of more liquid demand deposits and currency. Again, government revenue from the term-deposit part of the system goes to zero. For each possible fiscal deficit, therefore, the graph relating π to k must be U-shaped, with an interior solution for minimizing π where k is positive but less than 1. For $Z = 10$, the optimal solution is at point C, where the reserve requirement is set at a fairly high level to minimize the relatively high inflation rate and high rate of issue of base money. If the monetary technicians set reserve requirements either too low, as at point A, or too high, as at point B, the inflation rate will rise above the minimum at C. Intuitively, this is easily understood for point A, because the reserve requirement is too low and term deposits are insufficiently taxed, so that a higher inflation tax is forced on currency holders. It may seem counterintuitive to many readers, however, that higher price inflation results when the reserve requirement increases beyond C to B. The reason is that setting reserve requirements too high shrinks the term-deposit part of the system unduly and also diminishes the real government revenue based on it. Contrary to what simple textbook models of the money multiplier might suggest, increasing reserve requirements may be inflationary rather than deflationary! (The inappropriate but standard textbook model of the money multiplier may be an important reason why Chilean authorities in 1976 and 1977 kept the reserve requirement too high despite the marked improvement in their fiscal situation. As long as price inflation remained very high, they were reluctant to reduce it.) The apparent paradox is resolved if choosing the optimal reserve requirement is considered an exercise in the theory of optimal taxation for which the elasticities of response of depositors and borrowers are correctly weighed.

An equally serious error would be to leave large segments of the financial system with no reserve requirements at all. Important classes of deposit-taking financial institutions could be mistakenly classified as nonbanks not subject to the central bank's control. Real deposits would shift toward these unregulated intermediaries, people would avoid the inflation tax, and an unduly high rate of inflation would result, as depicted by A' in Figure 5.1.

As the size of the government's consolidated budget deficit is reduced, the U-shaped curves in Figure 5.1 shift downward and to the left: the optimal inflation and reserve requirement solutions shift from C to D to E. Not only does the minimum inflation rate fall but the optimal reserve requirement also becomes progressively smaller in order to maintain the correct tax balance between the market for currency and the market for term deposits.[1] If there is substantial economic growth, the minimum necessary price inflation can fall to zero before the public sector deficit is eliminated—point E along the graph $Z = 3$. Ongoing growth by itself generates just enough seigniorage to finance $Z = 3$ in a noninflationary fashion for given levels of prices and income (Friedman 1971). Indeed, further cuts in the deficit will generate price deflation in the economy, as shown by point G, if the monetary technicians stick with the pure strategy of minimizing inflation by maintaining reserve requirements at a significant level.

To eliminate inflation without going so far as to cause falling prices, one might want to truncate the optimizing procedure. Impose the additional condition that price deflation is to be avoided. Then, as the deficit is reduced below 3, the authorities respond by simply reducing reserve requirements. In Figure 5.1, reserve requirements are reduced from E to F to 0 with the significant additional advantage (not part of our formal optimizing procedure) of further liberalizing the capital market. At the origin in Figure 5.1, where k is 0, Z has been arbitrarily set at 1. Seigniorage from the currency part of the system is just sufficient to provide noninflationary finance for a deficit of this rather modest size.

Further reductions in the deficit below 1 will again cause deflationary pressure unless the monetary technicians reduce reserve requirements against demand deposits (not incorporated in our formal optimization procedure) or extend modest amounts of central-bank credit to the commercial banks. Either method will be sufficient to ensure that base money expands fast enough to prevent outright deflation as the public finances improve in the context of general economic liberalization.

SOME CONCLUDING CAVEATS

An important characteristic of a repressed economy is the tendency to run high, but unstable, fiscal deficits. However, our analysis of optimal inflationary finance omitted the important stochastic elements in the consolidated public sector deficit. For a given reserve requirement, the wedge between deposit

1. Philip Brock pointed out to me that insufficient conditions had been imposed on equations (5.9) through (5.11) to guarantee that in comparing steady states, the optimal k would decline as the fiscal deficit was reduced, however intuitively plausible that might seem. In his Stanford Ph.D. dissertation (1983), Brock has an ingenious argument showing that k and μ should be jointly reduced if the system is to remain dynamically stable as fiscal policy is improved. Sticking with steady-state comparisons, however, Remolona (1982) shows that in a more complete model of intertemporal optimization, where one worries about crowding out in the capital market as well as reducing inflation per se, optimally k will decrease along with the fiscal deficit.

and loan interest rates will be sensitive to inflationary pressure and thus will, to a limited extent, accommodate unexpected changes in such pressure. The absence of interest ceilings on the term-deposit part of the market gives the system additional flexibility. Nevertheless, whether or not the system is dynamically stable in response to stochastic fluctuations in Z is an important analytical question that remains to be answered.

Apart from the issue of stochastic instability in the fiscal deficit itself, our algebraic model assumed that the real rate of growth γ was given independently of the rate of inflation, the fiscal deficit, and how the reserve requirement k was actually set. This simplification enabled us to develop the idea of an "optimal" reserve requirement for minimizing inflation for a given revenue need on the part of the government. From the empirical analysis of Chapter 2, however, one would expect strong negative feedback effects on γ from higher price inflation or higher reserve requirements—both of which reduce real deposit rates of interest and the flow of loanable funds for new investment. This feedback effect remains to be analyzed in the context of a more general algebraic model. My guess is that such feedback effects would reduce the inflation-minimizing k below what the model in this chapter has suggested.

CHAPTER SIX

Macroeconomic Control

during Disinflation:

Chile versus South Korea

$\mathbf{D}$esigning a successful macroeconomic stabilization, where the economy moves from very high to low price inflation, is itself a major problem. From the starting point of a (typical) inflationary and partially indexed less-developed economy with uncontrolled government deficits, suppose that a major fiscal reform suddenly makes full monetary (price-level) stabilization feasible. Government expenditures, including credit subsidies financed by the central bank, are reduced and/or traditional tax revenues are increased. The otherwise quite different experiences of Chile and South Korea with inflation and disinflation in the late 1970s and early 1980s are useful benchmarks. Both achieved sufficient internal fiscal control to eliminate the need for the inflation tax as a means of public finance. Thus both could embark on credible programs for stabilizing their domestic price levels as a precondition for full-scale economic liberalization.

Even as improved fiscal policy reduces growth in domestic central-bank credit and optimum reserve requirements on bank term deposits fall (Ch. 5), there remain difficult problems of how to manipulate previously indexed wages, the exchange rate, and interest rates in the transition to a lower rate of inflation. As the economy evolves toward price-level stability, the government must consistently manage these key *nominal* prices in order to prevent serious *relative* price misalignments. What are the basic issues?

1. In order to disinflate, can "orthodox" tight money based on high real interest rates be effective?

2. To secure control over the real exchange rate, should access to foreign capital be limited?

3. Is traditional backward-looking indexing of wages or exchange rates consistent with price-level stabilization in the future?

4. Should governments depend on international commodity arbitrage at a fixed nominal exchange rate to stabilize the domestic price level?

To analyze these fundamental problems of how to keep exchange rates,

TABLE 6.1
Profile of the Chilean Tariff Reform

		Average Nominal Tariff Rate (Percentages)	Maximum Nominal Tariff Rate (Percentages)[a]
1973	July–December	94	500+
1974	January–June	80	160
	July–December	67	140
1975	January–June	52	120
	July–December	44	90
1976	January–June	38	70
	July–December	33	60
1977	January–June	24	50
	July–December	18	35
1978	January–June	15	20
	July–December	12	15
1979	June 30 onward	10[b]	10
1980		10	10
1981		10	10
1982		10	10

[a]With a few exceptions the maximum rate applies to all automotive vehicles. Small cars may be imported at the standard tariff rates.
[b]Of the 4,301 commodities or tariff lines that are classified for customs purposes, only 12 are exempt from any duties.
Source: Central Bank of Chile.

interest rates, and wages correctly aligned during disinflation, I shall use a historical case study approach. The failed Chilean stabilization attempt from 1978 to 1982 is treated first. Then some key differences with the more-successful, but less-demanding, South Korean stabilization of 1981–84 are pointed out.

ECONOMIC REPRESSION AND LIBERALIZATION IN CHILE: A BRIEF REVIEW

By the end of 1973, virtually every measure showed that the Chilean economy had become massively repressed. In foreign trade, extremely high tariffs on the order of 100 percent (Table 6.1) significantly understated the actual degree of protection. Exchange controls, quotas, and outright prohibitions proliferated over the whole range of both imports and exports.

Table 6.2 shows the basic macroeconomic and financial statistics for the Chilean economy from 1970 to 1982. Reaching almost 25 percent of gross national product (GNP) in 1973, the government budget deficit was out of control and had become fully monetized. But this understated the extent to which the central bank—either directly or indirectly—was forced to provide subsidized credit lines to a wide variety of enterprises and government agencies throughout the country.

Chile had a long history of using the central bank and a large state-owned commercial bank (the Bank of Chile) to provide credit subsidies for "develop-

TABLE 6.2
Macroeconomic Overview of Chile, 1970–82

	1970	1973	1974	1975	1976	1977	1978	1979	1980	1981	1982
Production											
GDP (% real changes)	2.1	5.6	1.0	-12.9	3.5	9.9	8.2	8.3	7.5	5.3	-14.5
Unemployment rate (%)	5.7	4.8	9.2	13.5	15.8	14.2	14.2	13.8	11.8	10.9	20.4
Gross domestic investment rate (% GDP)	16.7	7.9	21.2	13.1	12.8	14.4	17.3	17.8	21.0	20.7	9.9
Gross national savings rate (% GDP)	15.1	5.3	20.7	7.9	14.5	10.8	12.6	12.5	13.9	6.6	0.04
Balance of payments											
Exports (FOB billions U.S. $)	1.112	1.309	2.151	1.590	2.116	2.185	2.400	3.835	4.705	3.836	3.706
Imports (CIF billions U.S. $)[a]	956	1.288	1.794	1.520	1.473	2.151	2.886	4.190	5.469	6.513	3.643
Current account savings (billions U.S. $)	81	-294	-211	-491	148	-551	-1.088	-1.189	-1.971	-4.733	-2.304
Changes in reserves (balances in millions of U.S. $)	114	-21	-55	-344	414	113	712	1.047	1.244	70	-1.165
Total foreign debt (millions of U.S. $)	3.123	4.048	4.774	4.854	4.720	5.201	6.664	8.484	11.084	15.542	17.153
Fiscal											
Public sector expenditures (% GDP)	40.6	n.a.	39.7	39.5	37.0	34.7	34.2	32.4	30.3	35.6	43.3
Fiscal deficit (% GDP)	2.7	24.7	10.5	2.6	2.3	1.8	0.8	-1.7	-3.1	-1.6	2.4
Total change in monetary base (% GDP)	2.9	22.2	7.5	7.2	8.0	5.3	3.4	2.5	2.3	0.0	-0.02
Money and prices											
M2/GDP (%)	11.0	22.3	11.1	11.2	11.7	13.0	16.0	17.4	19.3	23.4	24.7
Annual real lending interest rates (%)[b]	-11.0	-76.1	-36.9	16.0	64.3	56.8	42.2	16.6	11.9	38.7	35.1
Annual change in CPI (%)	34.9	508.1	375.9	340.7	174.3	63.5	30.3	38.9	31.2	9.5	20.7
Annual change in WPI (%)	33.7	1147.1	570.7	410.9	151.5	65.0	38.9	58.3	28.2	-3.9	39.6
Real wage rate[a] index (1970=100)	100.0	60.8	60.2	63.9	82.9	86.2	85.9	87.2	96.5	110.6	107.1
Real exchange rate[a] index (1975=100)	102.6	99.5	88.9	100.0	86.6	83.6	91.0	79.9	69.4	69.7	87.9
Terms of trade[a] index (1960=100)	145.0	148	137	86	87	79	78	110	100	76	62

[a] In 1970 and 1973, import values are expressed CIF millions of dollars.
[b] Nominal (30–89 days) peso loan rates, deflated by official CPI.
Source: Luders 1985. World Bank, *World Bank Report,* 1984; Central Bank of Chile, *Economic and Social Indicators* and *Monthly Bulletin,* various issues.

ment" purposes to enterprises throughout the country. But under Salvador Allende's socialist government from 1970 to 1973, worker collectives seized operating control over most industrial enterprises and some large farms. Because wages rose sharply relative to the (nominally frozen) output prices, these enterprises began to run with large negative cash flows—which were then covered by new and extended credit lines from the banking system.

The result was massive inflation in the mid-1970s, partially repressed in 1973 by price controls but subsequently becoming open inflation with their removal. Because of the inflation, interest-rate restrictions, and heavy reserve requirements (more than 80 percent) on deposit-collecting banks, the financial system operated with negative real deposit rates of interest from 1973 into 1975. The domestic flow of loanable funds in any open, organized capital market was virtually nonexistent. In view of this economic chaos, as well as for political reasons, foreign capital (other than short-term trade credit) was completely unavailable to the Chilean economy.

In 1974, however, there began a remarkable series of liberalizing reforms and moves toward monetary and fiscal stabilization—the results of which are immediately evident upon glancing at Tables 6.1 and 6.2. Government expenditures were cut, income taxes were rationalized, and commodity taxes were consolidated through the imposition of a uniform 20 percent value-added tax. By 1978, the fiscal deficit was negligible, and surpluses developed in the next three years. (Sebastian Edwards and Alejandra Cox Edwards [1987] provide an excellent economic analysis and review of this traumatic period in Chile's history.)

Equally important, the government undertook additional draconian measures to liberalize the domestic financial system. It phased out automatic official credit lines to prop up failing industrial and agricultural enterprises. Reserve requirements on deposit-taking banks were greatly reduced, and by 1976 formal interest ceilings on deposits and loans were eliminated. Commercial banks, the principal financial intermediaries, were sold back to the private sector, thus creating a vigorous competitive market for deposits and loans. Interest rates rose sharply from negative to very high positive levels (Table 3.5) and thus encouraged financial growth (Table 6.2).

With the benefit of hindsight, however, we now know that interest rates became unduly high in real terms, as discussed in Chapter 3. This created severe adverse risk selection among nonbank borrowers and substantial moral hazard among the banks themselves (for reasons to be analyzed more precisely in Ch. 7). This failure to exercise proper supervisory control over the banking system was not, at the time, recognized as such but became an important contributing factor to the ultimate breakdown of Chile's otherwise well-designed program of economic liberalization, as we shall see.

Reforms were equally remarkable in the foreign trade sector. The first order of business, in 1974–75, was to unify the highly fragmented system of multiple exchange rates. Then, various quota restrictions or outright prohibitions on importing and exporting were converted to tariff "equivalents." Indeed, formal tariff protection for Chilean industry remained quite high in the early stages of the liberalization, but nontariff barriers had been pretty well eliminated by 1977. Then, most importantly, the government announced in 1977 a staged step-by-step reduction of the highest tariffs (protecting mainly finished goods) to a low uniform level to be completed in 1979. Table 6.1 shows how tariffs averaging over 90 percent in 1973 were scaled down to a flat 10 percent across all imported commodities by mid-1979—a reform that lasted through 1982.

Given the severe distortions that had developed in the Chilean economy by 1973, these new policies for freeing international trade and eliminating domestic financial repression seemed to be remarkably well ordered in a "textbook" sense. They were widely applauded by almost all economists who were then firsthand observers. Thus the numerous banking failures and severe downturn of the economy from late 1981 to 1984, leaving the economy with a huge debt overhang relative to the size of its shrunken GNP, are distressing not only to Chileans but to economists. (Subsequently the Chilean economy recovered and has grown strongly in the late 1980s into the 1990s.)

Granted, much of Chile's economic decline was due to adverse world economic conditions in the early 1980s: the unexpected deterioration in the terms of trade of non-oil primary products, the sharp increase in international real interest rates, and the unexpected appreciation of the dollar, which further contributed to the real cost of servicing Chile's external debt.

Nevertheless, a careful assessment of the monetary stabilization program, where price inflation was successfully reduced from several hundred percent per year in the mid-1970s to almost zero by late 1981, is in order. Did the authorities make any substantial technical errors in the administration of their foreign exchange and domestic financial policies? With the benefit of hindsight, what should they have done differently to support their general goal of liberalization?

Vittorio Corbo has developed the now generally accepted view of where Chilean financial policy went astray (Corbo 1985, 1986). In order to curb domestic price inflation, beginning in early 1978, the rate of depreciation in the nominal exchange rate was deliberately reduced below the differential between inflation in Chilean prices and that prevailing in the international economy. The apparent real interest costs of foreign borrowing in dollars fell below those prevailing in domestic financial markets in pesos. The resulting huge inflow of foreign capital forced an undue appreciation in the real exchange rate. In addition, this real exchange appreciation was exacerbated by the way in which wages were indexed—as Corbo emphasizes. In order to maintain the real purchasing power of workers' take-home pay, both minimum and "standard" wages covering most public and private sector activities in Chile were automatically written up in peso terms by the inflation in the consumer price index (CPI) experienced in the previous quarter. As long as inflation continues at more or less the same rate, this indexing procedure itself is neutral with respect to the levels of real wages. However, if inflation (and exchange depreciation) sharply decelerate, this "backward-looking" indexing procedure will cause real wages to increase rather sharply. And Table 6.3, taken from Corbo (1985), shows in column 4 the rapid rise in Chilean real wages in terms of tradable goods from 1976 through to the beginning of 1982. This caused a profit squeeze in Chilean industry and agriculture and defaults on domestic bank loans. The subsequent banking collapses in 1982–83 were worsened by previous regulatory lapses that had permitted the commercial banks to accumulate too many bad loans.

However, what exchange- and interest-rate policies the Chilean financial authorities should have implemented in the late 1970s remain to be identified. Let us review their policy options.

THE MONETARY STABILIZATION PROBLEM OF FEBRUARY 1978

What was the economic dilemma facing the Chilean authorities at the beginning of 1978, prior to their fateful adoption of an "active" (my terminology, McKinnon 1981b) downward crawl for the exchange rate? Although the government had virtually eliminated any need for the inflation tax as a means of public finance, in 1977 the rate of price inflation was still over 60 percent. Although it was substantially less than in 1975 and 1976, the authorities rightly thought this inflationary momentum to be unwarranted.

Prior to February 1978, the exchange rate had been "passively" (but only partially) adjusted to compensate for internal price inflation and to roughly balance international payments—with significant restrictions on inflows and outflows of private capital. Even so, a very sharp real appreciation of the currency took place from 1975 to 1977 (see Table 6.3). This increase in the real value of the peso was probably important in reducing price inflation from more than 300 percent in 1975 to less than 70 percent in 1977.

True, the peso was greatly undervalued in 1975 because capital flight forced a rapid depreciation of the currency. Yet, if the same ad hoc exchange-rate adjustments had continued after 1977, the real value of the peso could well have continued to increase. Few people now realize that the exchange-rate policy the Chilean authorities were following prior to February 1978 was not sustainable indefinitely.

What was needed was a "forward-looking" monetary policy that would stabilize the domestic price level and price expectations and at the same time prevent further appreciation in the real exchange rate. At the beginning of 1978, some substantial change in monetary and exchange-rate policies was

TABLE 6.3
Measures of Chile's International Competitiveness
(1979 II = 1.0)

Quarter	PM/PN (1)	PX/PN (2)	PT/PN (3)	PT/W (4)	PX/PM (5)	Nominal Exchange Rate[a] (6)
1975						
I	1.640	1.663	1.652	2.168	1.014	2.57
II	1.664	1.689	1.677	2.463	1.015	4.36
III	1.703	1.707	1.705	2.205	1.002	6.03
IV	1.752	1.777	1.765	2.208	1.014	7.80
1976						
I	1.732	1.774	1.753	2.218	1.024	10.48
II	1.529	1.522	1.526	1.923	0.995	12.43
III	1.340	1.370	1.355	1.628	1.022	13.91
IV	1.84	1.277	1.230	1.427	1.079	16.55
1977						
I	1.096	1.151	1.123	1.251	1.050	18.43
II	0.904	0.990	0.946	1.117	1.095	19.44
III	0.910	0.940	0.925	1.059	1.033	22.26
IV	0.954	0.968	0.961	1.171	1.015	25.99
1978						
I	1.016	0.967	0.992	1.106	0.952	29.11
II	1.016	0.907	0.960	1.078	0.893	31.25
III	0.999	0.875	0.935	1.047	0.876	32.69
IV	0.999	0.897	0.947	1.065	0.898	33.58
1979						
I	0.987	0.924	0.955	1.003	0.936	34.72
II	1.000	1.000	1.000	1.000	1.000	36.26
III	1.082	1.185	1.132	1.051	1.095	39.00
IV	0.984	1.103	1.042	1.032	1.121	39.00
1980						
I	0.939	1.118	1.025	0.920	1.191	39.00
II	0.925	1.092	1.004	0.864	1.178	39.00
III	0.917	1.017	0.966	0.832	1.109	39.00
IV	0.874	0.916	0.895	0.736	1.048	39.00
1981						
I	0.846	0.844	0.845	0.687	0.998	39.00
II	0.786	0.775	0.780	0.631	0.986	39.00
III	0.744	0.709	0.726	0.579	0.953	39.00
IV	0.723	0.681	0.702	0.569	0.942	39.00
1982						
I	0.696	0.606	0.649	0.532	0.871	39.00
II	0.713	0.611	0.660	0.549	0.857	40.34
III	0.937	0.837	0.886	0.755	0.893	50.01
IV	1.366	0.893	1.104	0.963	0.754	69.28

Source: Corbo 1985, 895.

Note: PN: price index for nontradables obtained from the Cortazar Marshall CPI. PM: import price index in pesos, obtained as a Divisia index of the exchange-rate-adjusted industrial components of the wholesale price index for Argentina, Brazil, Japan, West Germany, and the United States, using the structure of imports from each of those countries as a weighting base. The index is also adjusted for average customs duties. PX: export price index in pesos, measured as a Divisia index of major Chilean exports, excluding copper. W: Nominal manufacturing wage rate. PT: Geometric average of PX and PM with weights of 0.50 for each.

[a]The nominal exchange rate is the number of units of domestic currency required to purchase U.S. $1.

warranted to break the economy's inflationary momentum. The highly desirable fiscal reforms by themselves were not sufficient to establish monetary control.

THE DOMESTIC MONETARIST SOLUTION

One school of thought, actively advocated in Chile in 1977–78, was the standard Friedman-Meltzer approach of "domestic monetarism." This approach entails securing control over the domestic monetary base, revoking capital-account restrictions, and floating the exchange rate. Then some domestic monetary aggregate, such as M1 or M2, must be targeted to grow at a smooth rate consistent with future price-level stability and/or some deliberate pace of disinflation. A credible announcement effect would then directly reduce private inflationary expectations.

In my view, this strategy could well have proved more devastating to the Chilean economy than what actually happened. Because of the fast pace of financial transformation (the demand for real cash balances was rapidly increasing as inflation diminished), the authorities could not accurately estimate what the "correct" rate of growth in domestic nominal M1 and M2 should be. (And Table 6.2 shows that the ratio of M2 to GNP was indeed unstable.) This unpredictable growth in monetary aggregates is characteristic of any economy that is moving from a state of repression to a more liberalized financial system. Suppose the government directly tightened control over the monetary base and successfully reduced inflationary expectations. With an open capital account in the balance of payments, a massive shift in international portfolio preferences in favor of the Chilean peso would have occurred anyway—perhaps even earlier. The problem of excessive capital inflows would remain.

Because asset markets adjust much faster than goods markets, in 1978 a floating Chilean peso would have appreciated sharply, even in nominal terms. Although price inflation might then have fallen more rapidly in 1978 (despite the presence of backward-looking wage indexing), the gross overvaluation of the peso would have occurred much sooner and crushed the profitability of the Chilean export- and import-competing sectors even before the tariff reductions were completed in mid-1979.

In summary, in the course of moving the increasingly open Chilean economy from very high inflation to a stable price level, adopting a floating exchange rate in the 1970s would not have solved the fundamental problem of avoiding excessive capital inflows and real currency appreciation. Even the much milder U.S. price disinflation of 1980–82 led to a sharp appreciation of the floating dollar along with a depression in American tradable goods industries.

THE EXCHANGE RATES AS THE FORWARD SIGNAL

In February 1978, a successful monetary stabilization clearly required an unambiguous signal—around which private expectations could easily coalesce—that price inflation would be reduced to the international level in the near future. Quite plausibly, the authorities decided to use the dollar exchange rate as the intermediate target for Chilean monetary policy. This rate served as an indication of the intended rate of disinflation, and depended on using international commodity arbitrage as the instrument for achieving it.

The sweeping trade liberalization gave the authorities confidence (false, as it turned out) that domestic price inflation would quickly converge to the international level if the exchange rate was fixed. Because fiscal policy was such that the central bank could subordinate monetary policy to achieve any reasonable target for the nominal exchange rate, such a policy was credible and seemed potentially effective in stabilizing the price level.

This was the rationale for announcing and widely publicizing an active forward downward crawl, or *tablita,* for adjusting the exchange rate on a daily or weekly basis by very small amounts. The numbers going into the preannounced tablita were inevitably somewhat arbitrary: 24 percent depreciation in 1978 and 14 percent in 1979, after which the nominal exchange rate would be fixed indefinitely. The announcement effect was designed to allow private contracts denominated in pesos to anticipate the cessation of inflation.

Table 6.3 shows these decelerating movements in the nominal exchange rate converging in mid-1979 to a fixed exchange rate of 39 pesos to the dollar, which was sustained through June 1982. This tablita broke down with the exchange devaluations of 1982 in the midst of general economic decline.

THE INDEXING PROBLEM

This movement to an active downward crawl—or "forward" stabilization—in the nominal exchange rate by the Chilean government was not itself a policy mistake, as is often suggested. Rather the absence of suitably supportive capital-market and labor-market policies, as well as external stress, eventually caused the stabilization policy to fail.

Consider the labor market first. Corbo correctly emphasizes the inconsistency between the forward-looking indexing of the nominal exchange rate and the backward-looking indexing of money wages, which is often found in high-inflation economies. Chilean wages were linked to the past rate of inflation, which was very high relative to that anticipated in the future. Thus, as international competition from newly liberalized foreign trade and the ever-slower downward crawl in the nominal exchange rate slowed price inflation in the tradables industries, growth in money wages continued at a much faster pace.

Indeed, from early 1978 to early 1982, Corbo's data in Table 6.3 show that the ratio of tradables prices to wages fell more than 50 percent.

In retrospect, it seems as if money wages in February 1978 should have been put on the same forward-looking tablita as the exchange rate. Similarly, all other prices that were indexed to ongoing inflation, such as charges for the use of public utilities, should have been put on the same tablita.

Putting wages on the same forward-looking indexing procedure may not have eliminated the overvaluation problem entirely. Although wages would have been fixed in terms of the prices of tradable goods, the price of nontradables may have continued to edge upward. However, because wages are quite dominant in determining the cost of nontradable services, the sharp fall from 1978 to 1981 of the relative price of tradable goods, as shown in column (3) of Table 6.3, would not have been so pronounced.

Nevertheless, if the economy had tended to absorb large amounts of foreign financial capital when the exchange rate was pegged by the tablita, the domestic money supply would have expanded unduly and this inflationary pressure would have affected the prices of nontradables more than tradables. In the presence of massive capital inflows, even "correct" wage indexation would not have fully resolved the problem of avoiding exchange overvaluation.

In summary, it is now commonly accepted that better synchronization of those indexation procedures under government control in February 1978 would surely have prevented much of the gross overvaluation of the peso that we later observed. But why use the downward-crawling tablita rather than moving directly to a fixed exchange rate?

In the extreme case where the government controlled all nominal prices in the economy, inflation could have been halted immediately by decree. The authorities could simply have promulgated a fixed exchange rate, as well as fixing all other nominal prices under their control. No forward-looking tablita would have been necessary other than the announcement that the nominal exchange rate would remain fixed indefinitely. In effect, the tablita could have been completely truncated with no continued inflationary momentum in domestic prices.[1]

1. Are there any other circumstances in which a government could impose a fixed nominal exchange rate directly without fear of real overvaluation? Consider the last stages of extreme hyperinflation—such as that which occurred in Germany from 1921 to 1923. When the price level is increasing rapidly and erratically on a daily basis, hour-by-hour or even minute-by-minute exchange-rate quotations are the most efficient source of information telling people how fast inflation is actually proceeding. Everyone then keys on (indexes to) the exchange rate in determining domestic prices and wages. Significant backward-looking indexing tends to disappear and virtually all forward contracting uses foreign exchange as the numeraire (see Dornbusch 1985).

Consequently, a dramatic stabilization of the exchange rate will immediately stabilize domestic prices and wages—even if they are not directly controlled by the government. One must be cautious, however; a dramatic act such as the introduction of a new currency

In the newly liberalized Chilean economy of early 1978, however, the move to free trade was designed to restructure relative prices. Thus a general freeze of nominal prices of all goods and services would have been out of keeping with the very nature of the reforms—unlike wages, which were being controlled by the government anyway. Without such a general freeze, therefore, one could expect some price inflation to continue even if wages were put on the same tablita as the exchange rate.

In general, the greater the extent of forward contracting in pesos in private transactions, the stronger the case for stretching out the tablita for some months. Assuming the Chilean government was unwilling to undertake a general price freeze, the active forward crawl toward a fixed exchange rate within two years does not seem wrong—even with the benefit of hindsight— provided that other controlled prices in the economy were also on the same tablita.

SCALING DOWN NOMINAL INTEREST RATES IN LINE WITH THE TABLITA

In February 1978, should more comprehensive financial measures in the capital markets have been taken to assist the macroeconomic stabilization of the Chilean price level? Except to advocate more stringent (unspecified) controls on foreign capital inflows, authors writing on the experiences of the Southern Cone do not seem to have fully come to grips with this financial issue.

Clearly, everyone now agrees that money wages, along with other significant prices which the government controlled, should have been put on the same forward-looking tablita as the exchange rate. But does it then make sense to leave extremely high nominal interest rates—over 80 percent in 1978, as shown in Table 3.5—on peso loans in place when the government is planning such a fast convergence to price stability? Politically, Chilean workers would have been less likely to accept a scaling down of their nominal claims when nominal interest rates remained so high. Perhaps a standard nominal interest rate on peso loans, whose term structure was indexed to the tablita, should have been promulgated at the same time that the new exchange-rate policy was announced in February 1978. The authorities could have attempted to keep the standard loan rate between 10 and 14 percent in real terms, with real deposit rates 2 to 3 percentage points below this level. Real interest rates in Chile would then have been more in line with the successful Taiwanese experience discussed in Chapter 3.

To support a fiscally sound program for stabilizing the price level, what is the main constraint on scaling down nominal interest rates in the organized banking system in this fashion? The state of the balance of payments. If

---

along with a new fiscal policy might be necessary to convince people that the exchange rate is likely to remain stable.

exchange controls on capital account are absent or ineffectual, then governments must worry about capital flight. From 1978 to 1981, however, the opposite problem prevailed in Chile. Unduly large capital inflows threatened a loss of monetary control and an overvaluation of the currency. Indeed, the (falsely) high structure of domestic interest rates likely exacerbated the excessive absorption of foreign capital. Without worrying about capital flight,[2] the Chilean government could have easily scaled both deposit and loan rates of interest down to levels comparable to those in Taiwan. Clearly, some interim credit rationing would be necessary, but in principle one could do this by confining domestic lending to the highest quality (best collateralized) borrowers. By reducing the inflow of foreign capital, the program for stabilizing the domestic price level would have been strengthened. To be sure, however, such a scaling down of interest rates, with consequent credit rationing, was in conflict with the government's policy in the mid and late 1970s of rapidly privatizing and deregulating the commercial banks. Clearly, in the banking sector, Chile did not get its order of liberalization quite right.

With the benefit of hindsight, we are beginning to understand that full liberalization of the banks during a high and variable inflation is not warranted. Unduly high real interest rates will likely prevail in such circumstances, leading to adverse risk selection (as discussed in Chapter 7) both in the quality of the nonbank borrowers who come forward and in the banks' own behavior. These problems with prudential control over bank loan portfolios become magnified in stressful periods when the central bank is trying—one way or another—to impose "tight" money in order to disinflate successfully.

THE SOUTH KOREAN EXPERIENCE: 1981–1984

Are there precedents of other governments scaling down domestic nominal interest rates in the course of a major disinflation? The South Korean govern-

---

2. After 1985, Mexico greatly improved its fiscal policy and embarked on a similar program of exchange rate and price level stabilization as Chile had earlier. As in Chile, nominal interest rates remained very high even though the rate of price inflation slowed sharply. The very high real interest rates of 30–40 percent per year on government debt, much of which was held by the banks, threatened to undermine Mexico's public finances in an otherwise well-conceived economic program. Unlike the earlier Chilean experience, however, Mexico could not scale down these nominal interest rates on peso deposits unilaterally without provoking unsustainable capital flight. By the mid 1980s, the international debt crisis had dried up external sources of capital to all developing countries—and Mexico's greater proximity to the U.S. meant that exchange controls on capital account were unworkable.

Instead, Mexico had to depend on the help of external creditors under the "Brady Plan." By restructuring and reducing external debt, the risk premium on holding peso deposits diminished, and nominal interest rates eventually came down by 1990. But real interest rates in Mexico remain uncomfortably high given the high cost of servicing the internal debt within Mexico itself.

ment's successful price-level stabilization of 1981–84 provides one such example. The relevant interest-rate data are provided in Table 6.4.

Although much less than Chile, South Korea also suffered from inflation, which averaged over 20 percent during 1979–81. In real terms, its standard nominal loan rate of 20 percent (made somewhat greater by the use of compensating won balances) was slightly negative.

Then, with a big fiscal improvement and monetary stringency, South Korea's internal inflation rate was driven down to about 7 percent in 1982 and to only 3 percent in 1983 (Table 6.4). The South Korean authorities anticipated declining inflation by quickly reducing the standard loan rate in stages to 10 percent by mid-1982. Nevertheless, the loan rate became positive in real terms (see the last column in Table 6.4). Over the same interval, the standard short-term interest rate on won deposits was reduced from 14.4 to 6.0 percent.

It should also be noted that the Bank of Korea did not attempt to use its exchange rate as the forcing variable for domestic price-level stabilization, unlike Chile. Indeed, Table 6.5 shows that from 1980 to 1983, the won depreciated a bit faster than the reduction in the domestic inflation rate. In part because the South Korean foreign trade sector was not as fully liberalized as the Chilean, the South Korean government did not believe that international commodity arbitrage could be used to stabilize the domestic price level. Instead, the nominal exchange rate was managed by an informal downward crawl to adjust passively to declining domestic inflation. Thus, as price-level stability was secured, the syndrome of exchange overvaluation was avoided.

This scaling down of domestic interest rates as inflation slowed, while maintaining the rate of downward crawl in the won against the dollar to reflect the inflation differential between South Korea and the United States, prevented undue incentives to move foreign capital into the South Korean economy. Even so, the South Korean government maintained substantial controls on the capital account to prevent a further untoward buildup of international indebtedness during the liberalization process.

A RATIONALE FOR INTEREST-RATE MANAGEMENT

In the course of a major disinflation, why should interest rates on bank assets and liabilities be reduced by deliberate public policy? Shouldn't nominal interest rates be bid down by the market, be allowed to fall naturally, as inflation recedes?

First, one must address the question of correct macroeconomic signaling. Very high nominal interest rates above recorded inflation can easily be interpreted as a signal that most other people in the economy expect inflation to continue and the stabilization program to fail, even though the high nominal rates could be explained ex post on other grounds. Indeed, if enough firms borrow heavily at very high nominal rates of interest, it becomes more probable

TABLE 6.4
Nominal and Real Interest Rates in South Korea

Quarter	GNP Deflator (Rate of Change)	Curb-Market Rate[a] Nominal	Real[c]	Yields on Corporate Bonds Nominal	Real	Yields on Government Bonds Nominal	Real	Bank Lending Rate[b] Nominal	Real
1979									
I	20.1	44.0	23.9	26.1	5.9	23.4	3.3	19.1	−1.1
II	20.3	42.1	21.8	26.8	6.5	24.2	3.9	19.0	−1.3
III	21.4	40.7	10.3	26.9	5.5	25.5	4.1	19.0	−3.6
IV	22.6	42.7	20.1	27.1	4.5	27.5	4.9	10.0	−3.6
Year average	21.2	42.4	21.2	26.7	5.5	25.2	4.0	19.0	−2.2
1980									
I	25.5	50.8	25.3	30.5	5.0	30.3	4.8	24.3	−1.2
II	27.8	48.8	21.0	31.9	4.1	30.6	2.8	24.7	−3.1
III	23.7	42.5	18.8	29.7	6.0	27.9	4.2	23.7	—
IV	25.9	37.7	11.8	28.1	2.2	26.2	0.3	20.8	−5.1
Year average	25.6	45.0	19.4	30.1	4.5	29.8	3.2	23.4	−2.2
1981									
I	21.7	36.6	14.9	24.9	3.2	24.8	3.1	20.0	−1.7
II	17.0	35.2	18.2	22.8	5.8	22.2	5.2	20.0	3.0
III	17.1	33.8	16.7	22.9	5.8	21.8	5.7	20.0	2.9
IV	10.5	35.4	24.9	27.0	16.5	25.5	15.0	19.0	8.5
Year average	15.9	35.3	19.4	24.4	8.5	23.6	7.7	19.8	3.9
1982									
I	13.2	32.6	18.6	21.7	8.5	20.5	7.3	16.1	2.9
II	7.6	33.1	25.5	17.3	9.7	17.1	9.5	13.9	6.3
III	6.6	27.5	20.9	14.3	7.7	15.0	8.4	10.0	3.4
IV	3.7	29.0	25.3	15.7	12.0	16.7	13.0	10.0	6.3
Year average	7.1	30.6	23.5	17.3	10.2	17.3	10.2	12.5	5.4
1983									
I	4.8	24.1	19.3	14.9	10.1	14.4	9.6	10.0	5.2
II	2.2	27.5	25.3	14.0	11.8	13.5	11.3	10.0	7.8
III	2.2	26.8	24.6	14.0	11.8	13.4	11.2	10.0	7.8
IV	2.9	24.7	21.8	14.2	11.2	13.8	10.9	10.0	7.1
Year average	3.0	25.8	22.8	14.2	11.2	13.8	10.8	10.0	7.0
1984									
I	1.2	24.1	22.9	14.0	12.8	13.4	12.2	10.4	9.2
II	2.6	25.7	23.1	13.3	10.7	13.6	11.0	10.5	7.9
III	6.0	23.5	17.5	14.4	8.4	14.7	8.7	10.5	4.5
IV	5.1	25.4	20.3	14.9	9.8	15.2	10.1	11.1	6.0
Year average	3.9	24.7	20.7	14.2	10.2	14.2	10.2	10.6	6.6

Source: Cho 1985. Data taken from Bank of Korea and *Economic Statistics Yearbook.*
[a]Bank of Korea survey data.
[b]Interest rate on bank loans up to one year.
[c]Real interest rate = nominal interest rate − the rate of change of GNP deflator.

TABLE 6.5
Exchange Rates and International Competitiveness in South Korea
(Indices 1980 = 100)

	U.S. Dollar per Won	*Effective Exchange Rates*	
		Nominal	*Real[a]*
1978			
IV	125.1	117.7	94.8
1979			
I	125.1	120.2	99.6
II	125.1	123.8	107.1
III	125.1	123.4	107.2
IV	125.1	127.5	112.2
1980			
I	106.2	110.4	103.7
II	102.0	102.8	100.6
III	98.8	97.1	98.1
IV	93.1	90.6	96.5
1981			
I	93.1	88.3	96.0
II	90.8	90.0	100.1
III	89.0	92.2	105.8
IV	88.3	89.9	102.3
1982			
I	85.3	89.2	102.0
II	83.2	88.9	101.9
III	81.7	89.9	103.1
IV	81.4	89.8	102.5
1983			
I	80.4	85.5	99.4
II	78.7	84.3	97.2
III	77.2	83.8	96.1
IV	76.2	81.9	93.0
1984			
I	76.2	81.5	93.2
II	75.9	81.3	92.5
III	74.8	82.7	94.0
IV	73.9	82.7	93.4
1985			
I	72.2	83.2	94.2

Source: Aghevli and Marquez Ruarte 1985. Data taken from Korean Authorities and IMF Staff estimates.
Note: An increase indicates appreciation.
[a]Adjusted by relative movements in consumer prices.

that the government will keep the inflation rate high in the future in order to bail them out. This reinforces private fears that inflation will not wind down.

Second, when inflationary expectations are still high and uncertain, the problem of adverse risk selection at the microeconomic level in the Stiglitz-Weiss sense is particularly acute (Stiglitz and Weiss 1981). In contracting at any nominal interest rate substantially above the "normal" 10–20 percent range approximating average real rates of return, the borrower must bet on what the future inflation rate will be. He will then accept a riskier project in the hopes of a favorable high yield in case inflation does not bail him out and he has to default anyway. (See Chapter 7.)

Although government supervisory control over private banks can prevent undue risk taking at falsely high real rates of interest, this supervision does not guarantee that the government itself will not exert pressure to make bad loans! The price-level stabilization of 1981–84 was very successful, but the South Korean government's pressure on the banks in the 1970s was less benign. Because of its determination to support the development of domestic heavy industry and South Korean contractors undertaking major construction projects in the Middle East and elsewhere, the South Korean government coerced the banks into making risky long-term loans—many of which are now nonperforming. In the 1980s, the Bank of Korea still provided subsidized credit lines (official discounting at below-market interest rates) to various commercial banks to help them avoid bankruptcy by keeping those old 1970s loans on their books. Into the early 1990s, this overhang of old bad loans continues to hinder the full liberalization of the South Korean banking system.

IMPLEMENTING TIGHT MONEY IN THE TRANSITION FROM HIGH TO LOW INFLATION

In retrospect, it seems clear that Chile should have tightened up the domestic flow of bank credit more (including that financed by foreign borrowing), changed to forward-looking wage indexing, and relied less on the exchange rate as a lever to secure the price level. Because of acute potential problems with adverse risk selection, orthodox tight money relying on very high nominal (and real) interest rates could not work.

The Koreans implicitly recognized this in bringing about their successful price-level stabilization. Nominal interest rates were scaled down consistent with keeping real rates positive, albeit below market-clearing levels. Although the Bank of Korea also reduced reserve requirements as fiscal policy improved, central-bank credit was rationed to the commercial banks and foreign capital inflows were limited in order to secure the desired deflation without significant exchange-rate overvaluation. (Growth in money wages was also scaled down by the South Korean government.)

That is, tight money was imposed while real rates of interest were kept positive and fairly constant by decree. This meant that in order to disinflate, the South Korean banking system as a whole rationed credit to the private sector. However, because the South Korean government's fiscal deficits were simultaneously reduced (as was also the case in Chile), the real flow of loanable funds to the private sector actually increased, thus relieving the supply constraint on domestic output. No net credit squeeze on the private sector was necessary once the South Korean government and its various special agencies stopped directing the flow of bank credit to itself.

Given the equally good and perhaps even more favorable fiscal conditions existing in Chile, it seems—with the benefit of hindsight, of course—that in February 1978, the Chileans should have followed an internal interest rate, wage rate, and bank credit policy more like South Korea's of 1981–84. Then some of the burden of bringing about disinflation could have been taken off nominal exchange-rate policy, and reducing capital inflows during the price-level stabilization would have prevented such severe overvaluation of Chile's real exchange rate.

A CONCLUDING NOTE

Despite the difficulties enumerated above, the potential gains from successfully stabilizing the domestic price level while retaining competitiveness in foreign trade are enormous. South Korea's GNP growth and financial development for several years after the successful 1981–84 stabilization were truly remarkable.[3] The rapid deepening of financial flows within the South Korean economy made possible large net repayments of foreign debt through trade surpluses. Not only did bank deposits continue to increase sharply relative to GNP, but there was a considerable lengthening of the term structure of corporate finance.

The Chilean financial collapse of 1982–83 and the orgy of Chile's foreign borrowing in the preceding three years caused a sharp downturn in real output and left the economy with a huge external debt, which the central bank had to assume. Nevertheless, the liberalization process was only interrupted—albeit severely. Instead of reverting to protectionism, Chile retained its open stance in both foreign and domestic trade. With the subsequent devaluation of its currency made necessary by the cumulative overvaluation prior to the crash, exports are now growing rapidly, and growth in GNP has recovered. The modest ongoing inflation, a consequence of the central bank's deficits from servicing Chile's foreign debt, still inhibits the lengthening of the term structure of internal finance, but bank deposits as a share of GNP are again increasing, while the government continues to sort out the bad loan portfolios of most of the major banks. Chile's excellent economic position in the early 1990s seems to be at least as good as, or better than, that of any of the other major Latin American countries, none of which has succeeded in implementing such thoroughgoing trade, fiscal, and financial reforms.

Finance and trade liberalization, with borrowing and lending at substantial

3. But successful financial stabilizations need not last forever. In the transition to democracy in the early 1990s, the South Koreans are experiencing an internal wage explosion. Moreover, because of untoward pressure from the United States, they unwisely allowed their currency to appreciate sharply in 1988–89 and thereby greatly reduced their international competitiveness.

real rates of interest made possible by a stable price level, is not easy and is full of potential pitfalls. Nevertheless, it remains the only strategy capable of achieving successful economic development. That, of course, was the main message of my 1973 book, *Money and Capital in Economic Development*. It is perhaps a sign of advancing age, however, that I am now more inclined to emphasize the pitfalls.

CHAPTER SEVEN

Macroeconomic Instability

and

Moral Hazard

in Banking

In less-developed economies with low per capita incomes, open markets for common stocks, bonds, mortgages, or even commercial bills are typically insignificant. Information availability and economies of scale are insufficient for small farmers or merchants to issue their own notes or for shares to be publicly traded. Instead, private financial savings in less-developed countries (LDCs) are largely currency and deposits: claims on central banks, commercial banks, savings banks, postal savings deposits, and so on.

This absence of open markets in primary securities (particularly equities) creates more risk in the bank-based capital market. Combined with greater macroeconomic instability in LDCs, considerable tension is created in achieving a regulatory balance between the two traditional roles of the banking system:

1. The monetary function: providing a stable unit of account, store of value, and means of payment

2. Financial intermediation: transferring savings to public and private investors

Because of the third-party benefits that flow from preventing any impairment of the payments mechanism under (1), banks must be carefully regulated toward safety. And this inherently limits their active risk-taking, but still crucial, role in the capital market under (2). Hence individual savers perceive that the government is responsible for the safety of the financial (monetary) assets they own, whether or not there is some formal deposit insurance in place.

Governments rely on a wide variety of rules—capital and reserve requirements, restrictions on what can be lent to any one borrower, detailed inspections of the quality of asset portfolios to ensure proper loan-loss provisions for each risk category, and so on—to limit the capacity of banks to undertake risky investments. Sometimes, for safety reasons, banks are even state-owned, as in the Taiwanese case noted in Chapter 3 and as was true in South Korea well into the 1980s. Even so, if accounting information from enterprises is poor and equity or collateral difficult to judge, bank officers and government regulators have trouble distinguishing ex ante among borrowers in different risk classes.

Without addressing the complex task of how each of the above regulations might be optimally applied, let us focus simply on optimal interest-rate policy for the commercial banks. In this one-dimensional analysis based on interest rates, I initially assume that the other safety regulations are in effect.

Further narrowing the problem, suppose our hypothetical bank has a given supply of loanable funds from the deposit side (less required reserves) and can divide potential nonbank borrowers into a small number of risk classes within which each potential borrower is "observationally equivalent," that is, the subjective probability of default at any given interest rate is the same. The bank's one decision variable is how to set the lending rate of interest, uniform within each risk category, so as to maximize the expected net return per dollar lent.

Following Stiglitz and Weiss (1981), as the real interest rate charged to any one class of borrowers increases, so does the probability of default on loan contracts. Because of the nature of a fixed-interest-rate loan, borrowers get to keep any extraordinary profits if their project turns out well but can default and walk away from unusual losses. Thus, as the interest rate increases,

1. a higher proportion of riskier borrowers will come forward to accept the loan offer, whereas safer borrowers who are unlikely to default will drop out of the applicant pool; this is what Stiglitz and Weiss call "adverse risk selection";

2. any one borrower will tend to change the nature of his own project (insofar as the bank cannot perfectly monitor what he is doing) to make it riskier; this is what Stiglitz and Weiss call the "incentive effect."

Both effects will induce the bank to limit voluntarily the interest rate charged to any one class of borrowers in order to maximize expected profit. In equilibrium, there could be arbitrary credit rationing with a pool of unsatisfied potential borrowers who are observationally equivalent to those who get loans.

Stiglitz and Weiss simply assumed that their bank would behave in a risk-neutral fashion in reaching its rationing equilibrium. Even without regulation by some outside agency, banks in the Stiglitz-Weiss model would voluntarily limit the interest rate charged, while rationing credit, in order to avoid undue adverse risk selection and a decline in their expected profit net of defaults. But I shall show that this natural check on adverse risk selection need not hold if significant macroeconomic instability causes the returns on projects of the nonbank borrowers to be positively correlated with each other *and* the banks suffer from (enjoy?) moral hazard because their deposit base is insured by the government.

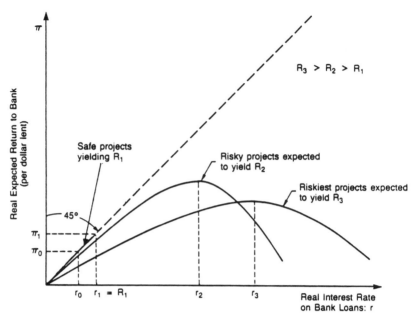

FIGURE 7.1. Bank Profit Maximization with Adverse Risk Selection and Statistically Independent Default Probabilities (Three Classes of Nonbank Borrowers)

ADVERSE RISK SELECTION WHEN THE MACROECONOMY IS STABLE

First, however, let us consider the simpler case of a stable macroeconomy (price level, output, real exchange rate, and so on), as implicitly assumed by Stiglitz and Weiss. Important aspects of their argument are illustrated in Figure 7.1, where the real loan rate, r, is plotted on the horizontal axis, and the real net (after defaults) yield per dollar lent, π, is shown on the vertical axis. In a stable macroeconomic environment, one can reasonably assume (with Stiglitz and Weiss) that the distribution of returns among the well-diversified projects of borrowers is statistically independent of one another; that is, there is no positive covariance among the profit positions of firms. Furthermore, suppose that the number of loan applicants in each risk class, R_i, is "large" so that there is a predictable number of defaults and a deterministic profit to the bank per dollar lent.

Figure 7.1 shows three distinct risk classes—R_1, R_2, and R_3—in ascending order of expected return and variance in that return on the borrower's project. Class R_1 is fully collateralized and perfectly safe with no variance in outcome, with the maximum interest rate the borrower can pay being $r_1 = R_1$. Because there is no adverse risk selection (or incentive effects), the bank's profits increase pari passu with the loan rate along the 45 degree ray from the origin until the maximum at r_1.

The graph R_2 covers riskier projects with a higher expected yield to the borrower. But R_2 lies below and to the right of the 45-degree ray because of incentive effects and adverse risk selection: profits to the bank (per dollar lent) increase more slowly than the loan rate. The maximum profit rate for the bank occurs when the loan rate is set at r_2, after which the influence of adverse risk selection on bank profits more than offsets any further increases in the rate of interest.[1]

Because the highest returns to the bank (net of defaults) occur when lending is restricted to the R_2 category in Figure 7.1, all borrowers in R_3 are completely rationed out—even though they have the most productive projects, albeit with the highest variance in internal returns. Because of adverse risk selection, the bank—with its fixed-interest loan contract—cannot charge an interest rate high enough to cover potential defaults in category R_3. In effect, the limited bank-based capital market cannot finance some of the economy's potentially more productive investment opportunities, as shown in more detail by Cho (1986). Cho demonstrates that further financial deepening in the form of an equities market would be necessary for risky projects in R_3 to receive adequate financing.

Notice that under the assumptions made so far, with the law of large numbers applying within each risk category of statistically independent borrowers and with the bank not being permitted to significantly concentrate its lending on any one borrower, *the bank's optimal strategy is independent of its own risk characteristics*. Because the net yield to the bank is not stochastic, it will choose simply to maximize profits by selecting a (limited) loan rate r_2 applying only to borrowers in category R_2—with arbitrary rationing (unless the bank runs out of this qualified pool of applicants). Without any official interest-rate ceilings, the bank's behavior will be inherently "conservative" without exhibiting the problems of moral hazard discussed below.

Of course, the government can "repress" this inherently conservative financial system by needlessly imposing an even lower interest ceiling (shown by r_0 in Fig. 7.1). This induces the bank to shift its loans to the perfectly safe, but less-productive, borrowers in R_1 and completely ration out borrowers in the other two higher-return areas of the economy. Starting from a position of

1. Note that if the banks were not subject to non-interest-bearing reserve requirements, and if "excess" returns to shareholders' equity above the loan rate were not significant, the net profits earned by the bank per dollar lent could be wholly paid out to depositors. Then the net profits on the vertical scale of Figure 7.1 could be interpreted as the approximate real deposit rate of interest. As in Stiglitz and Weiss 1981, this geometric model is heuristic and is not itself a complete picture of bank profit maximization, where the returns to bank shareholders are distinguished from the yield to depositors.

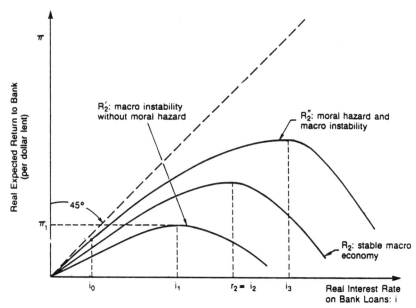

FIGURE 7.2. Moral Hazard in Maximizing Bank Profits: Macroeconomic Instability and Positive Correlation in Default Risks (One Class of Nonbank Borrowers)

loan-rationing equilibrium, financial repression still hurts if interest rates are forced below the level necessary to prevent undue adverse risk selection.

MACROECONOMIC INSTABILITY AND POSITIVE COVARIANCE IN PROJECT YIELDS

Consider how the behavior of nonbank borrowers and of the banks themselves might change if macroeconomic instability is introduced into our previous analysis of adverse risk selection based on the assumption of a stable macroeconomy. The forms that macroeconomic instability can take—changes in the real exchange rate, unexpected inflation or deflation, and so on—are many and varied, as discussed in Chapters 2 and 6. Within our narrow analytical framework, however, the introduction of macroeconomic instability is taken to mean (1) *increased variance* in yields (but without any change in mean) in the real returns of projects being considered by nonbank borrowers and (2) *positive covariance* among the expected returns to projects within any one risk class. All (or at least the majority of) projects will be adversely affected by poor macroeconomic circumstances, with collectively greater profitability in good times. To further simplify, let us confine the analysis to one preferred class of borrowers. The middle line in Figure 7.2 simply reproduces the R_2 profit function of the bank from Figure 7.1, which was drawn under the assumption of no macroeconomic instability.

Now assume no moral hazard within the bank itself. The structure of ownership or the nature of official supervision and control with sufficient required reserves against expected loan losses is such that the bank behaves as if it were averse to risk. Then increased macroeconomic instability (requiring increased bank reserves against defaults) is likely to shift the R_2 profit function in Figure 7.2 downward to the left to the new graph R'_2. Because of higher variance in returns from individual projects, increased macroeconomic instability will lower a risk-averse bank's optimal real loan rate and its own expected profits. Figure 7.2 shows that the optimal real interest rate associated with R'_2 is i_1, which is lower than i_2. And this new equilibrium with a lower real loan rate will, of course, require more stringent credit rationing.

But macroeconomic instability also means that the banks can no longer diversify away the risks they themselves face. Positive covariance among the project returns of the nonbank borrowers now introduces stochastic variance into the bank's own profit net of defaults. The law of large numbers no longer assures the bank of a deterministic yield. Although π in Figure 7.2 shows the *expected* return to the bank, the realized return at the end of the loan period could be considerably more or less because default rates among nonbank borrowers are now positively correlated. Thus even for a risk-averse bank with substantial loan-loss provisions, to keep the threat of bankruptcy minimal the regulatory authority might force the bank to select an even lower real interest rate, as shown by i_0 in Figure 7.2.

In summary, if banks themselves are properly regulated to be risk averse, macroeconomic instability will likely force lower real rates of interest and more severe credit rationing on the system.

MACROECONOMIC INSTABILITY AND THE AGGRAVATION OF MORAL HAZARD IN THE BANKS

Suppose now that the commercial banks are privately owned and that the government's regulatory apparatus for supervising risks assumed by the banks is fairly weak and without adequate loan-loss provisions. Moreover, the government has implicitly or explicitly committed itself to providing deposit insurance. As the Chilean and Argentinean experiences in the 1970s and the American banking experience in the 1980s and 1990s attest, such deposit insurance creates potentially severe problems of moral hazard within the banking system itself (Kane 1985).

Any one bank may well undertake very risky lending at unnaturally high real loan rates of interest on the twin presumptions that (1) favorable outcomes, where the nonbank borrowers succeed in repaying their high-interest loans, will lead to large profits for the bank's shareholders; whereas (2) unfavorable outcomes, with highly correlated defaults among the nonbank borrowers leading to massive losses by the bank in question (and perhaps even the banking system as a whole), will be mainly borne by the monetary authority. Even though the bank owners might lose their equity or ownership claims with an unfavorable outcome, most of the losses will be covered by the deposit-insuring agency. Therefore, ex ante expected profits from risky lending could well be very high because bank profits are not bounded from above in the case of a favorable outcome. In effect, the bank is the beneficiary of an unfair bet against the government; it gets to keep extraordinary profits without having to pay the full social costs of unusually large losses from risky lending.

Strangely enough, when the macroeconomy is stable, a completely diversified bank will be unaffected by such moral hazard because the default rates among the "large" number of nonbank borrowers are not positively correlated. The bank will simply maximize (nonstochastic) expected profit, as shown in Figure 7.1 and in the middle graph in Figure 7.2. (This result depends critically on the maintained assumption that regulation is sufficiently effective to prevent the bank from concentrating its lending to a few large borrowers.)

However, in the presence of macroeconomic instability, which inevitably creates positive covariance in the default rates of the bank's borrowers, moral hazard on the part of the bank itself becomes a very serious problem. With its own future profit now a random variable, our loosely regulated bank with inadequate loan-loss provisions has undue incentive to make high-interest (and therefore risky) loans knowing ex ante that a favorable macroeconomic outcome will lead to very high profits—and that it can walk away from heavy losses.

This interaction between bank moral hazard and macroeconomic instability is shown by the upper graph $R"_2$ in Figure 7.2. The vertical scale now represents the expected revenue per dollar lent *net* of anticipated bank losses to be covered (*ex post facto*) by the deposit-insuring agency in the event of unfavorable outcomes. The bank now behaves *as if* it wants to incur risk; its expected profits are uniformly higher than those of a risk-averse (properly regulated) bank because deposit insurance covers any unusual losses. Thus, with increased macroeconomic instability, a bank subject to moral hazard could well set its loan rate at a higher and riskier level, say i_3 in Figure 7.2. In order to cut their own expected losses from providing deposit insurance, however, the authorities could well try to overcome the bank's moral hazard by forcing it to charge a much lower, and safer, loan rate at, say, i_0.

The Chilean experience from 1976 to 1982 discussed in Chapters 3 and 6 exemplifies how uncontrolled interest rates coupled with (implicit) deposit insurance of the banks could lead to adverse risk selection among nonbank borrowers and severe moral hazard in the banks themselves when the macroeconomy is highly unstable. During this period, Chile was subject to large changes in the rate of price inflation and in its real exchange rate (Corbo 1985). Nevertheless, by 1977 Chile had (re)privatized commercial banks and removed interest-rate ceilings on deposits and loans, with a reduction in official supervision and monitoring of its commercial banks—a mistaken form of "liberal-ization."

Even in the highly developed capital market of the United States, federal deposit insurance is creating severe problems for bank supervisors in curbing undue risk taking by commercial banks as well as savings and loan institutions. In a developing country without an equities market and no well-developed accounting standards and where private (but insured) banks are the principal lenders, the probability of very high "real" (but phony) interest rates is much greater (Cho 1986).

OPTIMAL DOMESTIC FINANCIAL POLICY: THE IMPORTANCE OF A STABLE PRICE LEVEL

Failure to recognize the need for official action to limit bank lending rates was, in part, responsible for the financial collapses in the Southern Cone. Of course, proper bank supervision entails much more than simply setting interest ceilings, which is itself a second-best response. Preventing the concentration of loans to one borrower, limiting foreign exchange risk, requiring adequate reserves against default, and so on are the first line of defense against financial breakdown.

Nevertheless, the existence of moral hazard in banks, such as that induced by the presence of deposit insurance, implies that the government should probably impose a ceiling on the standard loan (and deposit) rate of interest as well as mandating a number of safety-first conditions such as stringent capital requirements. In the absence of such moral hazard the banks could be counted on to limit their own interest charges and behave conservatively by rationing loans. In either case, however, greater instability in the macroeconomy's price level, real exchange rate, terms of trade, and so on reduces the socially optimal real interest rates on bank loans and deposits.

That said, the empirical evidence provided in Chapter 2 underscores the importance of avoiding the opposite but all too common syndrome of financial repression, in which real interest rates are reduced too far below an appropriate loan-rationing equilibrium and are frequently negative in real terms when inflation is high and variable. To achieve high real financial growth, successful developing economies have combined domestic price stability with substantial, even if regulated, nominal rates of interest on both deposits and loans.

CHAPTER EIGHT

Protectionism

in

Foreign Trade:

Quotas versus Tariffs

In 1970, the National Bureau of Economic Research commissioned Professors Jagdish Bhagwati and Anne Krueger to coordinate book-length studies of ten developing countries: Turkey, Ghana, Israel, Egypt, the Philippines, India, South Korea, Chile, Colombia, and Brazil. Then in 1978, Bhagwati and Krueger each published a separate overview of how foreign trade practices common to the ten countries have influenced their economic development. Experiences with quotas, tariffs, and attempts to liberalize spanning the period 1950 to 1972 were systematically incorporated into the two synthesis volumes. Much of the analysis remains surprisingly relevant down to the present day.

In this chapter, I reproduce and update substantial portions of my review of the Bhagwati-Krueger work in order to bring out certain parallels between the use of directed quota allocations (licenses) in the flow of foreign trade and directed credits to preferred borrowers from the domestic financial system. Indeed, if the domestic financial system is repressed as described in Chapters 4 and 5, the incentive to introduce repressive quota restrictions in foreign trade is greatly accentuated.

In addition, I want to contrast a prototypical model of a repressed foreign trade regime, where free arbitrage with the outside world's goods and capital markets is largely blocked, with a more open economy where protectionism is confined to modest tariffs. This distinction between repressed and open foreign trade then sets the stage for the analysis of optimal exchange-rate and foreign payments policies in less-developed countries (LDCs) in Chapters 9 and 10 and the discussion of optimum foreign trade policy in a liberalizing socialist economy in Chapter 12.

THE NONEQUIVALENCE OF TARIFFS AND QUOTAS

A favorite demonstration of teachers of international economics is to show that, under certain assumptions, an omniscient government authority can replace a set of tariffs on imports with an allocatively equivalent set of quotas. Indeed, the formal literature, at the textbook level at least, has lumped tariffs and quotas together under the general rubric of "trade restrictions." In contrast, Bhagwati and Krueger actually define trade liberalization as a process of moving away from quota restrictions at, possibly, disequilibrium exchange rates to arrive at a system where only tariffs are used at an equilibrium exchange rate! India, which was rife with exchange controls, licensing, and import quotas, was, by their definition, illiberal; whereas Brazil, which in the 1960s did rely mainly on tariffs—some of which were very high—to protect domestic industry, was then considered more liberal. (Subsequently, into the 1990s, the general character of Indian trade restrictions has changed surprisingly little, but recurring financial instability in Brazil prompted a regression to severe quota restrictions in the 1980s.)

This idea of "liberalization," moving away from explicit quotas to explicit tariff protection, has its counterpart in the socialist economies of Asia and Eastern Europe in the 1990s—but with one modification. In the socialist economies, quota protection on imports that compete with domestic manufactured or processed goods is *implicit* in the system of exchange controls over currency transacting. In the absence of currency convertibility on current account, the state trading agency simply refuses to authorize imports when domestic supplies of the equivalent product are deemed "ample." Thus, in the transition from a socialist to a market economy, liberalization implies that this implicit quota protection be changed to explicit tariff protection before being gradually eliminated, as worked out in some detail in Chapter 12.

What then are the empirical and analytical roots of Bhagwati's and Krueger's concern to distinguish sharply between tariffs and quota restrictions throughout the two syntheses—and, to some extent, throughout the other ten volumes?

Consider the matter on a purely theoretical level first. What are sufficient conditions for perfect equivalence to hold? Take one import product that is "small" relative to the total trade bill so that it can be analyzed in partial equilibrium. Assume further that domestic producers and consumers are perfectly competitively organized, and they initially face a 50 percent ad valorem import tariff that raises the domestic price of like products by 50 percent and so reduces imports from 1,000 to 500 units. Now suppose the 50 percent tariff is replaced by an "equivalent" quota restriction that allows a maximum of 500 units to be imported. The only apparent difference is that license holders, instead of the government, receive a rental of 50 percent on the foreign price of each permitted import.

But, textbooks aside, the assumptions made thus far are *not* sufficient to guarantee equivalence, as Bhagwati emphasizes (1965, 1978). One must say how the additional import licenses are allocated. If they are auctioned off or simply given to a single person or firm—like a trading house or agency house with a history of importing that product—then a potential monopoly is created.

The exclusive license could generate a further rise in price by restricting supply. Alternatively, suppose licenses (and their economic rents) are apportioned to users by some economic criterion such as "capacity" for utilizing imported industrial materials. This immediately sets off a scramble by potential demanders to satisfy this criterion, for example, by expanding capacity more than in the tariff case. Only in the unlikely event that licenses are distributed widely and by economic criteria extraneous to the industry in question will one avoid some *endogenous* shift in the domestic supply or demand curve that distorts resource allocation beyond that occasioned by a simple tariff. And Bhagwati's major contribution was to carefully collate and document the incredible variety of endogenous distortions that arise out of the quota restriction systems to which the ten countries resorted in greater and lesser degrees.

FIVE PHASES OF QUOTA RESTRICTIONS AND OTHER EXCHANGE CONTROLS

Before reviewing the consequences for static and dynamic allocative efficiency of quota restriction regimes, let us get some idea of their origin and persistence in the countries. Bhagwati and Krueger delineate the cyclical intensity of the quota restrictions on both imports and exports in five phases, which need not be followed in a given historical order.[1]

Phase I is characterized by the imposition or sharp intensification of relatively undifferentiated or across-the-board import controls, usually undertaken to influence the balance of international payments. It might start in response to an unsustainable payments deficit resulting from prior inflationary pressure at a fixed exchange rate, perhaps due to the initiation of a large-scale development plan. Alternatively, it could result from a sharp drop in price of some major export or from unexpected capital flight occasioned by the buildup of external indebtedness, both of which would run down foreign exchange reserves. With no immediately protectionist intent, the government in this phase often imposes rules of thumb such as (1) this year's imports in every identifiable category can only be 80 percent of last year's, or (2) exporters must convert 90 percent of all foreign currency receipts into the domestic currency within thirty days. (Across-the-board tariffs, which usually require cumbersome legislative or parliamentary approval, are typically too slow or too uncertain to offset the macroeconomic impact of the initiating disturbance and achieve balance-of-payments equilibrium.)

Having committed itself to generalized exchange controls for reasons Bhagwati and Krueger do not analyze in any depth, our prototype country then succumbs in phase II to much stronger protectionist and dirigistic influences that Bhagwati and Krueger do analyze with remarkable thoroughness.

---

1. These phases are an augmented and analytically more developed version of the classification suggested in Bhagwati (1968).

Phase II is characterized by increased and more specific restrictiveness of the entire control system. Its hallmark is the proliferation of detailed regulations, administered by a large bureaucracy, to *differentiate* among alternative end uses of imports. Priorities are established to keep plants from closing from lack of spare parts or industrial raw materials and possibly to maintain supplies of basic foodstuffs for consumption. Import licenses are distinguished according to origin and destination (e.g., between wholesalers and final users) and according to very detailed type (capital goods, intermediate goods, and consumer goods). The net result is familiar in all ten countries: goods deemed "essential" by the bureaucrats come in at relatively low prices (relative to those prevailing in the domestic market) with large economic rents accruing to fortunate licensees; whereas inessential goods are kept out, thus increasing their domestic prices so as to provide enormous protection to "inessential" import substitution industries. At this point the administration of licensing procedures can become more sophisticated in the sense that taxes or special customs duties are often levied to soak up some of the economic rents accruing to particular import licensees—although others in the same commodity categories may be exempted. Moreover, specific exporters may get special subsidies to offset the overvalued domestic currency.

Although phase II has been virtually a stationary equilibrium for years in some countries, from time to time in others foreign exchange shortages become too severe (because of disincentives given to exporters) or too many obvious anomalies develop in the pricing and allocation of imports. Thus, pressure develops to devalue the currency and "rationalize."

Phase III is a major discrete devaluation, which occurred twenty-two times for the group of ten from 1950 to 1970, and its aftermath. But the degree of rationalization accompanying devaluation can vary enormously. Some countries used devaluation primarily to simplify the administration of foreign trade. Exchange controls can be relaxed, and more-or-less equivalent subsidies for exporters and surcharges on imports can be eliminated. Many of the devaluations in the ten countries were just this sort of tidying up operation. In other cases, however, the intent is to push the real devaluation much further in order to increase the export orientation of the economy and to reduce net incentives for import substitution by actually eliminating import quota restrictions. The devaluation may be part of a comprehensive package to restore the economy's access to external capital by reducing domestic prices and costs measured in terms of foreign exchange.

After phase III in one of its several manifestations, many countries regressed back to phase II; others continued the liberalization into *phase IV*. In phase IV, quota restrictions are greatly reduced and/or replaced by formal tariffs so that relative prices become more important in determining what is actually imported. The average premium on import licenses falls, and the dispersion in incentives to deviate from world trade prices is reduced. In the 1960s and early 1970s, Bhagwati and Krueger found that South Korea and Brazil maintained phase IV most systematically.

Finally, *phase V* is full currency convertibility on current account with quantitative restrictions on foreign trade not employed as a significant means of regulating the balance of payments. The pegged exchange rate is at its equilibrium level, and monetary policy and fiscal policy are consciously employed to maintain external balance. Bhagwati and Krueger found that perhaps only Israel, and then only in the early 1970s, precariously maintained this state of bliss.

Note that in the Bhagwati-Krueger formula, however, phase V could be associated with high tariffs and thus still be biased against exports. Also, substantial detailed controls on capital account, necessitating (implicitly) a pegged exchange rate, might still be retained in phase V. In the process of economic development, free currency convertibility seems to be either very hard to attain or not a highly regarded objective on the part of the authorities in poor countries. And why the elimination of capital controls comes last in the liberalization process is taken up more specifically in Chapter 9.

Empirically, each phase is hardly a sharply distinguishable entity. Nevertheless, Figure 8.1 nicely summarizes the temporal pattern of quota restrictions employed by the group of ten. What is particularly fascinating is the cyclical character of the phases, as one succeeds another in no well-established order.

THE MICROECONOMICS OF DISTORTIONS FROM QUOTA RESTRICTIONS

Let us now review in more detail Bhagwati's analysis of the tightly controlled regimes of phase II. With the possible exception of Israel, each of the group of ten had substantial experience with phase II: detailed exchange and quota controls on imports and/or exports that, in part, were meant to be protectionist in character by substantially altering the pattern of domestic resource use. On the import side alone, Bhagwati (1978, 13) notes and systematizes a bewildering variety of categories of quota restrictions:

    1. The regulation of imports by source

    2. The regulation of imports by commodity composition

    3. The regulation of imports by end use

    4. The regulation of imports by payments conditions

    5. Additional ad hoc regulations regarding surcharges (or multiple exchange rates) that determine the cost or usefulness of the license to import.

How then do these quota restrictions originate? Not all are indigenous. Although the industrial countries of North America, Western Europe, and Japan maintain more-or-less fully convertible currencies and honor the most-favored-nation (MFN) principle of the General Agreement on Tariffs and Trade (GATT), they have not applied this principle consistently in negotiating export outlets in LDCs. Aid tying, including the extension of export credits

I   II III IV V

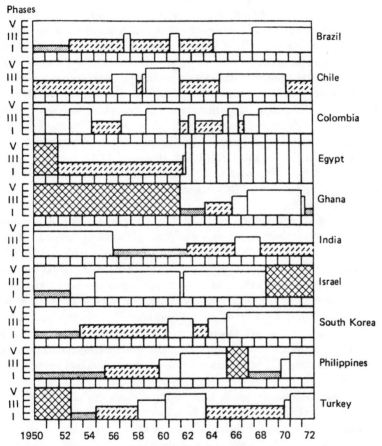

Note: In Egypt after 1961, the export and import trades became government monopolies, so that the phase system of classification no longer fits.

FIGURE 8.1. Phases of Exchange Control Regimes for Ten Countries, 1950–72. (*Sources:* Krueger: 1978b, 38; Bhagwati: 1978, 61.)

at below-market rates of interest, in effect requires recipient LDCs to regulate their imports by source or by payments conditions. America's attempts to improve its balance-of-payments position in the 1960s encouraged the proliferation of preferred lists of American goods from which aid recipients had to choose. Exports of American food grains to LDCs in the 1960s under Public Law 480 encouraged the proliferation of LDC import restrictions on like products that were not similarly subsidized. Dumping in LDCs of European commodity surpluses sometimes has similar side effects. Bilateral trade agreements with the centrally planned economies of Eastern Europe often had to be enforced by exchange controls. Into the 1980s and 1990s, major donor countries like Japan often include their "development assistance" as a subsidy element in ordinary commercial credits; thus such assistance can be obtained by the LDC in question only if it agrees to restrict its purchases from such credits to Japanese goods.

More passively, perhaps, the industrial countries have acquiesced to the massive violation of liberal trading principles by LDCs. Article XVIII of the GATT is a general escape clause that allows poor countries—at their behest—to impose any tariff or quota restriction for "developmental" purposes. Unlike the industrial economies, therefore, LDCs are not effectively part of the GATT legal mechanism for securing freer trade. However, LDCs generally receive MFN treatment for their exports to the industrial economies (with a few notable exceptions when particular LDCs become too successful in particular product lines, such as textiles).

Although these external influences have been important, the momentum for deepening quota restriction regimes into phase II is mainly internal. Starting from phase I or phase IV, Bhagwati and Krueger note remarkable protectionist pressure in virtually every country from Israel to Ghana to expand the list of prohibited imports, goods that in any way compete with existing or prospective domestic production. And such pressure is readily understandable in a general equilibrium sense if the domestic currency is chronically overvalued because some industries are already receiving protection, thus making imports look unduly cheap to others (McKinnon 1966). But this general equilibrium argument is, at the margin, a justification for new tariffs as much as for new quota restrictions.

At the microeconomic level, however, the really big difference in the economic impact of quota restrictions from that of tariffs arises in the regulation of imports by *end use*—Bhagwati's point 3 above. Here simple tariffs on imports cannot possibly (1) allocate according to functional end use (e.g., for use in production in industry A compared with industry B, investment versus consumption versus re-export) or (2) allocate among rival claimants for licenses (e.g., different regions, different firms, public versus private, one political party versus another) after functional end uses have been decided on.

In short, if one forecloses the possibility of a competitive auction among disinterested claimants, direct license allocations to specific end users become the common administrative response. Indeed, a truly disinterested bidder for the typical import license may not exist—let alone a large number in each license category. The outcome in phase II is that the import-licensing authorities—whatever their initial intent—begin to influence the whole internal flow of trade and commerce. Moreover, the distribution or redistribution of income through the assignment of license premiums becomes quantitatively very significant.

For example, for industrial intermediate inputs, those licensing authorities that are not corrupted typically do not want to concentrate licenses to import good X in too few hands. Lacking other criteria, they may try to distribute licenses evenly or "fairly" to all claimants that have used the product in the past. If licenses are not transferable, this could freeze the traditional industrial structure at small, possibly uneconomic, scales of output, where firms do not (cannot) compete with one another. (As seen in Chapter 3, this freeze on economic activity is similar to that associated with allocating heavily subsidized credits to small farmers by bureaucratic rules which also try to be "fair.")

Bhagwati and Krueger do a remarkable job in analyzing the distortions arising from the elaborate and complex quota restriction regimes they observed. Excess plant capacity, failure to absorb unskilled labor into the industrial labor force, rampant corruption and smuggling, the repression of exports, the absence of a market as opposed to bureaucratic competition among licensees, are all taken up and nicely analyzed, although quantitative estimates of such effects are hard to come by. As Bhagwati (1978, chs. 6 and 7) notes, the extreme inefficiencies and anomalies evident in the static allocation of resources do *not* seem to be offset by dynamic advantages of higher saving or greater entrepreneurial dynamism à la Schumpeter. Only Israel and South Korea succeeded, in the sample period, in consistently reducing, rather than increasing, the scope of their quota restriction regimes. The others were left with inefficient industrial machines that exhibited surprisingly high capital-output ratios and were not very competitive in world markets given their low wage structures.

THE RATIONALE FOR QUOTA RESTRICTIONS IN FINANCIALLY REPRESSED ECONOMIES

Neither Bhagwati nor Krueger discussed why the group of ten or other LDCs are so prone to incorporate quota restrictions as more or less accepted and acceptable economic policy. The authors' overwhelming criticism and empirical documentation of practices in phase II should be read by all concerned with economic development. Yet, if the economic results are so unfortunate, why do we observe phase II in so many LDCs in Latin America, Africa, and Asia—in addition to those explicitly studied by Bhagwati and Krueger—and also observe less-extreme quota restriction situations such as phases IV and I?

First, macroeconomic instability tends to generate a "demand" for quota restrictions. Domestic financial and price-level instability, which is usually associated with high and variable inflation, generates a (second-best) argument for quota restrictions per se because real and nominal exchange rates become highly variable and unpredictable (Edwards 1989). As analyzed in Chapter 2, this increased exchange risk has potentially deleterious effects on the productivity of domestic investment. Thus the authorities may try to mitigate this investment risk by protecting some of their producers with absolute quota restrictions because the protective effects of such restrictions are relatively invulnerable to exchange-rate changes. The same limited flow of imports is ensured no matter what happens to the exchange rate. In contrast, the protective effect from given import tariffs can easily be upset by a real appreciation of the domestic currency, causing domestic producers of import substitutes to incur unexpectedly large losses.

Second, what microeconomic arguments might explain the proliferation of quota restrictions even if the real exchange rate was assumed to be stable? The answer may lie in the realm of politics as much as in economics. For countries with rather weak constitutional limits on the assertion of economic power by the government of the day, favorable allocations of quota restrictions can reward one's political friends, and the denial of licenses (including the permission to export freely at an equilibrium exchange rate) can be economically devastating to groups who are politically unfriendly. Even if a formal quota restriction regime is put in place for strictly economic reasons, the pressures to distribute positive and negative patronage this way are difficult to resist.

Beyond simple patronage, however, many governments in LDCs are (were) self-styled socialists who view their legitimate mandate to be one of extending state control over domestic economic activity. Even military or sectarian governments, on what is thought to be the political Right, are often uninhibited interventionists. But these same governments are usually too weak in their formal administrative apparatuses, perhaps in part because of some residual constitutional restraints, to seize full control of domestic trade and commerce in the mode of the centrally planned economies of Russia and China before perestroika. Indeed, fully centrally planned economies practice a much more severe form of currency inconvertibility. Enterprises effectively operate with blocked cash balances even in the conduct of domestic trade. That is to say, enterprises must negotiate with the central-planning bureau before money can be spent to buy from *domestic* as well as from foreign sources of supply, as analyzed in more depth in Chapter 11. Moreover, the state trading agency, which monopolizes all international commerce in centrally planned economies, aims to mesh flows of imports and exports with the central plan.

Without such a strong planning apparatus for allocating resources directly, governments in our LDCs find that foreign trade is more easily controlled than domestic trade because of (1) the need of traders to change from foreign to domestic money (or vice versa) and (2) the long history of raising revenue by tariffs and licensing at a limited number of border-crossing stations and ports that conveniently encompass the economy. Hence, by this ideological argument, quota restriction regimes are an indirect but second-best method of exercising a socialist or otherwise interventionist mandate. Making the point more weakly, in the past most LDC governments were not ideologically inhibited from embarking on such detailed interventions.

Although I believe these purely political arguments apply in at least some of the group of ten, the lapsing into quota restriction regimes in a rather uncontrolled way in many others suggests that economic misdirection may be equally important. This misdirection has both fiscal and financial aspects. Let us discuss each in turn.

Suppose central planning and the concentration of economic power are not economic goals for their own sakes. Instead, the government is satisfied with a more decentralized market system *provided that* certain alleged economic distortions are adequately dealt with. Specifically, the government believes that inadequate market incentives exist for rapid industrialization. Because this is such a familiar theme in the literature of economic development, consider a summary tripartite classification:

1. Product-market distortions where, for example, there exist extramarket effects such as learning by doing or those associated with infant industries

2. Labor-market distortions where industrial or urban real wages are well above the opportunity cost of using labor in the rural parts of the economy

3. Financial distortions where, for example, no adequate capital market exists for mobilizing a rural surplus as a source of finance for new industrial development.

Governments in LDCs are prone to intervene on all three grounds. However, the theoretical literature has successfully criticized the fiscal inefficiency of using restrictions on *foreign* trade to compensate for what are essentially *domestic* economic distortions. Indeed, for categories 1 and 2 at least, Bhagwati himself (1971; see also Johnson 1965) has demonstrated that taxes and subsidies should be used to offset distortions directly in the markets where they appear. That is, for those new industries where technological spillover is very high and proportional to the level of production, direct production subsidies should be employed. If the urban wage is too high and there is surplus labor in agriculture, some kind of subsidy to industrial employment is preferred. At most, tariffs on competing imports can only be a second- or third-best policy. Finally, from Bhagwati and Krueger's convincing empirical demonstration, quota restrictions on foreign trade must be a distant fourth-best—or worst-possible—solution to the problem of overcoming domestic distortions.

But this still leaves open the question, why are quota restrictions so prevalent in practice? The problem is that this theoretical critique of using trade restrictions to correct domestic distortions implicitly presumes that governments in LDCs have control over their public finances. Precisely because governments cannot easily raise broadly based domestic taxes to support expensive development plans, "first-best" production or employment subsidies—categories 1 and 2 above—are out of the question. And frequent fiscal crises in LDCs often revolve around the problem of covering public sector deficits in a situation where capital markets are too rudimentary to permit government bonds to be sold directly to the nonbank public. Hence the authorities are frequently reduced to manipulating the flow of foreign trade and payments on the one hand and the flow of money and bank credit on the other.

But this hypothesis of domestic fiscal incapacity seems to be, at most, an argument for tariffs on competing imports, if one wants to compensate for distortions in categories 1 and 2. On balance, tariffs, which protect the final output of domestic producers, are no more difficult to administer than quota restrictions. Moreover, tariffs have the great advantage of being fiscally sound because part of the equivalent tax that consumers pay, in order to subsidize producers, is collected by the government, which needs the revenue anyway. Yet, Bhagwati and Krueger found few LDCs that made sustained progress away from quota restrictions to the use of tariffs and border tax adjustments.

A deeper economic explanation seems necessary. In a financially repressed economy, an open capital market barely exists and is incapable of channeling funds for investment into high-priority uses—category 3 above. Even in the highly protected import-competing sector, entrepreneurs find that they cannot effectively bid for bank credits. In this context, possession of an exclusive license to import some necessary intermediate good (industrial materials or capital equipment) performs an important dual role:

    1. The holder of a license gets a capital grant in the form of a premium that can be applied toward investment.

    2. The exclusivity of the license allows the holder to bid more easily for funds from the repressed financial system. The license is itself a form of collateral indicating that the enterprise in question is economically viable.

A simple protective tariff on final output does not confer exclusive advantages to particular entrepreneurs and thus is not so strongly geared to improving the financial position of an identifiable firm, that is, relaxing the capital constraint that it faces. Hence, I hypothesize that widespread financial repression provides some microeconomic rationale for the persistent use of quota restrictions in LDCs to encourage particular kinds of investment. (Of course, this argument is not inconsistent with political patronage being used as a basis for parceling out import licenses.)

Thus, the successful elimination of quota restriction regimes is more likely, and indeed may only be fully desirable economically, if packaged with a more general program to reestablish financial stability by reducing volatility in the real exchange rate on the one hand and improving the workings of the domestic capital market on the other. In the optimum order of economic liberalization, one might not want to eliminate all quotas in foreign trade, nor convert them to tarriff "equivalents," until a measure of financial stability has been achieved.

CHAPTER NINE

Exchange-Rate Policy

in Repressed

and

Open Economies

$\mathbf{F}$or an exogenously given fiscal deficit, Chapter 5 described how to minimize the rate of price inflation through appropriate use of the "reserve tax" on domestic bank deposits. The result was some unavoidable degree of domestic financial repression in the form of a wedge between deposit and lending rates of interest.

Suppose now that such an inflation-prone economy is open to foreign trade. How best might foreign exchange policy complement the domestic inflation minimization strategy outlined in Chapter 5 while also minimizing the incentives to impose highly distorting quota restrictions as described by Bhagwati (1978) and Krueger (1978b) and reviewed in Chapter 8?

The monetary technicians in the foreign exchange department of the central bank want to ensure that the inflation tax does not fall unduly heavily on the foreign sector: exports should not be disadvantaged. On the other hand, the management of the foreign exchanges—trade and capital flows—should not create additional inflationary pressure in the domestic economy. When both foreign trade and domestic finance are somewhat repressed, these goals can best be reconciled by (1) imposing exchange controls on outflows *and* inflows of private capital and by (2) roughly indexing the nominal exchange rate to offset inflation in order to keep the real exchange rate fairly constant.

However, once liberalization occurs so that the economy becomes more open to foreign trade on commodity account and domestic interest rates are freely determined, "passively" indexing the exchange rate and maintaining capital controls become more difficult and less desirable.

THE CASE FOR EXCHANGE CONTROLS IN A REPRESSED ECONOMY

Consider first the case for two-way exchange controls on international flows of private capital. The government itself could finance part of the fiscal deficit abroad by negotiating directly with foreign creditors. It was assumed above, however, that a substantial proportion of the fiscal deficit must be financed by taxing the domestic financial system. From the analysis in Chapters 4 and 5, real yields on currency and term deposits denominated in domestic money are depressed by this form of taxation, and depositors will substitute financial assets denominated in a "hard" foreign money (usually dollars) unless prevented from doing so. Hence, the tight controls on capital outflows so common in repressed economies are appropriate. Otherwise the deposit (tax) base on which the inflation tax is levied will shrink (Nichols 1974), and the rate of inflation escalates.

What is less obvious is that potential borrowers from the domestic banking system—with loans ordinarily denominated in pesos—would evade the tax by obtaining cheaper foreign credits denominated in dollars. Equation (4.5) in Chapter 4 showed how reserve requirements interact with the inflation rate to drive a wedge between domestic interest rates on term deposits and on loans. By forcing higher interest rates on borrowers, the government extracts more revenue for a given rate of inflation, and real yields to depositors hold up somewhat better. If, instead, businesses are free to borrow abroad, the domestic real loan rate is reduced, along with revenue to the government and yields to depositors. The term-deposit part of the domestic monetary tax base unduly erodes—and inflation becomes correspondingly higher—unless such private foreign borrowing is restricted.

Because the governments of repressed economies may consider themselves to be short of foreign exchange on a month-to-month basis, they often behave myopically: they encourage, rather than discourage, inflows of private capital—even though such inflows are artificially stimulated by domestic borrowers trying to evade the domestic inflation tax. Indeed, if the government is fixing the exchange rate, such private capital inflows directly augment official exchange reserves. But the loss of real revenue from the domestic financial system is manifest in the higher rate of base-money creation (inflation) coming through the foreign component of the domestic monetary base.

If private capital inflows are not restricted outright, they should be taxed by reserve requirements or similar measures such that the net tax burden on firms that borrow abroad is roughly equal to the wedge effect imposed on those that must borrow domestically (Brock 1984). Indeed, because the inflation-prone government is short of revenue, reserve taxes on foreign borrowing are the most efficient solution. If, however, inflows of foreign capital are not taxed or otherwise restricted, the monetary authorities may find that the external indebtedness of domestic firms builds up too rapidly—thus contributing to the "overborrowing" syndrome (to be discussed in Ch. 10) that was an important ingredient in the present international debt crisis.

Modern examples abound of countries taxing their domestic financial systems by inflation without realizing the importance of controlling foreign capital flows in order to maintain the tax base. To cite but two examples:

In late 1977, Israel precipitately abolished exchange controls on residents holding foreign currency or borrowing abroad, but the real size of its fiscal deficit remained unchanged. The domestic rate of inflation, which had been running at about 30 percent per year in 1974–76, then accelerated to over 100 percent per year in 1978–80. The smaller size of the domestic financial system required a much higher rate of price inflation in order to extract the same amount of revenue.

In 1977 and 1978, while still running a substantial (consolidated) fiscal deficit, Argentina loosened its controls on capital inflows and outflows. Then, in 1979–80, it reduced reserve requirements on all classes of bank deposits. These premature measures eroded the real size of the taxable part of the domestic financial system. The resulting inflationary explosion was temporarily forestalled in 1979–80 by fixing the exchange rate. Inevitably, the peso became overvalued. In 1981, when the fixed exchange rate broke down, domestic inflation accelerated dramatically.

As a postscript to these rather sad episodes, observers should remember that allowing an untaxed foreign currency component of the domestic financial system to develop within the country—the parallel circulation of foreign currency within the domestic economy—is just as bad as allowing free international inflows and outflows of capital. Not only Israel and Argentina but Peru, Mexico, Poland, and Yugoslavia permitted substantial "dollarization" of their economies in the 1980s. This greatly narrows the local-currency part of the domestic financial system and sets the stage for an unnecessarily violent inflationary explosion if and when fiscal control is lost. If the government develops an uncovered fiscal deficit that can no longer be financed abroad or by issuing dollar securities at home, the necessary issue of base money in domestic currency will lead to much greater price inflation because of the erosion of the real size of the domestic monetary system.[1]

Allowing untaxed dollar bank accounts to develop within the country can often be justified on the grounds of short-run expediency. For example, it can be used to encourage expatriate workers or capitalists to remit their foreign exchange earnings. But, once in place, a large foreign currency component in the domestic financial system has the characteristics of an "economic time bomb" (a felicitous phrase owed to Jacob Frenkel).

Clearly, monetary technicians should view exchange controls as an integral part of the financial management of a repressed economy. Only after very substantial fiscal, monetary, and foreign trade measures are taken to relieve that repression should such restrictions on international inflows and outflows of capital be lifted.

1. This issue will come up again in sharp relief in Chapter 11 in discussing whether a new "hard" ruble or foreign-currency-backed ruble should—in the 1990s—circulate along with the old soft ruble that the Soviet government is taxing by inflation in order to cover its fiscal deficit.

INDEXING THE EXCHANGE RATE

An immediate consequence of imposing exchange controls in a repressed economy is that the central bank must make the market for foreign exchange. Private foreign exchange dealers, banks, or multinational firms cannot do so, because exchange controls prevent them from moving capital into and out of the country. Potential private dealers cannot freely assume positive or negative positions in foreign exchange (against the domestic currency) and thus are not collectively capable of establishing a market-clearing exchange rate. Nonspeculative merchants are not by themselves capable of creating a stable foreign exchange market (McKinnon 1979b, ch. 7). Without direct government participation, therefore, the exchange market will be highly illiquid and hopelessly unstable.

Given the necessity of intervention, the government must still decide whether to establish an official parity or be a market maker within a no-par regime. How often and by what procedure should the exchange rate be adjusted, if ever? In a repressed economy the government should avoid discrete changes in the foreign exchange rate. The rate should be adjusted parallel to whatever degree of inflation tax the government is levying on the domestic financial system.

A passive downward crawl in the exchange rate (Williamson 1965) need not add to the price-level instability of an inflation-prone economy if foreign trade is substantially restricted by quotas and high tariffs and if capital flows are blocked by exchange controls. And many less-developed countries, with repressed financial systems, also repress their foreign trade (Krueger 1978b), as discussed in the previous chapter. Consider how a number of countries— Chile, Brazil, Peru, Portugal, and others—have sometimes indexed against domestically generated price inflation by continuously adjusting the nominal exchange rate in order to stabilize the real one.

Suppose E is the nominal exchange rate in pesos per dollar. P^* is the foreign price level in dollars, and P is the domestic price level in pesos. If P and P^* are broadly based general price indexes like the wholesale and consumer price indexes, commodity arbitrage in our repressed economy is too weak to link foreign and domestic price levels at the prevailing exchange rate. When quota restrictions and high tariffs are prevalent, the "law of one price" need not hold naturally. There is imperfect commodity arbitrage:

(9.1) $$P \neq EP^*.$$

In effect, quantitative restrictions convert most potentially tradable goods, whose domestic prices would normally be determined by international arbitrage, into "pseudo-nontradables," whose domestic prices are determined mainly by domestic supply and demand (McKinnon 1979a). Hence, domestic price inflation, as measured by the left-hand side of equation (9.1), may proceed independently of the right-hand side, unless the authorities consciously manipulate the nominal exchange rate to offset it.

Why might the authorities wish to continually raise E (depreciate the domestic currency) to offset domestic price inflation? Most repressed economies still depend heavily on unprotected export activities that must compete at world prices. In addition, even in a repressed economy, a few import-substituting industries may still face unrestricted competition from abroad. To stabilize the cost-price relationships for these few genuinely tradable activities, the authorities would like to maintain the real exchange rate, θ, at a predictable level:

$$(9.2) \qquad\qquad \theta = EP^*/P.$$

For a given foreign price level, any upward movement in P could be quickly offset by an upward adjustment in E (a depreciation or downward crawl of the domestic currency). The competitive position of exporters is then protected: the rigid real exchange rate ensures that a variable inflation tax does not fall unduly heavily on them. Exporters are taxed (along with everyone else) to the extent that they hold domestic currency or borrow from the domestic financial system, but they are not taxed when their foreign exchange earnings are translated back into the domestic currency. Unpredictable cycles in which overvaluation (high domestic inflation and a fixed exchange rate) is followed by a massive devaluation and a period of currency undervaluation are avoided.[2] In effect, an official commitment to indexing gives exporters valuable assurance that their domestic prices will not change capriciously relative to their costs of production. Because of this insulation from monetary or foreign exchange instability, investment in export activities can be undertaken more efficiently (as discussed in Ch. 2).

In the presence of a continuing and independently determined inflation in domestic prices, such indexing implies a passive, but variable, downward crawl (rise in E) in the nominal exchange rate. However, the authorities might have to make several adjustments when determining how much and how fast the exchange rate actually moves.

First, there may be more than one price index for measuring the inflation rate, rather than the unique P in our model. A broadly based index of tradable-goods prices would be preferable to a consumer price index. But if the latter is the only comprehensive index available, it is still worth using if price

---

2. This argument is a bit oversimplified. Insofar as there are substantial restrictions on imports coming into the domestic economy, even an equilibrium exchange rate associated with balanced trade will be biased against exporters. This bias can be eliminated only under full trade liberalization. An indexed exchange rate merely avoids an additional cyclical unplanned bias against exporting.

inflation is at all significant. However, discretionary adjustments in the nominal exchange rate may be necessary to compensate for "errors of measurement" in the underlying price indexes.

Second, there is the question of what adjustments should be made for international inflation. Often the price levels of trading partners do not move in unison. Some appropriately simple weighing system is not difficult to establish, but it may also call for periodic adjustments to compensate for imperfections in the weighting scheme.

Third, the authorities should not adjust the exchange rate discretely every month. Rather, if the domestic price index jumps 6 percent in a month, as announced on a single day, the required 6 percent adjustment in the exchange rate is best smoothed over thirty days, with adjustment of, say, 0.2 percentage points per day. In the classic mode of the crawling peg (Williamson 1965), this would minimize the propensity of traders to undermine the exchange controls by speculating on discrete exchange-rate changes. Each small movement in the rate is not worth the transaction costs of taking a speculative position.

Finally, if changes in the monthly price indexes are highly variable (say 6 percent one month and 2 percent the next) and the authorities have reason to believe that one month is "unusual," some ad hoc intermonth smoothing of the variable crawl is warranted.

However, the basic objective should be well advertised: to alter the nominal exchange rate with continual small adjustments at deliberate speed by whatever amount domestic price inflation exceeds that of the trading partners to whose currencies the domestic currency is pegged.

CURRENCY SUBSTITUTION AND FINANCIAL INSTABILITY: REPRESSED VERSUS OPEN ECONOMIES

Wouldn't a variable (indexed) downward crawl further exacerbate domestic financial instability? A fixed exchange rate, besides being an important political symbol, is often deemed necessary to stabilize price-level expectations and inspire confidence in the government's financial future. Although this traditional view is more-or-less correct for a completely open economy, it is invalid for a repressed economy that is insulated from financial and commodity arbitrage with the outside world and must resort to the inflation tax. Far better to regularize the inevitable exchange-rate adjustment in a series of small steps that are reported only in the back pages of the newspapers than to endure the occasional massive devaluation, following a squeeze on exporters, that is a threat to both political and economic stability.

First, consider why exchange controls on capital account facilitate the management of an indexed exchange rate. Suppose that our hypothetical price index is published on August 1 and shows 6 percent inflation for the month of

July, a substantially higher rate of inflation than the monthly average of 3 percent that has been experienced in the first half of the year. Everyone now knows that the government is committed to speeding up the rate of mini-devaluation—the downward crawl—into the "near future."

Suppose that, despite the continuing domestic inflation, the authorities in a completely open economy operate this indexing procedure *without* exchange controls. In the first half of the year, firms and individuals will have adjusted their portfolio holdings of currency and term deposits on the basis of a relatively low anticipated rate of inflation and exchange depreciation, the rates of interest on term deposits and loans having been determined endogenously. On August 1, however, the expected rate of smooth exchange depreciation suddenly increases. Because individuals have unrestricted access to foreign currency holdings, the demand for domestic money will fall sharply in favor of foreign-exchange assets.

More generally, destabilizing currency substitution will occur continually as the government varies the rate of downward crawl in the absence of exchange controls. (These short-run effects are in addition to the long-run shrinkage of the domestic monetary base caused by individuals who are avoiding the domestic inflation tax by holding foreign exchange assets.) For an open economy, then, the demand functions for currency and term deposits have to be respecified to include the expected rate of exchange depreciation as an important determining variable.

International currency substitution, in response to predictable exchange-rate changes in an open economy, may occur both directly and indirectly. Direct substitution out of domestic currency (and demand deposits) into foreign currencies is one channel, but one mainly confined to international traders with working cash balances both at home and abroad. Currency narrowly defined does not bear any protective market-equilibrating rate of interest to dampen such switching.

Less obviously, indirect substitution occurs within the domestic financial system as people move from currency to term deposits. With unrestricted international financial arbitrage, nominal rates of interest on domestic term deposits and loans increase in response to the anticipated faster exchange-rate depreciation. This induces the broad mass of domestic transactors to move out of currency, which has a high reserve requirement, into term deposits, which have a lower reserve requirement. Through this second and probably more important channel, the demand for domestic base money falls and capital flows out. Both channels are portrayed in Figure 9.1.

Clearly, unrestricted international currency substitution induced by predictable alterations in the speed of downward crawl in the exchange rate will seriously destabilize the short-run demand for domestic base money. And the indexing procedure proposed here would be predictable. Such indexing may well be dynamically unstable unless the government maintains the strict ex-

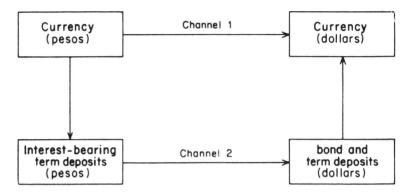

FIGURE 9.1. International Currency Substitution in an Open Economy

change controls on both capital inflows and capital outflows appropriate for managing a repressed economy.

Similarly, international arbitrage in the commodities market induced by an indexed exchange rate has different implications for an open economy than for a repressed one. Consider again a small increase in the domestic price index that produces offsetting indexed devaluations in the future. In an open economy, these mini-devaluations quickly feed back into domestic prices and accentuate the initial inflationary impulse, whether random or not, which then necessitates further mini-devaluations according to the indexing procedure. The rate of domestic price inflation is no longer an independent datum to which the exchange rate passively adjusts. Predictable exchange-rate movements themselves directly accentuate domestic price fluctuations in addition to destabilizing the demand for money. For an open economy, the intuitive opposition of government officials to such an indexing procedure is well founded.

For a repressed economy, however, international commodity arbitrage is (by definition) blocked. Feedback effects from passively adjusting the exchange rate to the domestic price level are largely absent, except for those few open categories of exportables and import substitutes that the government wishes to protect by maintaining their real exchange rate. Otherwise, the domestic prices of the more typical quota-restricted goods are well insulated from the immediate consequences of exchange-rate changes. Fluctuations in the exchange rate are reflected by fluctuations in the economic rents accruing to quota holders—the implicit or explicit market value of a license to import.

This simple point is illustrated in Figure 9.2, where the market for a typical restricted import good, X, is considered in partial equilibrium. Only 500 units of X may be imported over the time horizon for which its net domestic demand, D_1, is drawn. At point A, where D_1 is such that the domestic price is exactly equal to the foreign price at the beginning exchange rate, E_1, the value of an import license is exactly zero. Now suppose an inflationary surge in demand

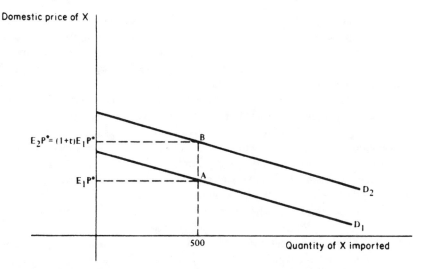

Note: E is the domestic currency price of foreign exchange; P* is the foreign price of good X; t is the ad valorem license premium; and D is net excess domestic demand for X.

FIGURE 9.2. The Domestic Price of a Quota-Restricted Commodity

to D_2 occurs that raises the domestic price of X and all similar goods. At point B, if the old exchange rate, E_1, holds, a premium of t percent develops on a license to import X. However, if our indexing procedure comes into play, the exchange rate is adjusted from E_1 to E_2. Notice that the only effect of the depreciation is to eliminate the license premium. There is no further upward movement in the domestic price of the commodity. Hence the exchange-rate adjustment does *not* reinforce the domestic inflationary momentum in the prices of import goods subject to quota restriction.

Unlike their colleagues in open economies, monetary authorities in a repressed economy seem well placed to manage an indexed exchange rate. Moreover, to keep the inflation tax as "pure" as possible, other officially controlled prices in the economy should be subject to the same quantitative indexing procedure. If the government is setting price ceilings on a few basic foodstuffs or official prices for public utilities or minimum wages, all should be subject to continual small changes of a similar nature. (This requirement presumes that most domestic prices are not set directly by the government, so that market-determined price inflation can provide an independent datum for the indexing authority.)

A CONCLUDING DISCLAIMER ON ECONOMIC REPRESSION

In less-developed countries and socialist economies in transition, the repression of foreign trade and of the domestic financial system is commonplace. International agencies and foreign academic advisers often react to this situation by advocating the liberalization of trade, financial, and fiscal processes. And if the difficult transition to a liberalized economy can be successfully carried out, the empirical evidence does indeed suggest that the economic welfare of the average citizen will improve dramatically (Ch. 2).

What is rational and desirable in a successfully liberalizing economy, however, may be counterproductive in a repressed one. The basic problem is the continuing fiscal deficit. If the deficit is not eliminated, liberalization can be economically disastrous, whether it is attempted by reducing reserve requirements, by removing exchange controls, or by slowing the rate of depreciation more than warranted by the indexing procedure. With an otherwise-uncovered fiscal deficit financed by the inflation tax, serious overvaluation will develop if the monetary authorities try to gain control over the domestic price level by slowing depreciation or fixing the exchange rate.

Accordingly, here and earlier in Chapter 5, we have advanced a second-best strategy for managing the economy. For a given fiscal deficit, we have proposed financial guidelines to minimize the necessary rate of inflation without unduly penalizing exporters and without crowding out the private capital market more than is necessary. Here are the main elements in this strategy:

1. Government authorities should eliminate general usury restrictions and directed credit subsidies to certain preferred borrowers, or replace them with untied subsidies that appear directly in the treasury accounts. Once other interest rates are freed, the true fiscal deficit can be calculated more accurately.

2. In the open part of the capital market, a comprehensive non-interest-bearing reserve requirement against term deposits should vary directly with the size of the fiscal deficit.

3. Flows of private capital both to and from the rest of the world should be subject to exchange controls or reserve requirements.

4. If the minimum necessary rate of domestic inflation exceeds that of the country's principal trading partners, the exchange rate should be indexed by a passive downward crawl.

Using this strategy and avoiding premature liberalization, our repressed economy can limp along in a second-best way without becoming dynamically unstable. The principal costs are a wedge in the domestic capital market between the interest rates for bank deposits and loans, a rigid real exchange rate that reflects the economy's inability to adjust the trade balance automatically to capital flows, and the continuing microeconomic distortions in the import-competing and export sectors with which we are so familiar.

CHAPTER TEN

The International

Capital Market

and Economic Liberalization:

The Overborrowing Syndrome

From the experience of Southern Cone countries (Argentina, Chile, and Uruguay) in the 1970s, our profession has become acutely aware of the problem of overborrowing in the course of an economic liberalization program. Chile is a very good example of an economy that liberalized seemingly correctly from 1976 to 1979. As described in Chapters 3 and 6, tariffs and quotas were eliminated from foreign trade, the fiscal deficit was turned into a fiscal surplus, interest-rate ceilings were removed, and bank reserve requirements were reduced. But then overseas borrowing by the newly liberalized private sector swamped the economy with external debt.

However, the case of the Southern Cone in the 1970s and early 1980s is hardly very pure. In this period virtually all less-developed countries (LDCs) overborrowed and then became mired in a debt crisis. This era was complicated by recycling from the oil shock on the one hand and then what I consider to be a major breakdown in the public regulation of the risk-taking of Western commercial banks on the other. The result was gross overlending by banks in the world economy at large and to the Third World in particular.

THE SOUTH KOREAN EXPERIENCE OF THE MID-1960s

A more uncomplicated example of overborrowing, without these other distractions, is the South Korean liberalization experience of the mid-1960s, well before the somewhat different South Korean liberalization of 1981–84 discussed in Chapter 6. Prior to 1964, South Korea had both severely repressed foreign trade and a repressed financial system with ongoing price inflation. The ratio of exports to gross national product (GNP) was less than 3 percent. Almost all foreign exchange earnings were U.S. military contributions or funds from the United States Agency for International Development (USAID). These earnings also provided much of the financial saving in the economy because household financial saving was negligible. Net inflows of private foreign capital were also negligible because foreign bankers considered the repressed Korean economy to be risky and unprofitable. The famous British economist Joan Robinson and her Cambridge colleagues used to compare North Korea very favorably with South Korea as a successful model for economic development!

Under pressure from USAID in 1964, trade reforms, including some liberalization of imports and a unification of the currency associated with a large exchange-rate devaluation, were implemented in South Korea. But then in 1965, under the influence of my colleagues Edward Shaw and John Gurley, of Stanford University, and Hugh Patrick, then from Yale, there was a major financial reform. The domestic capital market, which had been totally moribund, was suddenly brought back to life when interest rates were taken from very low pegs and put into high pegs—and so became positive in real terms. This was accompanied by a major fiscal reform: no change was made in the tax law but a different director was put in charge of the tax collection mechanism. Tax revenues doubled in the course of a year. So these reforms were very important, and they laid the foundation for the South Korean success in subsequent years.

By the end of 1965, when these reforms had taken hold and exports had begun to grow rapidly, the domestic price level was actually stable, with a rapidly rising flow of domestic loanable funds through the domestic banking system. Both the financial and the foreign trade reforms stimulated productive investment and output. By the middle of 1966, however, international lenders sharply changed their assessments of South Korea's prospects: the economy's apparent future profitability was greatly enhanced by the successful liberalization. These sharp shifts in portfolio preferences are not smooth—apparently because of the great herd instinct among international bankers.

So beginning in mid-1966, a large inflow of short-term capital suddenly hit the astonished South Koreans. An acute dilemma resulted for macroeconomic policy. If the government simply let the exchange rate appreciate, that would, of course, hit South Korea's nascent export industries very hard, something the authorities found unacceptable. However, if the government just persevered with the fixed exchange rate while being inundated with financial capital, it would lose control over the money base: inflation would come back, which it did in the late 1960s. The real exchange rate would still turn against exporters as the prices of nontradables were bid up, but the change would not be so precipitate.

Once lost, price stability in South Korea was not regained until the successful stabilization program of 1981–84 described in Chapter 6. In the 1970s, however, inflation followed by devaluation proceeded sporadically, along with some regression in domestic financial liberalization that was offset by continued heavy foreign borrowing. The burden of foreign indebtedness became troublesome in the late 1970s, although it was manageable in the Korean case because repression in foreign trade was minimal and exchange-rate bias against exporters was avoided by continual (mini-) devaluations (Krueger 1978b). Although South Korea in the 1970s had to rely much more on foreign saving than did Japan or Taiwan at similar stages of development because of the last two's more consistently liberal domestic financial policies and much higher real financial growth (Ch. 3), Korean exports continued to grow rapidly.

MARKET FAILURE IN THE ADJUSTMENT OF INTERNATIONAL ASSET PORTFOLIOS

The question is, what should the South Koreans have done in 1966–70, and the Chileans in 1977–81, when confronted with unexpectedly large and unsustainable capital inflows? Why, in a sense, did the international capital market fail in each period?

Once a country undertakes a successful stabilization cum liberalization program, where the profitability of the economy suddenly rises, then there is a once-and-for-all attempt by foreign lenders to take advantage of the situation and increase their claims on the newly liberalized economy. This inundation with foreign capital is possible even in the case of a pure trade liberalization, when there is no major financial stabilization occurring at the same time. But if there is a major financial stabilization in which the country moves interest rates from low pegs to higher pegs, as South Korea did in the mid-1960s, or removes interest ceilings altogether, as Chile did in the late 1970s, then the inflow of capital is greatly exaggerated.

So what is the nature of the market failure here? Initial expectations of future profitability turn out to be wrong. People look at the real exchange rate and interest rates immediately after the reform and project them into the indefinite future. They look at profitability myopically as individual lenders and borrowers, not taking into account what will happen if they all transfer foreign capital simultaneously. What seems profitable for any one of them today will become less profitable within a few years.

You might say that this is irrational. People should be able to project how the economy will behave, and understand that the real exchange rate will turn against exporters once capital inflows increase at the macroeconomic level. But these were once-in-a-lifetime experiences for the South Koreans in the 1960s and the Chileans in the 1970s and for most of the international lenders in each episode. Individuals are not usually far-sighted enough to anticipate what will happen to the general equilibrium of the economy in the future.

This problem is made more acute insofar as the financial flow into LDCs, even though it may be financing longer-term projects, is usually very short term. When the real exchange rate starts to turn adversely against exporters, just at that juncture the short-term finance may have to be repaid. Because this myopia exists in the international capital market, there is a very good case for doing what the Chilean government tried to do, namely, keep out short-term funds while allowing longer-term borrowing. However, the Chilean government was not stringent enough in preventing the accumulation of short-run indebtedness by Chile's private sector and in scaling down interest rates to limit moral hazard in domestic bank lending (Chapter 6).

In addition, we know that in any *purely private* capital market each individual borrower faces an *upward-sloping supply curve for finance*. That is not really a distortion. The more that is borrowed, the riskier the loan gets at the margin. The upward-sloping supply curve imposed by private lenders accurately reflects the increasing riskiness of the private borrower as he increases his exposure.

Consider instead the world of the 1970s and 1980s, where governments guarantee all credit flows. The host government in the borrowing country guarantees private foreign credits, either officially or unofficially. In the lending countries we have official export-import banks and deposit insurance for the commercial banks. Consequently, the normally upward-sloping supply curve for finance did not face *individual* private borrowers in the Third World during these two decades of huge accumulation of external debts. Because of the government guarantees that were involved, they could borrow at a virtually flat rate of interest.

There was a further undue incentive for private "overborrowing" in the international capital market in those countries whose domestic financial systems remained somewhat repressed. As I established in Chapter 9, ongoing inflation coupled with the use of the domestic reserve tax drives a wedge between domestic deposit and loan rates. In the absence of similar reserve taxes on inflows of foreign capital, domestic firms are artificially induced to borrow abroad.

If you combine these financial distortions—from government loan guarantees and the wedge effect—with the collective myopia over the economy's future profitability, capital inflows by private borrowers are further magnified at the time the (partial) liberalization occurs. Overborrowing in the Southern Cone in the 1970s was an order of magnitude worse than what happened to South Korea in the mid-1960s: the attempt to absorb large amounts of foreign capital very quickly in each case.

ENCOURAGING LIBERALIZATION WITHOUT THE ABSORPTION OF FOREIGN CAPITAL

What policy recommendations can we glean from these unsettling episodes? At the very minimum, official agencies such as the World Bank and the International Monetary Fund (IMF) should *not* try to induce trade liberalization by giving aid. If capital is injected at the time the liberalization occurs, that liberalization is much harder to sustain. The abortive efforts to liberalize trade in Pakistan and India in the 1950s and 1960s, where aid was sometimes used as a lever to induce governments in the subcontinent to expand the flow of imports into the economy, may have indeed failed for this reason. If this capital is allowed to come in, the real exchange rate turns against exporters and firms competing with imports and makes it unduly hard for them to adjust to the removal of protection, as I emphasized back in 1973 in chapter 11 of *Money and Capital*.

As far as possible, trade liberalization and financial stabilization should be a bootstrap operation that a country does for itself, possibly with technical assistance from agencies such as the World Bank. Exports and imports should remain in normal balance. A big injection of capital at the time the liberalization occurs finances an unusual increase in imports while decreasing exports and throws out the wrong long-run price signals in private markets. Because private lenders often magnify any such official injections of capital by the World Bank or IMF, free inflows of foreign financial capital should be allowed only at the end of an otherwise-successful program of liberalization. During liberalization, stringent controls on suddenly increased inflows (or outflows) of short-term capital are warranted.

There is, therefore, a strong case for not requiring a big fiscal prop from some outside lender. The need to bribe a country into opening its trade accounts often occurs because it has an uncovered fiscal deficit; the international agency covers it if the country agrees to liberalize and stop inflating from other sources. Then, to transfer the capital in real terms, the country must run a trade deficit at the outset of its liberalization, thus discouraging exporting. This is a bad combination if liberalization is to be sustained for more than a few months or a year. Fiscal policy should be brought under control before the move to liberalize foreign trade and the *domestic* capital market. Liberalization of the capital account of the balance of payments then comes last.

REFORMING THE INTERNATIONAL CAPITAL MARKET

Apart from these macroeconomic control problems within individual LDCs, there is the failure of the institutions of the international capital market per se. Government guarantees—both in the industrial economies that do the lending and in the borrowing countries—have created massive incentives to misallocate capital. How can one succinctly characterize the distortions involved?

1. Neither private lenders in industrial countries nor private borrowers in LDCs see normal commercial risks. Good or bad projects get the same government credit guarantees.

2. Commercial banks in the industrial economies have been unregulated in their risk taking in international lending relative to the much tighter regulations governing their domestic lending. This inadvertent regulatory loophole was, in part, associated with the development of the Eurocurrency market in the

late 1960s. Moreover, public agencies in the industrial countries, such as the U.S. Federal Deposit Insurance Corporation, give commercial banks undue incentive to take risks in the *unregulated* part of their loan portfolios without worrying about a run on their deposits. Consequently, commercial banks have completely preempted the inherently risky lending to LDCs. The dominance of commercial banks in the international capital market is an artifact of unbalanced regulatory policies in the industrial countries.

3. Mainly as a consequence of (1) and (2), there has been virtually no development of a "normal" long-term primary securities market where borrowers in LDCs sell bonds or equities to individual lenders in the wealthier economies.

Clearly, the private international capital market today looks very different from what it was prior to World War I. Then, the building of American and Argentinean railways was financed largely by the issue of long-term sterling bonds in London. Tea or rubber plantations were financed by the floatation of equities. A major bankruptcy in, say, a railway project, would put the bondholders out of pocket without jeopardizing the solvency of any major bank or the monetary system. Commercial banks were confined to discounting short-term trade bills associated with identifiable inventories or goods in transit. Merchant banks did the (risky) underwriting of bonds or equity floatations and on occasion provided risk capital directly to overseas investment projects (Arndt and Drake 1985).

Although sounding anachronistic, I think that the international market in private financial capital in the 1990s should be encouraged to return to something closer to its late-nineteenth-century format. This would happen naturally, of course, if official guarantees of private credits were phased out, deposit insurance was circumscribed, and the commercial banks' international and domestic activities were brought into better balance with respect to loan-loss provisions, capital restraints on lending heavily to one borrower (or guarantor), and so on. In the industrial countries, commercial banks, which are the custodians of the national money supply and the international payments mechanism, should not be in the business of long-term, high-risk lending.

Unlike the nineteenth century, however, official agencies such as the World Bank and IMF would still play an important role for those countries who remained poor credit risks, if and when the private flows of international finance were so liberalized. The World Bank's technical assistance and long-term project support for poor countries would remain invaluable, as would IMF's role as an international crisis manager on a shorter-term basis. Both would nicely complement the evolution of an active long-term international market in bonds and equities from which deposit-taking commercial banks were largely absent.

Of course, getting commercial banks out of the long-term international capital market cannot be accomplished any time soon. The existing debt overhang in LDCs is so large that only the banks have the capability—and strong enough vested interest—to refinance it. That said, one need not implicitly assume that the commercial banks should dominate the international capital market in the 1990s as they did in the 1970s. To avoid recurrence of another cycle of overlending by banks similar to that of the 1970s, major changes in bank regulations are imperative.

But what about the needs of the liberalizing socialist economies in the decade of the 1990s and beyond? Won't they require massive amounts of foreign borrowing that only the commercial banks as a group can mobilize rather quickly? In fact, I shall argue in the succeeding two chapters that if the socialist economies follow an optimum order of liberalization, their need for external capital is limited. As in the cases of Chile and South Korea or indeed any repressed economy moving toward freer trade, adjustment to international competition in a liberalizing socialist economy might well be easier if net inflows of foreign capital remain controlled and quite modest.

CHAPTER ELEVEN

Stabilizing the Ruble:

Financial Control

during the Transition

from a Centrally Planned

to a Market Economy

The political economy of the Soviet Union is in crisis. The old authoritarian model of allocating economic resources based on central planning has been discredited. But despite the enormous political shift in favor of restructuring, that is, perestroika, the financial conditions necessary for a workable market economy remain elusive. Instead, as fiscal deficits and the domestic money stock spiral out of control (Table 11.1), a potentially explosive internal inflation is forcing Soviet authorities to reimpose price and output controls. Gross national product (GNP) may well have fallen in the late 1980s and still appears to be on a downward path in the early 1990s.*

The analysis in this chapter of the breakdown of domestic financial control in the transition from a centrally planned to a market economy focuses on the Soviet Union. Nevertheless, many of the problems—if not all—abound in other socialist economies in East Asia and Eastern Europe trying to liberalize. Because the People's Republic of China (PRC) has undertaken a more systematic approach to liberalization since 1979 but now faces problems of financial control similar to those facing the Soviet Union, I will also draw on the more extended Chinese experience.

More fundamentally, however, my analysis of the present (1991) Soviet economic impasse rests heavily on the idea that there is indeed an optimum order of economic liberalization, as outlined in Chapter 1 and then developed in more detail in succeeding chapters on domestic financial and foreign exchange policies in developing countries, and that this optimum order also applies to the socialist economies in transition. However, in their remarkably brave attempt to move toward a market economy from 1985 to 1991, *the Soviets got the order of liberalization wrong.*

Where the Soviets went wrong was not any better understood by Western economists, who applied, and still apply, premature pressure to decontrol prices, float the exchange rate, privatize, and decentralize decision making before proper fiscal and monetary control over the Soviet economy is secured.

as opposed to peg?

* This chapter was written in late 1990, just before the breakup of the former Soviet Union in 1991.

TABLE II.I
Financial Statistics for the Soviet Economy

Year	Government Budget Deficit[a]		Government Debt[b]		Household Savings Deposits[a]		Enterprise Deposits[c]
	Billions of Rubles	% of GNP	Billions of Rubles	% of GNP	Billions of Rubles	Ratio to Retail Sales	Billions of Rubles
1979	n.a.	n.a.	64	n.a.	146.2	0.576	—
1980	12	1.9	76	12.2	156.5	0.579	—
1981	9	1.4	85	13.1	165.7	0.579	—
1982	15	2.2	100	14.4	174.3	0.589	—
1983	10	1.4	110	15.1	186.9	0.611	—
1984	9	1.2	119	15.7	202.1	0.639	—
1985	14	1.8	133	17.1	220.8	0.680	—
1986	46	5.8	179	22.4	242.8	0.731	—
1987	52	6.3	231	28.0	266.9	0.782	—
1988	81	9.3	312	35.7	296.7	0.810	100.0?
1989	92	6.9	404	43.4	337.7	0.837	100.0+?

[a]From Jan Vanous, ed., *PlanEcon Report*, February 21, 1990. Subsequently, Soviet officials have claimed that they are implementing emergency measures to bring the deficit down to 6.1 percent in 1990.

[b]Government debt seems to be defined as private savings deposits plus other government indebtedness to the State Bank plus very small amounts of government bonds in the hands of the nonbank public.

[c]Balances of state production enterprises with the State Bank. The estimate for 1988 is a minimal in the sense that the deposits of cooperatives and a wide variety of state agencies are excluded, and this "missing" money could amount to another 250 billion rubles.

Because the nature of monetary and fiscal processes in the "classical" Stalinist centrally planned economy was not (and is not) well understood by people who are familiar only with financial mechanisms in mature industrial economies, well-meaning advice and enthusiasm by outsiders for liberalization can easily be misguided.

The success of perestroika depends on monetary and fiscal discipline and that, in turn, requires a radically new domestic tax and banking system for the Soviet Union. Then, foreign exchange and tariff policies can be designed to move the economy toward freer international trade (Ch. 12). Before charting such a course in this chapter for stabilizing the internal purchasing power of the ruble so that domestic liberalization can proceed, however, let us trace the origins of the present impasse back to the nature of money and taxation under central planning.

IMPLICIT TAXATION IN THE SOCIALIST PLANNED ECONOMY

In the "classical" socialist economy, the Stalinist system of central planning, which was also the prototype for other communist countries in Eastern Europe and Asia, what is the nature of the fiscal process? How is revenue raised to support the ordinary functions of government—the military, the judiciary, education, the civil service, old age pensions, and so on? Although turnover taxes are sometimes levied explicitly on goods passing from the wholesale to retail level, the traditional tax-collecting mechanism was (is) largely *implicit*.

Under classical socialism the means of production—the capital stock of virtu-ally all significant economic enterprises—are owned and controlled by the cen-tral government. Thus enterprises' economic "surpluses" are effectively revenue in the fiscal sense. Depending on its revenue needs, the government simply sets average prices for goods and services at a healthy markup over money wages, although these profit margins may vary widely from one firm to the other. This average markup determines enterprises' collective economic surplus; it is auto-matically deposited with the State Bank and becomes revenue that could be used for general government support or reinvested in designated industries.

Thus, under central planning, *the Soviet government never had to formalize the nature of the tax system on which it was implicitly relying*. Discussion about principles of taxation, which is commonplace among Western economists, was largely unnecessary. There was no need for a general corporate profits or value-added tax, where the legal tax liabilities of enterprises were well defined. Calculating corporate depreciation allowances and debating whether interest payments should be deductible from taxable enterprise profits were not critical issues. Nor was any formalized personal income tax necessary. Because almost all workers were employed directly by state-owned enterprises, by keeping wages low the government effectively withheld a tax on personal incomes at the source.

True, turnover taxes were (are) collected from enterprises on many consumer goods before they are passed to the retail stage. Because of long-standing price controls, however, turnover taxes tended to reduce enterprise surpluses at the margin, and thus such levies became part of the surplus extraction process. As long as the economy remained centrally planned, this automatic sequestering of enterprise surpluses neatly avoided the resource costs and political pain of levying taxes explicitly.

With the advent of perestroika, however, this implicit tax-collecting mecha-nism tends to break down. First, as the effective ownership and control of industrial property passes from the central government to private farmers, independent industrial cooperatives, or local governments, the central govern-ment's implicit tax base—the surpluses of the enterprises it owns—naturally erodes. No formal tax-collecting mechanism (other than the hodgepodge of inconsistent levies on various activities at different rates that now characterizes Soviet tax policy) then exists for recapturing the loss in revenue.

Second, insofar as the remaining state-owned enterprises become more independent and profit oriented in making decisions outside the apparatus of central planning, the old government policy of simply appropriating enterprise surpluses becomes clearly incompatible with microeconomic incentives for these enterprises to operate efficiently. Why should managers strive to econo-mize on resource use if 100 percent of "profits" are to be expropriated? Realizing this, the Soviet government has allowed state-owned enterprises to begin accumulating innumerable "special funds" in the form of credit money

TABLE 11.2
Soviet Government Expenditures and Revenues
(as a percentage of GNP)

	1980	1981	1982	1983	1984	1985	1986	1987	1988	1989
Expenditures	—	—	—	—	—	49.8	52.2	52.3	52.5	51.6
Revenues	—	—	—	—	—	48.0	46.5	45.9	43.3	41.7
Deficit	1.9	1.4	2.2	1.4	1.2	1.8	5.7	6.4	9.2	9.9

Note: Data from Jan Vanous, ed., *PlanEcon Report,* February 21, 1990. Expenditures and revenues not separately available before 1985.

with the State Bank (Table 11.1); these funds may be spent for investment within the enterprise, for employee social purposes, or—with more strict limits—for a wages fund that is convertible into cash in order to pay workers. But each enterprise's spending is officially monitored and often restricted so that *the convertibility of this enterprise credit money into domestic goods and services (let alone into foreign exchange) is partially blocked.* Nevertheless, these funds are no longer part of "pure" tax revenue in the old sense, that is, a clear diversion of economic spending power from enterprises to the government. For a perceptive analysis of the decline in the Soviet government's fiscal position and the great difficulty in interpreting the government's accounts, see Shelton (1989).

Table 11.2 shows very clearly that from 1985 to 1989 the rapidly increasing Soviet fiscal deficit was mainly due to an increasingly serious shortfall in revenue, which decreased from 48.0 percent of GNP in 1985 (when Gorbachev assumed power) to 41.7 percent in 1989—a fall of more than 6 percentage points! This revenue shortfall is consistent with our basic hypothesis that perestroika itself tends to undermine the central government's traditional implicit tax-collecting mechanism based on appropriating enterprise surpluses.

But this Soviet fiscal decline need not be over. The PRC has been liberalizing over a much longer period (since 1978), although that might have ended in 1989. The data in Table 11.3 are taken from an important International Monetary Fund (IMF) study of the Chinese economy by Mario Blejer and Gyorgy Szapary (1989) and show that the revenues of the central government fell from 34.4 percent of GNP in 1978 to just 20.4 percent in 1988. Even more remarkable, the Chinese central government's revenue from enterprises fell from 20.6 percent of GNP in 1978 to just 7 percent in 1988. And, since 1985, the PRC's loss of monetary control with consequential inflationary pressure has been similar to that experienced in the Soviet Union.

In summary, as in the other liberalizing socialist economies of Eastern Europe and Asia, the Soviet government's ability to collect tax revenue has greatly diminished as a result of the liberalization itself: the growth of economic activity outside the state sector and the attempt to give state-owned enterprises better incentives to make their own investment and production decisions. Although the numbers are necessarily rather uncertain, Table 11.1 shows the

TABLE 11.3
Government Revenue in China
(in percentages of GNP)

	1978	1979–81	1982–84	1985–87	1988
Total revenue[a]	34.4	30.0	27.0	24.8	20.4
Revenue from enterprises	20.6	17.1	12.5	8.3	7.0
Profit remittances	(19.1)	(16.1)	(11.4)	(0.4)	(0.3)
Profit tax	(1.5)	(1.0)	(1.1)	(7.9)	(6.7)
Taxes on:					
Income and profits[b]	21.5	17.8	13.3	7.9	5.5
Goods and services[c]	11.3	10.6	10.1	10.6	9.1
Internatinoal trade	0.8	0.9	1.1	1.8	1.1
Other	—	—	1.5	3.2	3.0
Nontax revenue[d]	0.8	0.8	1.0	1.3	1.7

Source: PRC, Ministry of Finance, as compiled by Blejer and Szapary, 1989.
[a]Includes nontax revenue.
[b]Includes profit remittances.
[c]Includes product, value-added, and business taxes.
[d]Excluding profit remittances.

rapid buildup of the fiscal deficit—from 1.8 percent of GNP in 1985, when Gorbachev assumed power, to an estimated 9.9 percent of GNP in 1989. Correspondingly, the debt-to-GNP ratio increased extraordinarily, from 17.1 percent in 1985 to 43.4 percent in 1989.

Because a significant market in government bonds hardly exists, this outstanding debt was largely financed by borrowing against household savings deposits (Table 11.1) and by issuing coin and currency to households (the exact outstanding stock of which is unknown). Thus the government fiscal deficit is responsible for the major and rapidly growing amount of money and near money owned by households. But to understand the overall magnitude of the "monetary overhang" in Table 11.1, the huge stocks of partially blocked enterprise credit money (about which information is scarce) should be added, but on a less than one-for-one basis, to the more liquid cash and savings deposits of households. As estimated by Gregory Grossman (1990), Table 11.1 shows these balances of operating enterprises to be in excess of 100 billion rubles in 1989—an extremely conservative estimate because another 250 billion rubles seem to be held on deposit by "other" government entities since 1988.

PASSIVE MONEY AND CREDIT IN THE TRADITIONAL PLANNED ECONOMY

Beyond fiscal decline, what in the traditional system of money and credit might lead to a further loss of financial control with the advent of economic liberalization? Under central planning, the monetary system facing enterprises is necessarily *passive*. The flow of funds, duly recorded as debits or credits with the State Bank, fulfills an important auditing function to ensure that the purchases and sales of goods by each enterprise conform with the plan. However, neither the outstanding stock of the deposit money of enterprises nor their outstanding indebtedness to the State Bank inhibits bidding for real resources.

For example, if any enterprise has a "shortage" of credit money for buying the inputs it needs as approved by the planners, this shortfall is no constraint. The State Bank automatically advances the enterprise credit, at a zero or trivially low rate interest, to buy the inputs it needs to fulfill the duly approved plan.

Similarly reflecting this passivity, the "optimal" stock of enterprise deposit money for keeping inflation under control is indeterminate in a centrally planned economy. Unlike households, enterprises cannot freely spend the deposit balances they nominally own. With the traditional planning apparatus for controlling resource flows among enterprises remaining in place, however, the supply and demand for each producer good is more or less balanced directly.

The problem comes when the monetary system serving enterprises remains passive after liberalization begins, that is, after the apparatus of central planning is weakened. Once decision making is shifted to the enterprises themselves, they begin to behave as if they had no effective budget constraint in bidding for scarce resources. Indeed, the faster enterprise deposits with the State Bank can be drawn down, the less likely these surpluses will be hit with some arbitrary tax. Similarly, old established credit lines—particularly for loss-making state-owned enterprises—are likely to remain open at trivially low rates of interest. The result is that once a few producer goods are freed of centralized controls and can be bid for openly, their market-clearing prices might rise far beyond any level properly reflecting their relative economic scarcity.

Consider a rather dramatic recent example of well-established Soviet enterprises with soft budget constraints "overbidding" for foreign exchange. Everybody knows that the official commercial rate of exchange over the past twenty years—0.64 rubles for 1 dollar—greatly overvalues the ruble. Indeed, in late October 1989, the Soviet government introduced a new exchange rate for tourists that values the dollar at 6.26 rubles—a ten-fold devaluation. Then, on November 3, 1989, in a first-ever official, albeit quite small, auction for foreign currency, enterprises bid between 13 and 15 rubles per dollar (*Financial Times*, November 6, 1989)—twenty-two times the official rate! Does this market test imply that an appropriate official exchange rate should similarly be twenty-two times the old rate so as to value the ruble at just 6.7 U.S. cents?

Not at all. The dollar's ruble value was bid up so sharply because, in part, enterprises faced such weak domestic financial constraints. Market processes cannot work properly when budget constraints remain soft, because domestic money is too plentiful. If price controls are removed and open bidding for key producer or consumer goods becomes more common, the traditionally passive Soviet monetary system is likely to accommodate explosive, confusing, and demoralizing increases in prices, without any well-defined upper limits.[1]

DEADLOCK IN DECONTROLLING PRICES

How then have the Soviet authorities reacted to this "excessive" monetary demand for domestic goods and services by households and enterprises without adequate financial constraints? Relative prices have been wildly irrational. For example, energy resources have been grotesquely underpriced to enterprises and some basic foodstuffs have been underpriced to consumers. Reform of the traditional system of price controls, however, has been continually delayed and is now deferred until after 1991.[2] In late April 1990, the Soviet government officially announced—after intense internal discussions—that plans for further liberalization of the price mechanism were shelved because of fear of an inflationary explosion. Even those economists most committed to reform are hesitant to promote price decontrol until the necessary fiscal and financial constraints are in place.

> Stanislav S. Shatalin, an economist in Mr. Gorbachev's cabinet and an ardent proponent of change, [told] the daily Izvestia that the country must first take time to create a banking system, [new] fiscal and monetary policies and other measures.
> "Without all this, to introduce a market today would only be suicide," he said. (*New York Times,* April 25, 1990)

Indeed, price controls are being extended to cover previously independent cooperatives. Because of the monetary overhang, many of these cooperatives appear to be obscenely profitable. They charge prices many times those charged for similar goods and services (of limited availability) sold through traditional government stores. Beyond greater production efficiency, however, these profits may well reflect the ability of cooperatives to evade the price controls

1. János Kornai has made us familiar with the concept of the "soft" budget constraint on socialist enterprises. He emphasized how soft budget constraints make resource use by state-owned enterprises immune to changes in relative prices. If a (controlled) price change, say, an increase in the price of an important input, creates a potentially negative cash flow, then the (socialist) firm will simply borrow more from the State Bank, seek remission of taxes, or seek permission to raise the price of its own output—all without much changing the use of the now more expensive input (Kornai 1986a, 1986b).

The corollary of Kornai's important insight, emphasized in this chapter, is that in a world of enterprises with soft budget constraints but where the government stops setting prices from the center, any open bargaining process would leave both relative and absolute prices indeterminate.

2. Indeed, many authors, such as Ed Hewett in *Reforming the Soviet Economy* (1988, 356), have previously noted the peculiarity of delaying price reform to 1990–91 or beyond.

that are still largely enforced on state-owned enterprises. Thus much "rent seeking," corruption, and wastage of resources go into this evasion process as entrepreneurs try to arbitrage between the controlled and liberalized sectors of the economy.

Suppose, counterfactually, that this excess macroeconomic demand was absent. Then the introduction of cooperatives, private farms, or other enterprises that are free to set their own prices would generate lesser disparities with controlled prices in the state-owned enterprises. Not only would the current, unfortunately strong populist reaction against further privatization in the Soviet economy be muted, but the private or cooperative sectors would better reflect what "equilibrium" relative prices should be. In addition, such a balanced market could better sort out those liberalized enterprises that were more truly efficient in an economic (productive) sense from those that were simply living off the rents associated with a distorted price system. Surely a large fringe of legally established cooperatives, as well as much of the burgeoning activity in the "black" economy, would disappear once macroeconomic equilibrium was established.

In terms of the welfare theory of the second best, therefore, populist resentment with current Soviet efforts to liberalize is not entirely misplaced. In the face of a monetary overhang, economic efficiency could worsen as liberalization proceeds. The monetary imbalance makes the transition to a more market-oriented economy too difficult to orchestrate and makes the transitional welfare costs too heavy. Thus the Soviet and Republican governments are forced to continue existing price controls as a second-best method of pinning down the nominal price level, even though *relative* prices are badly misaligned and greatly distorting the economy (Shmelev and Popov 1989). (A fully liberalized economy, in which enterprises with hard budget constraints are free to determine their own prices, would, of course, by the best solution.)

STATE ORDERS AND WHOLESALE TRADE

With the price system thus paralyzed and price reform indefinitely deferred, how then are production and allocation decisions being made? The centerpiece of perestroika, the 1987 Soviet Law on State Enterprises and related legislation, was to make enterprises increasingly independent of the planning process (Aslund 1989). Detailed planning controls over thousands of commodities (traditionally exercised by Gosplan) were to be drastically truncated.

According to Academician Nikolai Fedorenko in 1984, Gosplan elaborated about 4,000 material balances, Gossnab[3] 18,000, and the ministries 40–50,000. The

---

3. Gossnab is the State Committee for Material and Technical Supplies. It is the trading agency directly responsible for distributing (and rationing) industrial inputs to producers—both in taking deliveries and in making allocations according to Gosplan.

number of balances increases lower down the hierarchy as they are disaggregated. Deputy Chairman of Gosplan, Leonard Vid, alleged that the number of material balances elaborated by Gosplan had been reduced to 2,117 in 1987 and that there would be only 415 in 1988. Vadim Kirichenko, who appears to be one of the last competent Soviet economists to believe in central planning, favoured a limited number of central balances—250–300 at the central level that would imply 3,000–5,000 material balances at the ministerial level. (Aslund 1989, 122)

The development of what reformists like to call "wholesale trade" was to be the counterpart of this stage-by-stage reduction in the centralized allocation of resources. Enterprises were to negotiate directly with each other on terms and delivery dates for supplies, without using Gossnab as intermediary. Goods could be legally bought and sold among state enterprises and private firms (mainly collectives of various forms) at negotiated prices that (presumably) could differ somewhat from the official ones. If new firms (cooperatives) in manufacturing are to succeed, they must be able to bid for industrial inputs or raw materials from existing state enterprises. (Entrants into personal service activities, such as beauty salons, would not suffer so much from being shut out of wholesale trade.)

The 1987 Soviet Law on State Enterprises intended that only a portion of each firm's output would be subject to state orders: traditional delivery quotas mandated by Gosplan. The remainder could then flow into a freer market at the wholesale level.

Unfortunately, the state enterprise law has not so far succeeded in developing wholesale trade and freer markets for industrial goods as promised. In 1987, Soviet economists projected that state orders would initially account for some 20–40 percent of the activity of traditional enterprises. Instead, throughout 1988, state orders absorbed closer to 85 or 90 percent. In 1989, the situation was no better with regard to producer goods; and on November 20, 1989, Leonid Albalkin, Gorbachev's principal economic adviser, announced emergency measures to reimpose rigidly comprehensive state orders on a wide variety of consumer goods including foodstuffs and basic household necessities, especially inexpensive items for children and pensioners (*Wall Street Journal*, November 21, 1989). Moreover, it appears that most enterprise deposit money remains effectively blocked except when used for officially designated purposes. Thus most managers of traditional enterprises have not perceived any real change from full-scale central planning. Apart from illicit trade, a substantially freer wholesale market—absolutely crucial in the transition from a planned to a market economy—does not yet exist.

Why didn't the 1987 Soviet Law on State Enterprises work as intended? Soft budget constraints on enterprises, government fiscal deficits, and the monetary overhang in households made failure inevitable.

In the face of generalized excess demand, the ministries that retained the responsibility for achieving a coordinated allocation of resources under their jurisdiction very likely were "forced" to use their remaining discretionary control over resource use to prevent economic chaos.[4] With irrational prices and soft budget constraints on enterprises, the predominance of state orders was necessary to prevent the mismatch of production decisions, including a further excessive buildup of inventories.

EXCESS INVENTORIES AND THE LOW PRODUCTIVITY OF CAPITAL

In the Soviet economy, to what extent is the low productivity of capital in general and in inventory accumulation at the enterprise level in particular a *financial* problem? Certainly, disappointing growth in real output antedates by more than two decades the accelerated loss of monetary control due to perestroika. Indeed, beginning in 1985, perestroika itself was largely a response to "the Breshnev years of stagnation" under the classical Stalinist planned economy. And with glasnost allowing increasingly more open scrutiny of Soviet statistics, realistic assessments of how low Soviet output is, and has been, are getting progressively more pessimistic:

> The actual condition of the Soviet economy is worse than that indicated by data either from the Kremlin or the [American] Central Intelligence Agency . . . said several senior Soviet economists today.
>
> The Agency said that the Soviet Gross National Product was about half that of the United States. . . .
>
> Viktor Belkin, a prominent economist from the Soviet Academy of Sciences, said that Soviet output was no more than 28 percent of American GNP and might be substantially less. (*New York Times*, April 23, 1990)

And since 1985, Soviet real economic growth seems to have slowed down even more. Overall GNP grew by less than 1.5 percent per year and actually fell by 1 percent or so in 1989 according to CIA estimates. GNP per capita seems to have been slowly falling in the 1980s on the order of 1–2 percent per year—with the recent decline being a bit sharper.[5]

Nevertheless, the problem is *not* the conventional one of mobilizing financial intermediaries to increase aggregate saving. All observers agree that the Soviet investment (saving) effort as a share of national income has been truly enormous for many decades. For the first half of the 1980s, Shmelev and Popov (1989, 149) estimate net Soviet investment (saving) has been over 20 percent of net national income, whereas the comparable figure for net national investment in the United States would be less than 6 percent. Nor is there any reason to believe that this discrepancy was any less in the late 1980s. Indeed, the Soviet saving-investment effort in the postwar period probably exceeded Ja-

---

4. John Litwack suggested this particular—fairly benign—interpretation of bureaucratic behavior.
5. Jan Vanous, ed., *PlanEcon Report*, February 21, 1990.

pan's. Why then did the payoff from this enormous capital investment turn out to be so abysmal?

The sheer impossibility of efficiently allocating hundreds of thousands of industrial goods and raw materials by central planning now goes without saying. Without a market mechanism for evaluating equilibrium prices for inputs and outputs, planners must specify some form of gross output targets for each enterprise and then allocate inputs from other enterprises according to crudely specified "norms" of what usage should be. Enterprises then have no incentive to economize on inputs in meeting their gross output targets, which themselves are not subject to effective quality control through market discipline. In their insightful book *The Turning Point: Revitalizing the Soviet Economy* (1989), Shmelev and Popov have a long chapter entitled "Black Holes That Swallow Resources." They provide incredible detail on the specific irrationalities and waste from perverse managerial responses to ministerial or Gosplan directives.

But this massive (social) waste of resources in enterprises is an outcome not only of quantitative central planning per se. It is also affected by the system of money and credit. Because all the details of resource use cannot be planned from the center, managers have considerable discretionary latitude in their use of supplies—latitude that has increased since perestroika began. *Without any liquid domestic monetary asset bearing an attractive real rate of return, however, enterprise managers will opt to hold excess inventories of all kinds:* raw materials, semifinished goods, their own outputs, and then "fixed" assets, such as excess capacity in plant and equipment, semifinished structures, and so on. With "hidden" price inflation being on the order now of 5–10 percent per year, and without an offsetting rate of interest being paid on enterprise deposits with the State Bank, which are semiconvertible and subject to being frozen or otherwise restricted, firms will naturally opt to build up excess inventories as *a substitute monetary store of value.* These excess commodity stocks and spare production capacity serve as a hedge against threatened shortages of key material inputs if official allocations prove inadequate or late. Or, if some unanticipated shortage arose, excess stocks of other commodities could be informally bartered in the extensive "gray" markets among enterprises for those parts the firm really needs, or even for consumer goods to distribute directly to its employees.

If the firm has access to further credit from the State Bank at a trivially low rate of interest, this tendency to hold excess inventories will be exacerbated. Similarly, if the credit is designated for fixed capital investments, construction projects will be delayed because of the low opportunity cost of not bringing them to completion.[6] Unfinished structures are themselves something of an

6. John Litwack has suggested that the apparent proliferation of unfinished construction projects in the formal accounts may be somewhat exaggerated because the soft credits have actually been diverted to other uses.

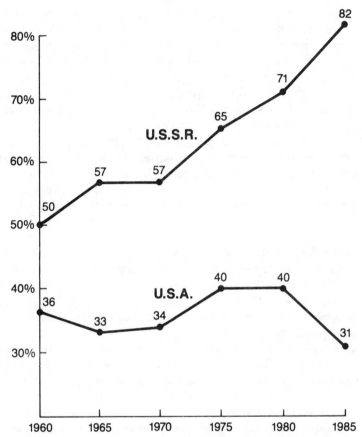

Note: U.S.S.R.—Year-end inventories excluding collective farm inventories (almost 9 percent of national income in 1986), percentage of utilized national income. U.S.A.—Year-
end inventories, percentage of national income in the business sector; national income of
business sector calculated on the assumption that its share in the total national income is
the same as in the GNP.

FIGURE 11.1. Inventories: Percentage of National Income. (*Source:*
Shmelev and Popov 1989, 305.)

inflation hedge—albeit much less liquid than commodity inventories. In part
because excess enterprise stocks continue to proliferate, the incremental Soviet
net output-capital ratio seems to be approaching zero.

    Shmelev and Popov (1989) calculate that Soviet industrial inventories rela-
tive to national income rose from 50 percent in 1960 to 82 percent in 1985,
compared to just 31 percent in the United States in 1985 (Figure 11.1). In
addition, farm inventories are also relatively high and rising in the Soviet
Union. Because Soviet inventories are increasing faster at the margin, Shmelev
and Popov further estimate that "almost 6 percent of created national income

goes toward increasing inventories in our country in the 1980s, while in the United States this figure is less than 1 percent" (1989, 135). Although comparable American data are not available, Figure 11.2 shows the remarkable increase in unfinished Soviet capital and construction projects from 1986 to 1989—with projects actually brought to completion declining somewhat. During this period the stock of unfinished construction rose at an average annual rate of 11.4 percent and in 1989 was equivalent to twenty months' worth of total investment in plant and structures.

Because "wholesale" markets are not open at equilibrium prices, the liquidity of enterprise deposits is reduced. In the long run, the syndrome of excess accumulation of inventory and fixed capital is thereby worsened. In the presence of a monetary overhang, however, any attempt to open wholesale trade could greatly exacerbate this syndrome of excess stock holding in the short run:

> Yet it will be difficult for us to move away from the direct, central allocation of capital goods to a system of wholesale buying and selling for the simple—ostensibly contradictory—reason that enterprises currently have too much money at their disposal. As soon as they would be allowed to buy what they please, the acquisitive instinct they have developed over the years would come into play, and they would increase stocks out of all proportion.
>
> Such apprehensions are not simply speculation. A large scale experiment conducted in 1984–1986 has shown that as soon as enterprises were given the go-ahead to make special purchases, they bought equipment and material for the "rainy days" ahead. The value of the stock (inventories) in all our enterprises exceeds 460 billion rubles—almost as much as the State's entire annual budget! Moreover, the stocks are growing twice as fast as production. Because enterprises acquired material resources largely by credit, there were years when enterprise production increased by 3 to 4 percent and debt by 10 to 15 percent. As a result, there is an enormous amount of spare money not geared to the real requirements of production. For this reason alone, the introduction of wholesale trade is necessary, and must go hand-in-hand with the reform of finance and credit discussed at the 27th CPSU Congress. (Aganbegyan 1988, 36)

Before proceeding much further with perestroika, therefore, the domestic Soviet monetary and fiscal systems need to become an active constraining influence on the ability of enterprises, households, and governments to bid for scarce resources. Going one step further, any new system of money and credit should prompt massive dishoarding by enterprises of excess commodity stocks in open wholesale trade at equilibrium prices while encouraging more efficient use of existing fixed capital and curtailing cheap credit for new projects. Indeed, the general dishoarding of excess inventories, to be replaced by new domestically convertible enterprise money, could be an important part of

GROSS INVESTMENT IN FIXED CAPITAL, CAPITAL PUT INTO OPERATION AND CHANGE IN UNFINISHED CONSTRUCTION

(IN BILLION RUBLES AT 1984 COMPARABLE PRICES)

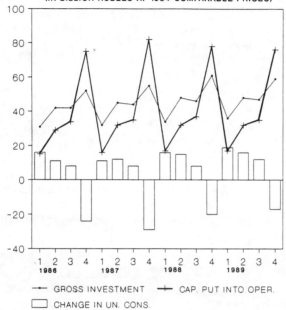

DEVELOPMENTS IN THE STOCK OF UNFINISHED CONSTRUCTION

(IN BILLION RUBLES AT 1984 COMPARABLE PRICES)

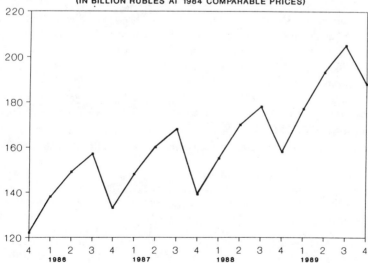

FIGURE 11.2. Unfinished Soviet Construction Projects. (*Source:* J. Vanous, ed., *PlanEcon Report,* February 21, 1990, 28.)

a macroeconomic process of disinflation that simultaneously increased the productivity of capital.

In our multicountry empirical analysis in Chapter 2, we showed that raising the real deposit rate of interest and stabilizing the purchasing power of (enterprise) money substantially increased the productivity of physical capital in a wide variety of developing countries. Although the current circumstances in the Soviet Union are somewhat different, there appears to be even more scope for improving the efficiency of the existing capital stock if Soviet enterprises had access to more attractive monetary assets.

Securing sufficient financial control to promote such disinflation in the Soviet Union requires, first, the imposition of fiscal and monetary constraints on the ongoing cash *flows* of both enterprises and households and, second, monetary measures to deal with excessive existing *stocks* of various monies or near monies. We shall discuss each in turn.

TAXING VALUE-ADDED INSTEAD OF ENTERPRISE PROFITS

On the tax side, resolving the flow problem is conceptually straightforward although politically difficult. To help limit the excess issue of new money, major reforms in enterprise and personal income taxation are needed to eliminate the Soviet government's fiscal deficit. The rapid fiscal decline can only be retrieved by a massive effort to, first, cut government expenditures, particularly the massive resources devoted to defense[7] and food subsidies, and, second, replace the old implicit revenue system and the more recent ad hoc levies with a comprehensive and uniform system of *explicit* business and personal income taxes according to well-established canons of taxation.

At the very outset of the liberalization process, a socialist economy should restructure enterprise tax arrangements so that (1) revenue does not fall simply because "ownership" and management of industrial enterprises devolve away from the central government's direct control and (2) the new tax system is fully consistent with hardening the budget constraints of enterprise by avoiding the arbitrary expropriation of enterprise surpluses.

For satisfying principles 1 and 2, elsewhere I have suggested (McKinnon 1989b) that the value-added tax (VAT) is best suited to be the main pillar of a reformed system of enterprise taxation. A VAT permits the central government to tax all forms of enterprise income *uniformly*. Profits, interest, rents,

7. For the 1980s, Rowen and Wolf (1990) estimate that Soviet military expenditures narrowly defined were about 15–17 percent of Soviet GNP; broadly defined, military expenditures could have been as high as 22–28 percent! If one remembers that American defense expenditures were only 6–7 percent of American GNP at the height of the Reagan buildup, these estimates of the Soviet defense burden are staggering. But cataloging this and other potential areas for the Soviet government to reduce expenditures, although critical for the success of the fiscal reforms, exceeds the scope of this paper.

wages, and salaries could all be taxed at a flat rate, say 20 percent, without having to make distinctions among them. Indeed, the accounting conventions for making such distinctions have yet to be established in socialist enterprises.[8]

The VAT could be particularly advantageous for a socialist economy in transition. First, because it avoids the conceptual and accounting difficulties associated with defining "profit" that plague business income taxes, the VAT has the great advantage of being neutral with respect to any corporate form that might develop in the liberalized enterprises. By levying the VAT on all enterprises—whether state-owned, cooperative, joint-stock, or sole proprietorship—the Soviet government can collect revenue without precommitting itself to any particular set of legal ground rules defining ownership and control, rules that currently seem to be in a state of flux. The creation of thousands of new small firms or cooperatives—some of which will compete with the large state-owned enterprises—would not then undermine the revenue position of the Soviet government.

Second, the VAT would be neutral between domestic and foreign trade. If applied on the "destination" principle, imports would be taxed at the same uniform rate as domestically produced goods. Government revenue would rise automatically as foreign trade was liberalized and imports increased. Provided that the exchange rate was "right" (a big issue to be discussed below), enterprises with access to foreign inputs, including joint ventures with foreign firms, would not be so heavily advantaged over those that did not have such access.

In contrast, the proliferation of new enterprises in the PRC—many of which operate in free-trade zones or have come under the control of the state and local governments—has undermined the ability of the central government to collect tax revenue and weakened its control over the flow of credit in the Chinese economy. Indeed, one of the main arguments against the introduction of uncontrolled free-trade zones is that the central government would find it more difficult to collect taxes. For example, customs officials normally collect the VAT levy on imported goods as they cross the border; but in a pure free-trade zone, goods would come through the initial port of entry without being checked by customs. By the late 1980s, the resulting inflationary pressure forced the Chinese to begin retrenching on liberalization and to reintervene in enterprises that had previously been given their independence.

Third, with an easily understood (uniform) VAT in place in the Soviet

8. The tax collector need not actually calculate wages, profits, interest, and so on as separate categories. Instead, in order to determine the enterprise's gross tax liability, he need only verify that the firm is correctly stating its gross sales—to which the uniform rate of (tentatively) 20 percent is applied. Then, to get tax credit on intermediate goods—raw materials and capital goods—purchased from other enterprises, the taxpayer enterprise must itself provide proof that the 20 percent VAT had been paid on these supplies. If such documentation is complete, the enterprise's net tax liability can be correspondingly reduced.

Union, each potential new firm would know its tax liabilities before deciding whether or not to go into business. Thus, ex post changes in the tax rules to recapture "surpluses" in the most profitable enterprises could be minimized or even avoided altogether. For fully liberalized enterprises that are financially independent (to be discussed more fully below), *taxes on profits could then be officially abandoned.* Because of the unfortunate history of the Soviet and other communist governments seizing profits arbitrarily, eliminating profits taxes altogether would be a highly visible—not to say draconian—step demonstrating the Soviet government's commitment to a more stable future tax regime for enterprises.

However, if a firm's output prices are tightly controlled, the VAT may not be collectible because it could not be shifted forward and incorporated in the price paid by the final user. In fact, the incidence of the tax could be shifted backward and could reduce the firm's profit on a one-for-one basis. Many enterprises that might be profitable after paying their VAT in the absence of price controls might find themselves with a negative cash flow if the VAT was levied with price controls in place. The authorities would find they had not escaped from arbitrary profits taxation or the seizure of surpluses. Indeed, with an arbitrary and therefore disequilibrium pattern of price controls in place, the *only* feasible method of taxing enterprises may well be the seizure of surpluses, or "profits," in the old Stalinist mode.

Hence, *the introduction of a broad and uniform VAT cannot be effected without simultaneously decontrolling enterprise prices.* Thus do successful monetary and price reforms facilitate the collection of enterprise taxes, and vice versa.

THE TAX POSITION OF HOUSEHOLDS

Although a carefully designed VAT on enterprises would be a major fiscal resource, a broadly based personal income tax would also raise badly needed revenue. After standard deductions to keep the poorest people off the tax rolls, a substantial, but uniform, basic rate of the order of 25–35 percent could be levied on the *consolidated* personal income, including wages and interest or profits actually paid out to each household.

In the present state of the Soviet economy, however, much household income is imputed in the form of some good or service being given directly to individuals without charge rather than income actually paid out in the form of cash. For example, many people pay trivial rents for substantial housing services. Similarly, the social funds in enterprises often provide substantial returns—through canteens and so on—to employees at their place of work. Because of the monetary overhang and resulting long queues at retail shops, Soviet enterprises often distribute a wide variety of consumer goods directly to their employees. Until all these noncash sources of household income are properly priced out, their value should be estimated for inclusion in the base of the personal income tax. Realized capital gains accruing to households would also be included in the base of the personal income tax, provided that the marginal tax rate was kept moderate as suggested above. However, neither unrealized capital gains of households nor capital gains by enterprises would or should be in this particular tax net.

Specific commodity taxes on consumer luxuries (alcohol, gasoline, jewelry, and so on) at the retail level would also be necessary for revenue purposes. Insofar as the base for the personal income tax remains weak at the beginning of perestroika, a wide range of such specific consumer levies could generate additional revenue. And like the personal income tax itself, these specific commodity taxes should apply to informal distribution channels—factory sites, for example—as well as to formal retail outlets.

In the order of economic liberalization, these consumer excises should be formally in place (like the VAT itself) at the time prices are decontrolled. Under the preexisting price controls, special consumer excise or sales taxes were largely implicit. In addition to the old turnover tax, the prices of vodka or cigarettes or other sumptuary consumer goods were kept artificially high (above the costs of production). Thus large surpluses were generated within the enterprises producing sumptuary goods—surpluses which then simply reverted to the state as implicit tax revenue. (The same phenomenon can be found in China and other centrally planned economies in Asia.) To prevent the serious erosion of government revenue when prices are decontrolled and competition in the production of these goods is permitted, an explicit and comprehensive system of consumer excises should be in place.

Finally, "negative" commodity taxes, the vast array of subsidies for particular consumer and producer goods, should be discontinued or phased out. This policy would help balance the government's budget and further reduce the discretionary power of the Soviet government to intervene ex post facto once markets have been ostensibly liberalized (more on this below when the mechanisms of monetary reform are discussed).

In summary, the issues involved in tax reform are conceptually straightforward in a technical economic sense. The key idea is to identify a tax base for enterprises and households that is as broad as possible—covering all forms of income—and then tax it moderately. Unfortunately, successful implementation would require major new administrative bureaucracies for collecting both the VAT and the personal income tax. And achieving the necessary political consensus is undoubtedly difficult. Nevertheless, the reformers have no choice. Such a comprehensive new tax system is simply a necessary condition for perestroika to succeed.

Do the above suggestions for tax reform in evolving socialist economies differ from what might be advocated for any advanced industrial economy where market processes, including borrowing and lending in the capital market, are better established? The only substantial difference lies in the treatment of profits accumulated within enterprises. I suggested that the liberalizing socialist economy avoid levying a separate profits or capital gains tax on domestic enterprises that were otherwise properly registered for paying their VAT. For many years, the Soviet system could run better without the equivalent of a "corporate" profits tax typically found in mature capitalist economies. Without a separate profits tax on retained earnings, self-financed capital accumulation *within* those enterprises that were liberalized could be better promoted as the centerpiece of a general monetary program for hardening the transition economy's system of money and credit—the all-important conundrum to which we now turn.

HARDENING THE SYSTEM OF MONEY AND CREDIT: BANKS AND THE LIBERALIZED ENTERPRISES

"For decades the country's credit system catered to the projects thought up by the State Planning Agency and the Ministry of Finance, while the State Bank acted as a kind of cash-desk handing out the money. And when the money ran out, the mint went into action spinning the flywheel of inflation and encouraging enterprises to be careless spenders and spongers" (*Business in the USSR,* July–August 1990, 36).

Let us call nonfinancial enterprises "liberalized" when they are free to make their own output, employment, input, price, and wage decisions. (The distinction between state-owned and private liberalized enterprises will be made more precisely below.) During the transition to a full-fledged market economy, how should liberalized enterprises in industry and agriculture be limited in their access to credit from the banking system?

Mature market economies use quite different methods for imposing a capital constraint (i.e., a hard budget constraint) on decentralized enterprises. In Appendix 1, the financial structure governing Japanese corporations is compared with the structures prevailing in West Germany and the United States. These mature capitalist economies differ enormously in how property rights are defined and in how external creditors such as banks influence corporate decision making. They provide no wholly desirable model of corporate governance, and their financial structures are too complex to be immediately applicable to newly liberalized Soviet enterprises.

Moreover, the sorry history of bank lending in partially liberalized regimes—such as Yugoslavia, Poland, Hungary, and the PRC in the 1980s—shows the severe moral hazard from state banks overlending to enterprises that local or central governments wish to sustain or promote. Loss-making enterprises were the main absorbers of credit. In the initial stages of perestroika, therefore, unambiguous restrictions on bank borrowing by liberalized enterprises are necessary to prevent capital from being wasted. Equally important, these guidelines should also reflect the degree of macroeconomic imbalance (inflationary pressure and deficits in the consolidated budget of the government).

Suppose we start with a prototype Stalinist financial system where all deposit-taking and lending activities are concentrated in a single State Bank, with the passive credit-granting characteristics described above. Then perestroika in farming and industry begins with some enterprises becoming "liberalized" whereas others remain "traditional," that is, under the thumb of some planning ministry with access to credit from the State Bank. In an optimum order of liberalization, how might domestic banking arrangements (foreign borrowing will be discussed later) evolve with respect to the liberalized sector? Imagine two successive stages in the transition.

Stage 1: Liberalized enterprises are confined to self-finance and to borrowing from the nonbank capital market.

Then, after a lapse of some years when the (decontrolled) price level has been stabilized and the sums the government must borrow from the banking system are much reduced, the financial system could enter the next stage.

Stage 2: Commercial banks begin limited and fully collateralized short-term lending to liberalized enterprises according to the "Real Bills Doctrine."

Consider first the economic rationale for stage 1. Because of the passive nature of banking under central planning, Soviet bankers have very little experience with assessing domestic credit risks and foreign bankers have little knowledge of the Soviet economy. At the outset of the liberalization process, therefore, there is a strong case for making liberalized enterprises—whether state-owned, cooperative, or private—ineligible for bank credit. In stage 1, both rural and urban enterprises would be forced to rely mainly on (untaxed) retained earnings for investment finance.

Such reliance on self-finance is the simplest technique for imposing financial restraint on liberalized enterprises. Bankruptcy would be virtually automatic if their internal cash flows became negative for any significant length of time. The effective wages paid to workers, as well as the (implicit) yield to all owners of the firm's equity, would vary directly with the firm's success in the open market with the goods and services it buys or sells. Self-finance has the great advantage of bypassing the difficult problem of how to establish a more elaborate corporate structure (the different possible forms of accountability to outside lenders are discussed in Appendix 1). However, self-finance is only viable for enterprises in competitive industries if their output prices have been fully decontrolled and they can negotiate freely over inputs.

As the nonbank *private* capital markets develop—say, rural credit cooperatives or urban markets in short-term commercial bills—the severe credit constraints on liberalized enterprises would be naturally relaxed. But these private lenders would also face bankruptcy if they made bad loans or charged interest rates below "market" levels. Compared with lending by the state-owned or state-insured banks, moral hazard in lending would be dramatically reduced. Through the judicial system, however, the government would retain the important role of ultimate enforcer of private debt contracts.

The deposit side of the State Bank's balance sheet would assume heightened importance for the liberalized enterprises even though they could not borrow from the State Bank. If checks were cleared efficiently with free domestic convertibility of enterprise deposits into domestic coin or currency and commodities, and if a substantial positive real interest rate was paid on time and saving deposits, the self-financed accumulation of *productive* capital would then be greatly facilitated (McKinnon 1973). Indeed, the key to reducing excess inventories in Soviet enterprises and the general excessive hoarding of physical capital would be to pay (liberalized) enterprises an attractive real deposit rate of interest—say, 5–8 percent per year in the mode of Taiwan and Japan (Ch. 3).

In addition, the efficiency of the fledgling private capital markets would depend heavily on the liquidity provided by checkable deposits in the State Bank and on the success of the monetary authorities in stabilizing the price level so as to provide a stable-valued unit of deferred payment in private debt contracts.

This suggestion for confining liberalized enterprises in the Soviet Union (and possibly in similar socialist economies) to self-finance and to the nonbank capital market is more draconian than most successful monetary stabilizations occurring in less-developed countries (LDCs). For example, the two South Korean monetary stabilizations (in 1964–65 and in 1981–84, as discussed in Chs. 10 and 6 respectively) were associated with increases in real deposit rates of interest and an immediate recycling of the increased flow of loanable funds through the South Korean commercial banks back to industry and agriculture. But two important factors militate against this immediate recycling in the Soviet case: the first is the much greater Soviet monetary overhang, which somehow must be corrected, and the second is the complete absence of a commercial banking tradition of seeking out high-yield projects by creditworthy borrowers.

SELF-FINANCE IN PRACTICE

When new enterprises are constrained to self-finance, are there historical precedents for economic development proceeding satisfactorily? Small-farmer agriculture seems to provide the best examples, in part because agriculture is particularly well suited to decentralized economic incentives.

Beginning in 1979, the Chinese government began giving farm families long leases on small plots of land that had previously been managed collectively. After paying a tax in kind to the commune (in recent years also payable in cash), farmers were free to market any additional produce for what they could get in unblocked domestic currency. This experiment succeeded in virtually doubling agricultural output by 1984.

Chinese financial arrangements supported the rapid monetization of agricultural trade *without* significant injections of bank credit. Since 1979, the Agricultural Bank of China (ABC) has established branches throughout the country. These accepted savings deposits but did virtually no direct lending to farmers in the early 1980s (although the ABC did some lending to nonfarm enterprises established in rural areas). However, through collecting deposits and issuing currency in rural areas and then lending to the People's Bank of China, the ABC transferred financial resources on a large scale to other sectors of the economy.[9]

Under the auspices of local authorities, nonbank rural credit cooperatives (RCCs) did provide some credit for collective agricultural purposes and rural industry but not much for individual farm households in the early years of the reform. Apart from credit in kind for particular inputs against future crop deliveries, cooperative credit reached between 10 and 25 percent of rural households (Feder et al. 1989). But the RCCs were self-contained financial units that did not issue "money." More important, the rapid rise of monetary liquidity (i.e., "owned" cash balances) in the rural areas meant that most small farms did not feel themselves to be credit constrained.

In summary, there are two key financial aspects of this successful rural reform in the PRC: (1) The small farm units could not borrow from banks and were carefully circumscribed in what other nonmonetary credit they received. (2) The price level was quite stable in the early 1980s, unlike the present situation. Farmers had the option of holding a stable-valued domestic currency to finance their buildup of working capital.

Factors 1 and 2 were complementary. This (implicitly) tight financial control over the liberalized farm enterprises, which included most of the population, prevented the central bank from creating money faster than the growth in demand for monetary liquidity. Indeed, because the monetization of Chinese agriculture in 1979 was very limited, over the next five years farmers were willing to build up their cash balance positions relative to their growing incomes. This had the inadvertent, but highly fortuitous, effect of providing noninflationary finance for the increasing government fiscal deficits from 1979 to 1984 (Table 11.3). Closing this virtuous circle, the consequential absence of general price inflation made it easier for individual farm units to finance internal investments out of their own holdings of cash balances.

Beginning in 1985 and into the early 1990s, however, the Chinese lost monetary control, and price inflation surged because (1) too much bank credit flowed to loss-making urban enterprises, including township enterprises under

9. I am indebted to Lawrence Lau for discussions on these points.

the control of local governments and new activities in free-trade areas such as in the bustling special economic zone of Guangdong and the experimental area around Wenzhou;[10] (2) the fiscal position of the consolidated central and local government accounts continued to deteriorate (Table 11.3); and (3) by 1985 farmers had more or less reached their "equilibrium" cash-to-income ratios so that they were no longer willing to finance the rest of the economy in a noninflationary manner. And if cash balances become less attractive to hold because of high inflation, the earlier successes in commercializing agriculture through on-farm self-financed investments—the virtuous circle—will be in jeopardy.

Another example of financial restraint, largely in the form of self-finance imposed on farms and urban enterprises alike, was the Soviet Union's own experience in 1922–28 with the New Economic Policy (NEP). As small enterprises and farms were leased out to private citizens, decision making was decentralized throughout the rural and urban economies. Even the larger state-owned trusts were required to balance their cash flows without resorting to bank credit. Thus did the successful currency reform of 1922–23 become feasible. Because the Soviet government managed to balance its own fiscal accounts even as the cash drain to loss-making enterprises was stopped, the depreciating old ruble could be replaced by a new currency called the *chervonetz,* which retained a stable value *and* remained internally convertible until the reversion to central planning and price controls in the late 1920s. (Nove 1969, 83–118).

As long as the lending resources of the State Bank are more or less fully absorbed by the government so that no (noninflationary) room for bank borrowing by liberalized enterprises exists, then decentralizing the State Bank into a central bank and a number of commercial banks is rather pointless. After all, if the rationale of this institutional transformation is to allow decentralized commercial banks more independence in attracting deposits and expanding loans, macroeconomic stability could be undermined through excess money issue. Again, the loss of monetary control in the PRC in the mid-1980s seems in part due to the premature creation of "commercial" banks whose lending policies were outside the control of the central bank. In Poland in the late 1980s, near hyperinflation coincided with the premature commissioning of a new system of commercial banks.[11]

10. See "Straining at Beijing's Tether," *The Economist,* December 10, 1988, 31–33. In fact, the recent Chinese experience with free-trade zones illustrates that although new activities can indeed be established very quickly, they may also contribute to a general loss of monetary control because of their failure to pay taxes and their absorption of too many scarce inputs, including bank credit, from the rest of the economy.

11. I am indebted to Professor Arnold Harberger of the University of California at Los Angeles for pointing out this ill-advised feature of financial reform in Poland prior to the more-successful Polish price-level stabilization of 1990.

LIMITED COMMERCIAL BANK LENDING IN STAGE 2: THE REAL BILLS DOCTRINE

But suppose sufficient fiscal control is achieved. At a stable price level, the lending resources of the consolidated State Bank now exceed the government's borrowing needs. The implicit reserve requirement against the monetary liabilities of the consolidated State Bank no longer need to be a full 100 percent in order to keep the price level stable. Then deconsolidation of the monolithic State Bank into a central bank and independent commercial banks, in the mode of more-mature market economies, is not only warranted but highly desirable.

In order to protect the integrity of the payments system, however, close government supervision of newly independent commercial banks would still be necessary. To prevent bank panics or runs, the deposit base of the commercial banks would be actually or implicitly insured by the government—if only because the central bank acts as lender of last resort. To minimize the resulting moral hazard in commercial bank lending, what then should be the regulatory guidelines in stage 2?

After some years of our hypothetical stage 1, where liberalized enterprises could not borrow from the banks, private financial markets for transferring savings from "surplus" to "deficit" households or enterprises would begin to appear. Because liberalized enterprises would be free to lend to each other (e.g., by extending trade credit) secondary markets in the corresponding financial instruments are likely to be among the first to develop. Trade bills of borrowers with good reputations could be sold off to third parties. This is the beginning of a market in commercial bills at equilibrium open-market rates of interest. One could even imagine bill brokers, or discount houses, centralizing and unifying the market in the tradition of the late nineteenth century. However, these would not be banks, because their liabilities would not be money. Even though a well-established finance company might issue interest-bearing notes and even keep them on account for the general public, these would not be checkable or part of the system of money transfers controlled by the State Bank. And the State Bank would want to keep it that way until monetary control was secured and the price level was stabilized.

Once monetary control was established and the fiscal deficit became manageable, a private bill market could provide a natural vehicle for licensed commercial banks—subject to a formal capital requirement—to begin lending in the private financial markets at competitive rates of interest. Indeed, established bill brokers might be the most technically qualified applicants with sufficient capital for commercial bank licenses. Checkable and interest-bearing deposits could be offered to the general public—part of the general system of check clearing run through the State Bank—provided that these authorized banks invested in a diversified portfolio of commercial bills with well-defined secondary markets and with more or less the same term to maturity as their deposit liabilities. Although interest rates would be freely determined on both deposits and loans, because the new commercial banks would be confined to investing in a diversified portfolio of "rated" money market instruments, risk taking would be quite limited. In effect, they would be much like what are called "money market mutual funds" in the United States, where the discretionary powers exercised by managers of these funds are relatively minor. Moreover, once such banks (mutual funds) entered this market and began to bid for the existing stock of bills, the supply of eligible commercial paper from nonfinancial enterprises would naturally increase.

If the reduction in the consolidated deficit of the government permits, a subset of these banks could be authorized to lend at short term to (smaller) enterprises whose debt is not directly marketable. Such specialized lending would involve a loss of liquidity by the bank and would require extensive credit investigations by bank managers with appropriate skills and training. To ensure the safety of the deposit base of this class of commercial bank, reserve requirements held on deposit with the State Bank would be warranted. In addition, the regulatory authority could well impose the condition that such lending be fully collateralized: that there be fairly liquid assets such as inventories or accounts receivable that could be seized should a default occur.

In summary, both money market mutual funds where marketable commercial bills are held directly and bank lending fully collateralized by the short-term assets (working capital) of nonbank borrowers satisfy the old Real Bills Doctrine. In each case, the scope of commercial bank lending is limited to financing "safe" but productive short-term assets of minimal risk. By being very restrictive as to the asset quality and liquidity of the fledgling commercial banks, no additional restrictions on deposit and lending rates of interest would seem necessary for limiting risk taking (compare the analyses in Chs. 3 and 7). And one can imagine a continuous transition where direct lending by the State Bank to the government and (loss-making) traditional enterprises diminished, and the domain of productive lending by commercial banks at market interest rates to liberalized enterprises expanded.

It should be emphasized, however, that this adherence to the Real Bills Doctrine is primarily a *microeconomic* control device to ensure the quality of bank lending to liberalized firms. By itself, this doctrine is insufficient to ensure macroeconomic equilibrium: balancing the supply and demand for money to stabilize the domestic price level. At the macroeconomic level, the state banking system would still have to control the overall supply of liquidity across both the traditional enterprises with blocked bank accounts and the newly liberalized firms with domestically convertible money (see below).

"WILDCAT" BANKING IN THE SOVIET UNION

So much for our idealized reform as laid out in stages 1 and 2. What path to financial liberalization has the Soviet Union actually been following? From

TABLE 11.4
Credit Facilities of Banks in the Soviet Union as of January 1, 1990

	Short-Term		Long-Term	
	Billions of Rubles	%	Billions of Rubles	%
Promstroibank (industrial construction)	78.8	27.7	18.7	18.1
Agroprombank (agriculture)	147.6	51.9	69.7	67.5
Zhilsotsbank (municipal services)	32.4	11.5	7.0	6.8
Vneshekonombank (foreign trade)	19.3	6.8	6.1	5.9
Sberbank (personal savings)	0.3	0.1	—	—
Commercial and cooperative banks	5.7	2.0	1.8	1.7
Total	284.1	100.0	103.3	100.0

Source: Babicheva et al. 1990, 38.

1988 to 1990, the deconsolidation of Gosbank (what had been the consolidated State Bank) looks very different from the optimum order of liberalization sketched above. Despite escalating fiscal deficits and the failure to eliminate price controls on most industrial products, banking functions throughout the Soviet economy are being rapidly decentralized in a way that makes a further massive loss of monetary control more likely.

In 1988, the government began to break Gosbank's monopoly and introduce more specialized credit-granting intermediaries for industry and agriculture. As indicated in Table 11.4, these and other functions have been handed over to five large specialized banks: Promstroibank for industrial construction, Agroprombank for agriculture, Zhilsotsbank for municipal services, Vneshekonombank for international banking, and Sberbank for personal savings (*Financial Times,* March 12, 1990). This new structure itself is still sufficiently concentrated—if these banks were to remain owned and managed by the central government—that the central banking authorities need not lose control over the total flow of credit. In 1990, however, President Mikhail Gorbachev gave "individual republics the right to jointly manage banks on their territory" (*Financial Times,* July 30, 1990).

More astonishing to the casual outsider is the rapid proliferation in 1989–90 of what are loosely called commercial banks, but which in fact are financial entities sponsored by the traditional enterprises, which, presumably, still operate with soft budget constraints.

Enterprises which had been used to passing on all the money they had earned, without complaining, to the powers above, began to collect their resources and use them actively. Commercial banks appeared. Today they number 280. They grant

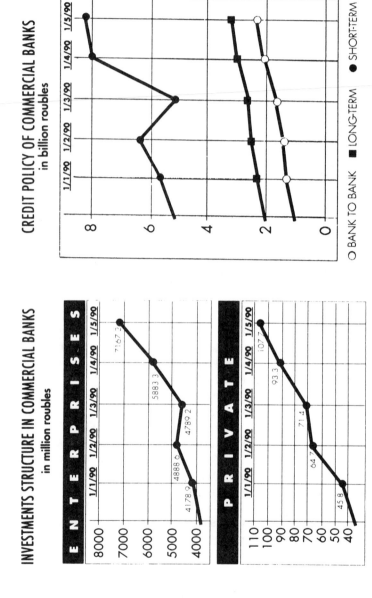

FIGURE 11.3. Soviet Cooperative and Commercial Banks. (*Source:* Babicheva et al. 1990, 39.)

loans to businesses in need, but since they have no state backing, they have to charge an interest rate of 15 to 20 percent. . . . Far from all the new banks remain credit institutions, even though lending would be highly profitable for them. . . . They are created using industrial capital, and have an inclination towards trade and middleman operations; they find scarce goods, buy them up, and then sell or barter them. (Babicheva et al. 1990, 36)

These new commercial and cooperative banks were responsible for only 2 percent of outstanding total bank credit as of January 1, 1990 (Table 11.4). Nevertheless, in 1990, they have been growing exceedingly fast, and their credit outstanding to the existing state enterprises and organizations sector is about eight times as great as their lending to "private" cooperatives (Fig. 11.3), although their stated objective is to finance the latter. In a game without rules, new deposit-taking banks are just as likely to be commodity traders or equipment lessors as credit-granting organizations. It is a modern, Soviet version of wildcat banking.

Although far too early to more than speculate about their consequences, these radical institutional changes involve uncomfortable trade-offs. At the microeconomic level, the new Soviet "commercial banks" are striving to fill important gaps in the operation of nascent markets for commodities and equipment in the best tradition of Adam Smith. And the development of efficient wholesale trade is of central importance for the ultimate marketization of the Soviet economy. At the macroeconomic level, however, the proliferation of unregulated quasi-monetary intermediaries could well further undermine the central government's control over its fiscal and monetary policies:

1. Insofar as traditional Soviet enterprises are now placing (some of) their cash surpluses with "commercial" banks that they (rather than the State Bank) control, effective "tax" revenue to the central government is correspondingly diminished.

2. Insofar as other traditional or partially liberalized enterprises can borrow outside the State Bank (or its five specialized subsidiaries), their soft budget constraints are further softened.

3. As a consequence of (1) and (2), the economy's stock of monetary liquidity—checkable claims on the new commercial banks *and* on the state banking system—spiral further out of control.

Clearly, if macroeconomic control is ever to be established to prevent explosive price inflation, the tax obligations of both traditional and liberalized enterprises must be better defined. The latter's access to credit must be limited to the *nonbank capital market* as sketched above for our hypothetical stage 1. Gosbank should move quickly to distinguish between new financial firms that are (1) truly banks issuing checkable deposits or providing cash on demand and (2) nonbank commodities traders, leasing companies, or bill brokers. Those that are clearly banks in the monetary sense of (1) should be sharply regulated and the licensing of new ones prevented. (By way of compensation, Gosbank could also make the state banking system more efficient. They could improve check clearing and other commercial services and increase interest rates on time deposits and loans to substantially positive levels.) On the other hand, nonbank trading companies in the sense of (2) should be encouraged, insofar as they are not simply agents of traditional enterprises with soft budget constraints.

LIBERALIZED ENTERPRISES AND STATE OWNERSHIP

Returning to our analysis of a hypothetical optimum order of economic liberalization, what should the relationship be between private and state-owned enterprises in the liberalized sector? All private enterprises, that is, those in which the residual profits accrue to private owners, should be in the liberalized sector. Otherwise, if price controls and quantitative restrictions on outputs and inputs remain, privatization is counterproductive and rather pointless. Once markets are decontrolled markets and macroeconomic equilibrium is established, small-scale private capitalism—small shopkeepers, farmers, artisans, and so forth—could flourish and grow rapidly. After some years, larger-scale private industrial activity would naturally develop as the most successful entrepreneurs accumulated larger amounts of capital that permitted a substantial expansion of their operations. But as János Kornai (1990) emphasizes, capitalism does not spring into full bloom automatically as a result of implementing extreme liberalization measures. It must be nurtured from small beginnings in which a sorting process eventually identifies good entrepreneurs from their less-successful colleagues.

In an optimally organized transition, therefore, some liberalized enterprises may well remain government owned. For example, the government need not immediately break up large-scale manufacturing activities that are going concerns and could possibly be viable in a competitive environment. If the private capitalist sector is still small scale with no concentrations of wealth in the hands of honest individuals with proven entrepreneurial skills, no efficient means for the privatization of large manufacturing complexes would yet exist—although that would not preclude the future sale of some state-owned enterprises at "fair" market prices. Indeed, the tendency of the fiscal position of the government to deteriorate because of the liberalization itself militates against any "giveaways" of industrial assets or the housing stock.

In the meantime, any state-owned enterprise that is free to determine its own output prices and bargain freely over input prices, including wages, could well be treated like a private firm and could be subject to a full-scale VAT. Such liberalized but state-owned enterprises would be cut off from government tax forgiveness, access to subsidized inputs, credit from the monetary system, and so on in order to ensure a hard budget constraint similar to that imposed

[handwritten annotations in top margin:]
Reform Strategy
) private → no access to
Liberal → - tax forgiveness (apply VAT)
SOE → - subsidized inputs (access to nonbank capital)
- credit from banks / no involvement w/ commercial banks

on private firms, as in stage 1 above. Like private firms, they could have access to the nonbank capital market but could not operate or sponsor commercial banks.

The important caveat is that *the state must assert its role as owner*. The state must be the recipient of any residual profits and generally must demand a fair claim on the firm's capital, perhaps after a once-and-for-all recapitalization as per Lipton and Sachs (1990b). Like a private owner protecting his capital, the government would have to oversee wage bargaining within the state-owned firm in order to hold down wage claims to the minimal market level necessary for securing needed labor inputs. Given the precarious fiscal position of most socialist governments, the net profits of state-owned enterprises are best returned to the government, which would have the incidental advantage of gradually reducing the size of the state-owned sector relative to the private one.

Why shouldn't state-owned firms be self-managing or simply turned over to worker cooperatives in the Yugoslavian manner, where any residual surplus accrues to those who currently work for the firm? In his important paper "Issues in the Introduction of Market Forces in Eastern European Socialist Economies" (1990), Manuel Hinds demonstrates that neither the capital market nor the labor markets will work right if firms are self-managing and the ownership of capital is ambiguous. Consider a typical socialist enterprise with a large capital stock previously financed by government loans or grants. Then, in a liberalized environment, the enterprise is (mistakenly) set at liberty by the government to be purely self-managed. Hinds demonstrates that internal pressure to pay excessive wages (in cash or in kind) to managers or workers would tend to decapitalize the firm, unless the government reasserted its ownership interest. Workers (or managers) would behave as if they had a claim on the assets of the self-managed enterprise. But the firm's current employees could only exercise this otherwise illiquid claim if (1) above-market wages and salaries are paid out to existing employees, who in turn must remain tied to the firm if they are to collect and (2) new entrants—employees who would potentially share in this economic surplus—are excluded.

Thus, self- or worker-managed enterprises are induced to deplete the capital stock through "excessive" wage payments, as Kornai (1990) observed in Hungary. This has also been a well-known feature of Yugoslavian labor-managed firms for many years. True, existing workers could be given equity claims on the enterprise's capital stock rather than higher wages. That might solve the problem of wasting capital or interfering with labor mobility. But directly giving the capital away to the existing labor force would be manifestly unfair because some workers in highly capitalized or natural-resource-based enterprises would be unduly enriched. More important, the government's precarious fiscal position would be further impaired if it failed to earn revenue from its accumulated capital stock.

Thus, in the proper order of liberalization, the government must claim the residual profits of state-owned firms, even those in the liberalized sector. And this is the maintained hypothesis in the following summary of alternative financial arrangements for liberalized and traditional enterprises in the transition period.

FINANCIAL CONSTRAINTS ON LIBERALIZED AND TRADITIONAL ENTERPRISES: A TRIPARTITE CLASSIFICATION

Before the transition to a full-fledged market economy is effected, both liberalized and traditional enterprises would coexist under somewhat different monetary and tax regimes. In Table 11.5, I have tried to summarize what financial arrangements would be *consistent* with the degree of liberalization, that is, mode of operation, of each class of enterprise. Three relatively gross classifications are distinguished.

1. *Traditional enterprises,* which are state owned and subject to direct price controls on their outputs and perhaps to direct materials allocations for some inputs, including credits from the state banking system. They could include both natural public goods such as utilities, energy-producing resource-intensive industries, and infrastructure activities such as roads or irrigation facilities. Then, too, industrial "basket cases"—those running with negative cash flows in a domestically liberalized environment but which the government could not immediately close down for social reasons—would also be classified as traditional.

This distinction between liberalized enterprises with hard budget constraints and traditional enterprises need not preclude substantial rationalization of relative prices in the latter. For example, in the energy sector, which one would expect to remain under state ownership and control much like a public utility, a sharp increase in the economy-wide price of energy to approximate world levels should be charged to the liberalized enterprises at the outset of the transition process. Otherwise, they will continue to use energy wastefully. Higher energy prices would allow the government to better collect (tax) the economic rents (surplus) associated with the exploitation of this valuable natural resource. (When the economy is open to foreign trade, however, temporary tariff protection might then be appropriate for energy-using industries facing higher costs—see Chapter 12 below.)

2. *State-owned liberalized enterprises,* where output and input decisions—on prices and quantities—are freely determined by the enterprise management in pursuit of higher profits after paying its VAT. But the government would exert its ownership claim over the return to capital (residual profits) as described above.

3. *Private liberalized enterprises,* where there are no government restraints on enterprise behavior in making output, price, and wage decisions in the

TABLE II.5
Alternative Domestic Financial Arrangements for
Enterprises in Transition

	Traditional Enterprises[a]	Liberalized Enterprises	
		State-Owned	Private
Taxation	Expropriation of surpluses	Uniform VAT	Uniform VAT
Deposit money	Restricted convertibility[b]	Domestically convertible[b] interest-bearing	Domestically convertible[b] interest-bearing
Credit eligibility	State Bank	Nonbank capital market	Nonbank capital market
Wages	Government-determined	Government-determined	Market-determined
Residual profits	Accrue to government	Dividends to government; retained earnings for reinvestment	Dividends to owners;[c] retained earnings for reinvestment or lending to other private enterprises

[a]Traditional enterprises are those whose output and pricing decisions are still determined by a central government authority or planning bureau, with centrally allocated inputs and credits from the State Bank to cover (possible) negative cash flows.

[b]"Convertibility" here means the freedom to spend for domestic goods and services only—and not necessarily convertibility into foreign exchange.

[c]Dividends would be subject to the personal income tax when paid out to private owners, but retained earnings would not be taxed.

pursuit of higher profits except for the obligation to pay the VAT at the enterprise level and to cooperate with the government authorities in the collection of consumer excises and the personal income tax (through tax withholding) on any wages, interest, dividends, or capital gains payouts to individuals.

For each of our three enterprise classifications, the columns in Table 11.5 list mutually consistent tax, monetary, credit, wage, and profit arrangements. Each set of financial arrangements is more or less self-explanatory from our previous analysis. For example, it may well be infeasible to collect a broad-based VAT from traditional enterprises, although that would be the prime mode of enterprise taxation in the liberalized sector.

Note, however, that the different treatment of money and credit in traditional versus liberalized enterprises has implications for macroeconomic control in the system as a whole. Traditional enterprises could borrow from the State Bank at a positive real rate of interest, although they would be strictly rationed by centralized government oversight. Nevertheless the earnings of the State Bank from such government-sanctioned borrowing should be positive in order to pay a positive real yield to depositors in the liberalized sector. But the deposits of the traditional enterprises themselves would remain blocked, only partially convertible for domestic purposes, as part of the centralized financial control exercised by the government. In effect, the bank accounts of traditional enterprises would be simply part of the general government's treasury accounts. These are naturally subject to centralized official oversight and, in Western economies, are typically *not* counted as part of the general money supply in the hands of the nonbank public. That is, these blocked balanced would be excluded from any general monetary measure such as M1, M2, M3, and so on that is normally considered to influence the spending behavior of the nonbank sector.

However, credits to traditional "basket case" enterprises remaining under state ownership and control should be phased out as soon as possible, either by dismantling the enterprises themselves or by forcing them to liberalize. The domain of liberalized enterprises, with hard budget constraints using domestically convertible rubles, would expand relative to traditional enterprises, with soft budget constraints under centralized control. For some years to come, however, the lending resources of the deposit banks would be fully utilized financing the government's current deficits (to be phased out one hopes) and capital expenditures for rebuilding the economy's depleted infrastructure in transportation, the environment, and so on.

The domestically convertible deposits of the liberalized enterprises and, of course, coin, currency, and savings deposits held by households would now constitute the generalized monetary aggregates to which the government would look in trying to contain inflationary pressure in the economy. Indeed, the monetary circuits of liberalized enterprises and households would now be fully integrated. There would be no official restrictions on transacting between them. Either could hold coin and currency and the same classes of deposits.

Transacting between traditional and liberalized enterprises would certainly occur, but they would be subject to the official payments (convertibility) restrictions on the former. Indeed, insofar as the traditional enterprises ran payments deficits vis-à-vis the liberalized enterprise and household sectors (probably covered by loans from the State Bank), then the economy's generalized supply of fully convertible money, as measured by M1, M2, or M3, would increase. Inflationary pressure would be correspondingly greater— much in the same way that a general government deficit financed by bank borrowing would expand the supply of domestically convertible money in the system.

In summary, the key to control over the supply of effective domestic "money" in our partially liberalized economy is to measure the *consolidated* net deficits of the general government and the traditional enterprises and then to take fiscal and other restrictive measures to keep that net deficit as small as possible. I have assumed that a generalized domestic market in government bonds does not exist so that the consolidated fiscal deficit cannot be offset by selling government bonds directly to the nonbank public. Moreover, neither liberalized enterprises nor households can borrow from the banks, so that the government need not worry about additional money creation from this direction. Therefore, to eliminate price inflation and establish macroeconomic equilibrium in stage 1, the main policy instrument to control monetary *flows* would be this consolidated public sector deficit. In stage 2, however, the development of open markets in commercial and (perhaps) treasury bills would provide an additional avenue by which the central bank could control the supply of domestically convertible money.

A ONE-TIME ADJUSTMENT IN MONETARY STOCKS?

Resolving the stock problem—the excess monetary overhang—is conceptually much trickier. Nothing much can be done before the necessary fiscal and credit market reforms for correcting the economy's flow imbalances are implemented. Then, once the yield on deposit money available to both liberalized enterprises and households was made much more attractive, a determination would have to be made as to how great the monetary overhang actually was, presuming that the current price level was, on average, to be maintained when price controls were removed.

If a once-and-for-all stock adjustment seemed necessary, a natural place to start would be with the quasi-convertible deposit money owned by those state-owned enterprises who opted, or were forced, to become liberalized. In the process of their recapitalization, both their debts to and deposits with the State Bank (in all their many categories of wage funds, working-capital funds, social funds, and so on) could be written down in a balanced fashion, although the government would retain the residual claim on the subsequent profits of those enterprises that remained state owned. Then each newly liberalized enterprise could be given a small starting fund of "new" rubles that were unrestricted for making *domestic* payments in any category and which were fully convertible into coin and currency.

After this recapitalization, however, the newly liberalized enterprises could not borrow from the State Bank or other state enterprises (as in stage 1). To build up their liquidity for making investments over the longer term, liberalized enterprises that were still state-owned would be forced to raise their profitability by raising output prices, shedding labor, reducing their use of raw materials, and so on so that (untaxed) retained earnings increased in the steady state. To ease their initial liquidity squeeze in the short run, many would strive to auction off their excess inventories in the now-burgeoning wholesale markets for all manner of industrial goods. Because such liberalized enterprises, whether agricultural or industrial, would be forced to build up their cash balance positions for some years, they would help finance the remaining deficit sectors of the economy in a noninflationary manner. And the dividends from the remaining state-owned enterprises should improve the government's fiscal position.

Restructuring the cash positions of enterprises, while ignoring households, may or may not be sufficient to deal with the inflationary overhang for the economy as a whole. (Empirical data on the stock of currency held by households are not currently available.) If not, then the liquidity of households could be reduced by replacing a portion of their outstanding ruble balances with less-liquid government bonds, although still at an attractive rate of interest in real terms. Because of the acute political and administrative difficulties, however, tampering with the cash position of households is best avoided. Indeed, simply raising the interest rate(s) and lengthening the maturities on savings and time deposits available to households *and* to liberalized enterprises (in the hypothetical new monetary regime) well above any expected inflation may be sufficient to prevent net cash dishoarding and to eliminate inflationary pressure.

However, increasing real interest rates on savings and time deposits, the liabilities of the State Bank, implies a corresponding sharp increase in the costs of servicing the central government's outstanding debt, even if enterprise deposits are written down as suggested above. In effect, the past cumulative deficits of the Soviet government were largely financed by issuing savings deposits (Table 11.1) and coin and currency through the state banking system to households. Thus, financing an increase in interest rates on savings deposits without adding to the government's deficit would require (1) a general increase in the yields on government-owned assets and bank loans to enterprises or (2) an increase in general tax revenue from households and enterprises. As part of a general program to raise the productivity of capital in the economy, (1) is clearly the preferred route for financing the higher payout to depositors.

If neither increased yields on government-owned assets nor new tax revenues are available for paying higher deposit rates of interest, there remain three uncomfortable alternatives for eliminating the monetary overhang in households.

The first is simply to remove price controls to bring about a once-and-for-all general price inflation similar to that attempted in Poland in the first half of 1990. Because people cannot estimate how far the inflation will go, however, great uncertainty is introduced into the fledgling market economy; relative price signals become confused. Nevertheless, if flow constraints are successfully imposed—the government budget is balanced and tough credit controls are in place—the price inflation itself will eventually eliminate the monetary overhang and then diminish after a period of some turmoil.

The second alternative is a once-and-for-all cancellation or write-down of outstanding cash balances and savings accounts throughout the economy, including households. "Old" rubles are canceled as legal tender and "new" rubles are introduced at, say, a 1:5 ratio. In effect, there is *currency replacement*. The objective is to roughly stabilize the price level in new rubles even as decontrol allows free variability in relative prices. This second route eliminated repressed inflation in West Germany in 1948. The West German experience is often referred to as a model for eliminating the current largely repressed inflation (monetary overhang) in the Soviet Union in the early 1990s. However, the special political and very favorable fiscal conditions prevailing in West Germany in June 1948 indicate that this second route is unlikely to be feasible in the Soviet Union today, as I demonstrate in Appendix 2.

Third, a plethora of schemes to introduce some form of new "hard" ruble that would circulate for a time *in parallel* with the old "soft" ruble have been proposed by both foreign and Soviet economists. Typically in these schemes, the new currency would, unlike the old ruble, establish its hardness by being directly convertible into foreign exchange or its equivalent at a fixed rate. For example, both Jude Wanniski (1989) and Wayne Angell (1989) have suggested introducing a new gold-backed ruble that would be stable-valued because of free arbitrage (presumably on both capital and current account) with the gold prices of foreign goods and services.

At a meeting in Moscow in October 1988, the International Task Force on Foreign Economic Relations submitted a working paper authored by George Soros, Ed Hewett, Wassily Leontief, and Jan Mladek proposing that the Soviet economy be partitioned into a market-based "open sector" that is sharply differentiated geographically or by industry from the traditional economy based on central planning. This hypothetical open sector of the Soviet economy would, by allowing free foreign and domestic trade, have a different and more flexible relative price structure from the frozen disequilibrium prices prevailing in the traditional economy.

What would be the monetary mechanism in this hypothetical open sector? The original Soros proposal suggested that a new hard money, the *valutny* ruble, circulate in the open sector and be freely convertible at a fixed rate into foreign exchange. Some workers would even be paid partly in valutny rubles and partly in traditional rubles depending on where or for whom they were employed. But the large fiscal deficits that the Soviet government now generates are financed by the issue of old rubles. In short, it uses the inflation tax. However, the consequential rate of inflation depends on the willingness of people to hold old rubles, the real stock of which is the "tax" base, as described in Chapter 5. This willingness to hold old rubles would be quickly undermined if the valutny ruble (or some other form of foreign exchange certificate) began to circulate in parallel as illustrated in Chapter 9. People would dump old rubles in favor of the harder currency. With this shrinkage of the tax base, the rate of inflation in old rubles (the tax rate) would have to increase to cover any given fiscal deficit. This could lead to hyperinflation in the old currency. And once the old ruble was driven out of circulation, the Soviet government would find itself without any means of internal finance to cover its huge budgetary deficits. It would then be forced to overissue the hypothetical valutny ruble, thus undermining its purchasing power and convertibility at a fixed rate of exchange.

In addition, the deliberate creation of a large open sector with different regulations and different relative prices from the remainder of the Soviet economy would aggravate corruption and resource misuse as people tried to arbitrage away the differences. By deflecting attention from the current *domestic* fiscal and monetary disarray, therefore, such suggestions for introducing harder monies to circulate in parallel with the old ruble do more harm than good.

So there is no quick fix. The introduction of a new hard currency—perhaps fully convertible into foreign exchange—cannot negate the need for achieving domestic fiscal balance on the one hand and better control over domestic money and credit on the other. Once these fundamental flow conditions are satisfied, however, introducing an entirely new currency would be redundant and unnecessarily disruptive. It is better to reform the old one by unifying the monetary circuits of liberalized enterprises and households to secure full *domestic* currency convertibility, as described above. Then, as prices are decontrolled throughout the Soviet Union, some combination of higher real interest rates on domestic bank deposits, severe constraints on bank borrowing by enterprises, and a one-time inflation of officially recognized prices toward their current black-market levels would seem the most promising scenario for eliminating whatever monetary overhang of traditional rubles households had accumulated.

RESTRICTING INTERNATIONAL CAPITAL FLOWS

With domestic commodity markets so liberalized, the economy could move with deliberate speed toward free ruble convertibility on current account and toward a meaningful unified exchange rate to balance foreign trade. The appropriate strategy for freeing foreign trade in goods and services, with the possible use of bridging finance in the form of (controlled) net capital inflows from abroad, is analyzed in detail in Chapter 12.

However, extending unrestricted ruble convertibility to the capital account would come later in the transition—and possibly much later, as indicated by the analyses in Chapters 6 and 10. Indeed, with the current state of financial repression in the Soviet Union, or even with the limited liberalization of the domestic capital market envisaged in our idealized stage 1, abolishing exchange controls on capital account is undesirable. On the one hand, it would invite massive capital flight. Liberalized Soviet enterprises and households would strive to build up their liquidity in harder foreign monies. On the other hand, those enterprises with overseas connections would tend to overborrow because of the (implicitly) high wedge between deposit and loan rates. The monetary domain of the ruble would shrink and inflationary pressure would increase (Ch. 9). Fledgling domestic entrepreneurs without such overseas connections would be severely disadvantaged. Until domestic financial processes are fully liberalized with a normal flow of bank lending at equilibrium interest rates, therefore, the nascent ruble-based capital market should be protected by exchange controls on (gross) outflows and inflows of foreign portfolio capital.

However, foreign technological expertise can still be efficiently utilized, even if massive international capital flows are avoided. As in the Japanese experience of the 1950s and 1960s, foreign technologies could still be absorbed through the licensing of domestic Soviet partners, joint ventures, and the like, even though financial capital inflows remained small. But domestic price-level stability and high internal financial growth (described in Ch. 3) were key ingredients enabling Japanese entrepreneurs to absorb and license foreign technologies without incurring any significant net buildup of foreign debt.

THE WRONG KIND OF MONETARY REFORM: AN ADDENDUM

In early 1991, after this manuscript was virtually completed, the Soviet government did try a quick fix on the economy's monetary overhang. The authorities had become increasingly desperate about empty shelves and severe shortages of consumer necessities in the official price-controlled outlets, high price inflation in the legal cooperative market outlets where prices are only "monitored," and very high inflation in rapidly proliferating black-market activities. Thus on January 23, 1991, the government announced that

1. Ruble bank notes in large denominations of 50 and 100 rubles were no longer legal tender—perhaps one-quarter to one-third of the outstanding supply of currency was thereby canceled;

2. People were given just three working days to turn in large ruble notes (presumably for smaller denominations or for credit to their savings accounts) up to a maximum governed by a worker's monthly salary—which averaged 257 rubles per month in 1990—or 1,000 rubles, whichever was less. Pensioners were restricted to converting a maximum of 200 rubles.

3. Personal savings accounts (which in practice are very large relative to the coin and currency held by households—Table 11.1) were frozen. Individuals could withdraw no more than 500 rubles per month from these accounts.

Insofar as they can demonstrate that their large notes were acquired by bringing hard currency into the country, foreigners were exempted from these restrictions on money changing; and individuals who were about to make a documented large-scale purchase from an official outlet could still transfer the money. The authorities claimed that they were mainly out to confiscate the cash hoards of black-market traders and profiteers who deal in large denomination notes.

However, many of the Soviet Republics, including the huge Russian Republic, immediately moved to undermine or soften the decree. Within each republic's jurisdiction, banks were variously required to extend the number of days for transferring money, and to increase the amounts that could be transferred in different categories. Indeed, because they didn't trust savings accounts, pensioners turned out to be major holders of large denomination bank notes—and their great economic distress was the most obvious.

The full empirical consequences of this dramatic monetary action cannot be assessed before this book goes to press. The reform could even be reversed. Nevertheless, in light of the analytical framework provided in this chapter, whether or not the reform is conceptually well founded *ex ante* can be assessed.

Over the years, the Soviet government has continually intervened to freeze or confiscate the cash positions of state enterprises. Even cooperatives, which were supposedly made independent by the 1987 Law on Cooperatives, were subject to having their cash positions frozen or intervened. What then was novel about the degree of January 23, 1991? The direct confiscation and reduction in the internal convertibility of household and small enterprise money that had heretofore been on a separate monetary circuit that was not restricted. (True, goods might not be available in government shops, but there had been no restraint on spending household money *per se*.)

In effect, this most recent decree cuts in the *opposite* direction to our "optimum" program for stabilizing the Soviet price level while simultaneously increasing the productivity of capital in the Soviet economy. The optimum program, as sketched above, focused on the desirability of raising the stock demand for money as well as on curtailing the flow imbalances that created excess supplies of money. Indeed, the idea was to extend the domain of internally convertible rubles to encompass liberalized enterprises—to unify the monetary circuits of households and firms. Then by increasing interest paid on deposits, reducing expected inflation, *and* eliminating the threat of arbitrary seizure and confiscation of the monetary holdings of households and liberalized enterprises, the increased demand for money would itself tend to reduce inflationary pressure. Households and enterprises would sell off their excess inventories of physical goods in order to build up their real cash balances.

Although aiming to reduce the monetary overhang from the supply side (by cancelling outstanding money), the decree of January 23, 1991 could well reduce the (future) stock demand for money even more. Households and enterprises will be even more loathe to hold rubles because of their heightened fear of expropriation, and instead will strive harder to hold their wealth in the form of "excess" inventories of physical goods and foreign exchange. Thus, if the demand for rubles was to fall by more than the outstanding stock is reduced, net inflationary pressure from the monetary "reform" could actually increase. Either way, however, the economy will become more demonetized and the productivity of physical capital could well fall further.

In addition, the Soviet government did not supplement the one-time adjustment in the stock of rubles with any significant action to stem the economy's more fundamental flow imbalances: the fiscal deficit and the overextension of bank credit that will inevitably lead to more inflationary pressure in the future.

Because people know then that the one-time stock adjustment of January 23 will not correct the ongoing inflation in the longer run, their current demand for rubles is further undermined.

APPENDIX I
Financial Structure and Managerial Control:
Some Notes on Japan, West Germany, and the United States

Even among mature capitalist economies, there is no consensus on what constitutes an optimal financial structure governing corporate enterprises. Japan, West Germany, and the United States differ enormously in who effectively owns major corporations and in the restraints external creditors impose on managements.

In Japan, the common shareholders exercise virtually no influence, because the common stock of any one company is owned mainly by related companies in the same industrial group (*keiretsu*). Decision making is accomplished on a broad consensus basis within each firm, where workers themselves participate by having their wages tied to the firm's profitability. The management process is audited in great detail by each firm's principal external creditor. Its "main bank" not only organizes the firm's access to the capital market but also appoints some directors. Should the firm get into difficulty, the main bank can force changes in its management even before bankruptcy occurs.

West Germany is similar to Japan insofar as a main bank—usually one of the German "big three"—undertakes detailed auditing of what the firm does and can request changes in management. Common shareholders again need not have a decisive voice, because they do not even have a majority on the board of directors, which by German law must include representatives from labor as well as "outsiders." Even so, consensus decision making is not as pronounced as in Japan, and the wages of German workers tend to be quite rigid because they are set on an industry-wide basis and, unlike Japan, do not vary with the fortunes of the particular company for which a person works. Although the West German economy is otherwise very successful, its high and rigid real wages are the principal cause of the high rate of German unemployment—a malady that also afflicts most other Western European economies.

In the United States (as in Britain), by contrast, commercial banks (but not necessarily investment banks) have an arm's-length relationship with the firms to which they lend. Commercial banks cannot own equity claims on nonbank enterprises and are not represented on board of directors unless the firm is in bankruptcy. Firms may borrow from more than one bank and typically do not submit to continuous internal auditing by outside creditors. To compensate for their lack of managerial control over the borrower, American commercial banks depend more on direct collateral to secure their loans. Traditionally (before the distortions caused by deposit insurance), the commercial banks would only lend at short-term for the accumulation of working capital. Under the old Real Bills Doctrine, such short-term loans were directly secured by the borrowing firm's liquid assets: accounts receivable or inventories of raw materials and finished goods, which were marketable items the bank could seize in the event of a default.

The legal owners of American corporations are the common shareholders. But, in part because such shareholding has become increasingly diversified or controlled by mutual funds that are unwilling to audit what firms do, control over the typical firm's assets has devolved to the "executive suite," that is, an inner group of managers or sometimes only the chief executive officer. This shift in effective property rights has caused great turmoil in the American financial structure, as manifested in the mergers and acquisitions frenzy of the late 1980s. The incumbent managements and outside raiders vie with each other to strip the assets of the company for their own personal gain. Outside creditors, whether mutual funds or banks, have inadequate power to restrain this behavior. One consequence is an unfortunate shortening of the time horizon over which investment takes place and a lessened ability to invest in new technologies with a long lead time.

APPENDIX II
The West German Monetary Experience of 1948

In 1945, under wartime price controls, the West German economy faced a huge monetary overhang from excessive money issue during the war.[12] Because the four-power occupation authorities could not agree on how many additional reich marks (in the form of occupation currency) to issue, this monetary overhang was then considerably augmented from 1945 to early 1948. Because price controls were also continued, suppressed inflation became acute. The West German economy languished, with output actually falling.

Then, on June 20, 1948, the West Germany monetary overhang was elimi-nated by directly canceling most of the outstanding stock of monetary purchas-ing power. No longer legal tender, the old reich mark could only be traded on a 1-for-10 basis for new deutsche marks, with the controlled price level in "marks" initially remaining largely in place. Other monetary assets and liabili-ties were scaled down commensurately (mainly 1 to 10); and, in addition, each family was given 60 deutsche marks starting money. Then, with the monetary overhang removed and little net inflationary pressure on the overall

12. For an extensive retrospective analysis of events leading up to the 1948 West German reform and its aftermath, see Richter 1979.

price level, general price decontrol quickly followed within the next few months. With relative prices now free to vary and clear individual markets, the stage was set for the West German postwar recovery.

Although the current suppressed inflation in the Soviet Union resembles that prevailing in West Germany in early 1948, key fiscal differences exist.

First, in 1948 West Germany, a full-fledged tax-collecting mechanism was in place. An elaborate system of turnover and profits taxes on businesses was complemented by a stringent personal income tax. Indeed, the Allied occupation authorities were determined to impose a level of taxation in West Germany that was at least as high as that prevailing in the United States or Britain. Thus, when the West German economy began to grow after June 20, the revenue elasticity with respect to income tax collections was (much) greater than unity.

Second, it is important to realize that the currency replacement of 1948 not only was a monetary reform but was also implicitly a fiscal reform. Prior to June 20, the old reich mark circulated as legal tender across all four military zones. Because of disputes between the Allied and Soviet military authorities, however, excess money issue (in reich marks) continued. After June 20, therefore, the new deutsche mark was issued only in the three Western zones, and that on a strictly limited basis. What later became the German Democratic Republic (East Germany) was suddenly excluded, with the Soviet military authorities eventually issuing a new money of their own. By suddenly restricting monetary circulation from four zones to three, the Allied authorities could avoid overissue of the new deutsche mark. In this special sense, the introduction of the new currency was a great "fiscal" improvement. (Moreover, to be successful, the planning for this massive currency substitution had to be kept secret from the German people—something an occupying military force is capable of doing.)

On both counts, the fiscal circumstances within the Soviet Union in the 1990s are much less promising. A major currency replacement, although very traumatic, would only temporarily reduce the monetary overhang. The large fiscal deficits—inability to collect taxes—would quickly lead to excessive stocks of the new money. Unlike the West German experience of 1948, simply replacing an old currency with a new one in the modern Soviet circumstances would not itself constitute a fiscal improvement.

CHAPTER TWELVE

Foreign Trade, Protection,

and

Negative Value-Added

in

a Liberalizing Socialist Economy

A sustained movement toward free foreign trade in goods and services is crucial for the successful transition from a socialist to a market economy. From our examination of tariff and quota protection in less-developed countries (LDCs) (Ch. 8), no government can maintain detailed controls over the flow of foreign trade without seriously interfering with market mechanisms in the domestic economy—particularly in socialist economies, where monopoly power and industrial concentration are major problems. Table 12.1 shows the high degree of industrial concentration in important manufacturing industries in the Soviet Union. In addition, efficient international specialization is highly desirable in its own right for all the conventional reasons.

This chapter focuses on the optimum order of liberalization in foreign trade presuming that domestic financial equilibrium has already been secured and that commodity prices in domestic markets have been largely decontrolled, as described in Chapter 11. With hard budget constraints, "liberalized" enterprises produce and trade in open markets the thousands of goods and services that constitute the bulk of the domestic economy. The currency is unified and fully convertible for *domestic* transactions: the liberalized enterprises no longer operate with restricted bank deposits in buying or selling domestic goods and services. The monetary overhang has been largely eliminated (Lipton and Sachs 1990a) and the (decontrolled) domestic price level is fairly stable.

But domestic liberalization need not be complete before moving toward freer foreign trade. The government could still be intervening to set a few key prices and wages in "traditional" enterprises, as defined in Chapter 11. To curb monopoly power in highly concentrated manufacturing industries (Table 12.1), these enterprises might well continue under centralized wage and price controls until an effective degree of foreign competition is established. In energy and other raw materials producing industries, the government as principal owner of the natural resource would naturally set domestic prices until these industries were integrated into world markets. Finally, for reasons developed in

TABLE 12.1
Industrial Concentration in the Soviet Union

Simple Monopolies

Product	Producer	% of Total Production
Consumer goods:		
Sewing machines	Shveinaya Association, Podalsk	100
Automatic washing machines	Elektrobytpribor Factory, Kirov	90
Transport:		
Trolley buses	Uritsky Factory, Engels	97
Forklift trucks	Autopogruzhchik Association, Kharkov	87
Diesel locomotives	Industrial Association, Voroshilovgrad	95
Electric locomotives and trains	Electric Locomotive Plant, Novocherkassk	70
Tram rails	Integrated Steel Works, Kuznetsk	100
Metals:		
Reinforced steel	Krivoy-Rog-stal, Krivoy Rog	55
Construction equipment:		
Concrete mixers	Integrated Mill, Tuva Works	93
Road-building cranes	Sverdlovsk Plant, Sverdlovsk	75
Locomotive cranes	Engineering Plant, Kirov	100
Oil, chemicals, and chemical engineering:		
Polypropylene	Neftkhimichesky Combine, Perm	73
Deep-oil-well sucker rods	Ochesk Engineering Plant, Ochesk	100
Sucker-rod pumps	Dzerzhinsky Engineering Plant, Baku	100
Hoists for coal mines	City Coal Machinery Plant, Donetsk	100
Coking equipment	Kopeisk Engineering Plant, Chelyabinsk	100

Products Produced by Two or More Factories Run by the Same Ministry

Product	Producer	% of Total Production
Power engineering:		
Hydraulic turbines	Metallurgical works, Leningrad; turbines plant, Kharkov; pipe-building factory, Syzran	100
Steam turbines	Metallurgical works, Leningrad; turbines plant, Kharkov; turbo-motor plant, Sverdlovsk	95
Metals:		
Electrolytic tin plate	Magnitogorsk and Karaganda	100
Rolled stainless-steel pipes	Pipe factories, Nikopol and Pervouralsk	95
Consumer goods:		
Color-photography paper	Positive Film, Leningrad; and Positive Film, Pereslavi	100
Freezers	Freezers Association and Plants, Kishinev and Krasnoyarsk	100

Source: The Economist, August 11–17, 1990, 67.

Chapter 11, exchange controls on international capital flows would remain in place indefinitely.

Presuming that these domestic preconditions are more or less satisfied, what then should be the optimum order of liberalization in foreign trade? In a large, fairly closed economy like that of the Soviet Union, how quickly should *current-account* convertibility expose domestic industries to foreign competition in comparison to the smaller economies of Eastern Europe?

In their swift "cold turkey" adoption of free trade with full current-account convertibility in 1990, both East Germany and Poland experienced rapid industrial decline: the collapse, or threatened bankruptcy, in an astonishingly wide variety of manufacturing and agricultural industries that turned out ex post facto not to be internationally competitive. True, their sudden attempts to expose domestic enterprises to market forces coincided with their sudden moves to free trade—rather than first liberalizing their domestic economy. (Indeed, in very large socialist economies such as those of the Soviet Union and China, liberalizing the domestic economy first is likely to be easier than in the much smaller, and more naturally open, economies of Eastern Europe.) Even if not a pure test of our "optimum" order of liberalization, however, the Polish and East German experiences reflect the severe adjustment problem associated with a precipitate move to free trade that is this chapter's main concern.

Is successful adjustment to free trade mainly a question of getting the exchange rate "right"? Apparently not. Poland and East Germany each pursued a quite different exchange-rate policy. In July 1990, East Germany entered economic union with West Germany at what seemed, by previous black market standards, to be an overvalued exchange rate: one east mark for one west mark. In contrast, in early January 1990, Poland embarked on its remarkable opening to the West, in which the zloty was deliberately undervalued at 9,500 to the dollar—a sharp devaluation from the 6,500 zloty to the dollar that had prevailed. In order to eliminate the monetary overhang as domestic prices were decontrolled, this undervaluation was designed to force a one-time inflation on the Polish economy. The sharp inflation in the first three months of 1990 was remarkably successful in eliminating queues and securing a balance in supply and demand in most domestic commodity markets (Lipton and Sachs 1990a), and Polish output fell less sharply than East German.

Thus the problem of industrial decline seems to be much more than an exchange-rate question—although that remains important. At first glance, the great difficulty of East Germany and Poland in expanding (new) export activities as import substitution industries contract seems to refute the law of comparative advantage. Even if average industrial productivity were low, conventional textbook wisdom had it that the comparative efficiency of at least some major domestic industries soon would assert itself. And some reasoning such as this lay behind the willingness of the Polish and German policymakers to move so quickly toward unrestricted foreign trade.

In this chapter, we examine alternative theories of comparative advantage based on differing (implicit) views of the industrial structure prevailing within socialist economies before the move to free trade occurs. The first is the standard *Ricardian model* for ranking existing domestic industries by *comparative efficiency* vis-à-vis their counterparts in the outside world. Goods are produced directly from basic labor with fixed production coefficients, which, however, may differ between trading partners.

The second I shall call the *substitution model* because it is based on the circular flow of production where goods and services can be combined in variable proportions. Producers of finished manufactures use labor and capital to add value to industrial raw materials and energy in combinations reflecting the highly protected domestic market. Once the socialist economy is open to unrestricted foreign trade, this second approach admits the possibility of *absolute inefficiency* in existing domestic manufacturing and agricultural processing activities. At the beginning of the transition, industries producing finished goods might well exhibit *negative value added* at world market prices, whether or not they turn out to be viable in the long run once free trade is attained.

Which analytical model of industrial organization one chooses empirically is important in selecting an appropriate adjustment policy for the transition to free trade. The optimal speed with which protective barriers—tariffs versus quotas—should be dismantled, the desirability of bridging finance (the large *net* absorption of capital from foreign lenders during the transition), and the choice of an exchange-rate regime might all be conditioned by the (implicit) analytical model that policymakers adopt. Let us discuss each in turn.

THE RICARDIAN MODEL OF LABOR PRODUCTIVITY

What does the traditional Ricardian theory of comparative advantage, which emphasizes technological differences among countries, tell us? Let us take the leading example—virtually an economic parable—of East and West Germany suddenly moving from no trade to free trade.

In economic autarky for each country, the Ricardian model posits well-defined domestic production technologies for the whole range of potentially tradable goods. Each good is produced directly from basic labor—the sole factor of production—so that the analysis of capital accumulation or the circular flow of intermediate products is bypassed. Before trade is opened, the model assumes that each industry in West Germany could be exactly matched with a counterpart industry in East Germany producing qualitatively the same good. However, the industries of the two countries differ in technological proficiency (conventionally indexed by labor productivities) in varying degrees for different industries. Let a_i and b_i be output per worker in the ith industry for West and East Germany, respectively. Define the index i such that $i = 1$ is the relatively most efficient East German industry, through all m tradable goods to $i = m$, which is the most efficient West Germany industry, such that

$$(12.1) \qquad a_1/b_1 < a_2/b_2 < \ldots < a_k/b_k < \ldots < a_m/b_m.$$

On average, suppose that output per worker in West German tradables industries is, say, twice as high as in East Germany and that this is counterbalanced by the wage level in West Germany being twice as high. Consumption tastes in the two countries are identical and homothetic in income and prices so that expenditure shares for each commodity are constant, as worked out in considerable technical detail in the Ricardian model with a continuum of goods (Dornbusch, Fischer, and Samuelson 1977). Further assume that consumption demand is evenly balanced[1] across all m industries such that one could find some intermediate industry k where $a_k/b_k = 2$ and which, having equal production costs in both countries, produces goods that are just on the borderline of not being traded. That is, once inter-German trade was opened, all goods in industries where $a_i/b_i > 2$ would be produced only in West Germany, and those where $a_i/b_i < 2$ would be produced only in East Germany. When there was no net capital flow between the two Germanys, that is, balanced trade, then

$$(12.2) \qquad \sum_{i=1}^{k-1} (p_i x_i^b) = \sum_{i=k+1}^{m} (p_i x_i^a),$$

where p_i is the (common) price of the ith commodity, and the x^a are exports from West to East, with the reverse being true for x^b.

Monetary mechanisms, including the nominal exchange rate and price level, in this simple full-employment Ricardian model are only implicit. However, there is a natural interpretation of the "real" exchange rate, denoted by θ, as the ratio of real wages between the two Germanys in free-trade equilibrium. For the kth industry, which is the dividing line determining the flow of trade, output could equally well be produced in either country. Wage costs of

---

1. I want to avoid any elaborate discussion of the theory of reciprocal demand, which would be misplaced concreteness at this stage of the analysis of a socialist economy that is "small" in world markets. For an extensive welfare analysis of the terms of trade and reciprocal demand between two comparably sized trading partners in the Ricardian context, see Dornbusch, Fischer, and Samuelson 1977.

producing the kth output would be the same whether it was produced in West or East Germany such that

$$(12.3) \qquad p_k = w_a/a_k = w_b/b_k, \qquad \text{or} \qquad \theta = a_k/b_k = w_a/w_b,$$

where w_a is the common wage throughout West Germany and w_b is the common wage throughout East Germany (presuming that all labor does not immediately move to the high-wage area). Thus, the real exchange rate θ is just the ratio of labor productivities in the marginal kth industry and is also the wage ratio. Under balanced trade in our particular example, $\theta = 2$ reflects the fact that real wages are twice as high in West as in East Germany: the average difference in technical efficiency across all m industries. In effect, an increase in θ represents a real appreciation of the shadow West German mark, or a real depreciation of the shadow East German mark. An increase in θ thus expands the number of tradables industries where East Germany is the low-cost producer relative to West Germany.

In advocating an abrupt, complete move to free trade, most economists implicitly take the real exchange rate, in the textbook Ricardian model, to be a sufficient control variable to secure the necessary adjustment. No matter how technically inefficient East German industry might be on average, one could always find a θ sufficiently high, that is, an East German real wage (measured at world market prices) sufficiently low, that industries 1 through $k-1$ could begin exporting profitably and absorbing labor at the outset of the liberalization process. In East Germany soon after the jump to free trade, the major problem of contracting and closing down industries $k + 1$ to m would still be traumatic. (The mirror-image adjustment is faced by West Germany.) However, in this Ricardian view, the buoyancy of increased East German output in their internationally competitive industries would go a long way to ease the industrial distress.

CAPITAL TRANSFERS AND INDUSTRIAL ADJUSTMENT IN THE RICARDIAN MODEL

Do capital flows affect the acuteness of the problem of industrial adjustment? Continuing with the parable of the two Germanys, massive capital transfers—on both private and government account—have flowed from West to East in order to ease the adjustment problem. Putting aside the long-run effects on the capital stock and labor productivity (which are outside the simple Ricardian model), we are left with the short-run effects of the transfer itself on the pattern of industrial production. For the transfer to be effected, East Germany must run a trade deficit with West Germany corresponding to its increased expenditures made possible by the transfer. Would such a deficit then worsen the industrial contraction in East Germany?

If we limit our simple Ricardian model to *tradable goods only* as described above and simply take money out of the hands of West German taxpayers (or pension funds) in order to subsidize increases in spending by East Germans, then *the capital transfer per se will not change the free-trade pattern of production or relative wages.* Because tastes are identical and expenditure shares are constant for the two Germanies and all disposable income must be spent for tradable goods, the decline in demand by West Germans for goods 1 to *m*, will be exactly offset by increased spending by East Germans for these same goods. Thus neither country's production pattern will deviate from the free trade equilibrium prevailing in the absence of a capital transfer.[2]

Starting from free-trade equilibrium, let $T > 0$ be the amount of the capital transfer and the East German trade deficit at current prices. Then equation (12.2) can be modified to show the East German trade deficit equal to the capital transfer:

$$(12.4) \qquad T = \sum_{k=k+1}^{m} (p_i \tilde{x}_i^a) - \sum_{i=1}^{k-1} (p_i \tilde{x}_i^b),$$

where p_i is the common price of the *i*th commodity as before. But $\tilde{x}^a$ is now the increased level of exports from West Germany, where $\tilde{x}_i^a > x_i^a$; and the $\tilde{x}^b$ are the reduced level of exports from East Germany, where $\tilde{x}_i^b < x_i^b$. Nevertheless, *production* in industries 1 to *k* in East Germany and *k* + 1 to *m* in West Germany would remain unchanged, the same as in the absence of the capital transfer. Thus the capital transfer itself imposes no additional adjustment burden of industrial redeployment.

However, suppose now a *nontradables sector*—say, local services on which a substantial proportion of each country's disposable income is spent—exists in each country. In fact, from our assumptions of identical tastes and homothetical utility functions for each country, we could imagine each Germany spending $0 < \alpha < 1$ of its disposable income on tradables and $(1 - \alpha)$ on nontradables. In practice, $(1 - \alpha)$ could be 40 or 50 percent. Then upon the receipt of the capital transfer, some of the increased East German spending will be diverted away from tradables 1 to *m* to the nontradable good, which we shall denote by *n*. (The mirror-image adjustment occurs in West Germany.)

So production in the nontradables sector in East Germany would expand relative to both its previous autarkic equilibrium level and relative to its level under free trade without the transfer. Thus, *the initial effect of the capital inflow is to force a further contraction in the range of tradable outputs produced in East Germany.* Remembering that aggregate demand from the two Germanys remains initially unchanged for each tradable good in the face

2. For a formal demonstration that production remains unchanged in response to a capital transfer in a Ricardian model with only tradable goods, again see Dornbusch, Fischer, and Samuelson 1977.

of the transfer, the nontradables industry in East Germany can only expand by bidding up real wages so as to attract labor away from tradables, thus forcing up the international prices of those tradables produced in East Germany. The result is a further contraction in the range of tradable outputs produced in East Germany (Dornbusch, Fischer, and Samuelson 1977). As represented earlier in equation (12.1), the borderline good (between exporting and importing) shifts to the left:

$$(12.5) \qquad a_1/b_1 < a_2/b_2 < \ldots < a_j/b_j < \ldots < a_k/b_k < \ldots < a_m/b_m.$$

The index j now denotes the new borderline industry, and $j < k$ after the capital transfer. Moreover, the real exchange rate of East Germany—its relative wage—appreciates.

$$(12.6) \qquad \theta' = a_j/b_j = w_a'/w_b' < a_k/b_k = w_a/w_b = \theta,$$

where the primes represent equilibrium in the presence of nontradables.

For any socialist economy in transition to free trade, in the Ricardian context, what might we then conclude about the use of bridging finance from abroad to assist or smooth structural readjustment in the exposed domestic production of manufactured goods and primary products? The absorption of large *net* amounts of foreign capital, whether through direct government-to-government aid or through private channels, is probably best avoided. Apart from the problem of servicing foreign debt in the future, the absorption of large net capital inflows from abroad at the beginning of a liberalization program will flood the economy with foreign goods. Because a large trade deficit is necessary to effect the real transfer, the relative prices of internationally tradable goods will be artificially depressed in the fledgling market economy. Older industries, already facing the difficult problem of winding down many of their existing activities, will find their transitional problems made more acute by this "subsidized" international competition. Potential new entrepreneurs looking for areas in which to invest might try to avoid manufacturing, and even agriculture, altogether in order to concentrate their new investments in domestic services (such as housing, restaurants, or equipment leasing) that are more naturally sheltered from international competition.

Although many such investments in services are beneficial in that they fill immediate gaps in what the economy should eventually provide, neglecting potential export activities will create a foreign exchange constraint on future development once the transitional inflow of foreign capital is phased out and foreign debts have to be serviced. This distorting effect of a massive capital inflow on economy-wide resource allocation that reduces international competitiveness in manufacturing is reminiscent of the "Dutch Disease" facing a country exporting some valuable natural resource whose world price suddenly increases.[3]

THE SUBSTITUTION MODEL AND EFFECTIVE PROTECTION OF VALUE-ADDED

Whether under free trade or economic autarky, the Ricardian model assumed that all goods are, or can be, produced according to predetermined production technologies from basic labor. Alternatively, let us now consider the circular flow of production in a "typical" socialist economy. Goods are produced from intermediate products as well as labor and capital, and there are substantial substitution possibilities for combining them. In this substitution model, technological capabilities, including labor productivities, are conditioned by the preexisting structure of protection before liberalization occurs.

In the traditional Stalinist economy, virtually all domestic production of more or less "finished goods"—those sold directly to consumers or sold back to industry as plant and equipment—was insulated from foreign competition. Because the ruble was inconvertible into foreign exchange on current account, protection for domestic manufacturers (including processed agricultural goods) was absolute. The state trading agency refused to authorize competing imports unless there were pronounced domestic shortages of similar products. Although there were no formal tariffs or quota restrictions in any legal codes, the *implicit* level of protection was as high as if quota restrictions had eliminated competitive pressure from abroad. At some equilibrium exchange rate (to be discussed below), domestic prices for finished goods (after discounting for their normally poorer quality in the protected setting) were typically higher than their foreign counterparts. Thus, in its general repercussions on economy-wide resource allocation, this price wedge is similar to the effect of a high tariff on the importation of competing finished goods.

At the same time, exports of energy, raw materials, and limited amounts of manufactures (largely military equipment in the Soviet case) were largely determined centrally by "a vent-for-surplus" doctrine. That is, after domestic needs for, say, energy, at low domestic prices had been more or less satisfied, the residual (quite a large residual in the Soviet case) was then sold abroad at much higher, world market prices. The effect was similar to imposing an export tax on energy that drives the domestic price below that paid by foreign buyers. Energy in all forms, together with nonfood raw materials which were similarly "taxed," amounted to over 60 percent of Soviet exports in 1989 and over 75 percent if one omits "protected" military sales from the export base.

---

3. The distortions arising from trying to absorb large amounts of foreign capital into an imperfectly open economy (i.e., where free arbitrage in all goods and factor markets was not yet well established) constituted one of the main themes of chapter 11 in my *Money and Capital in Economic Development* (1973). Some of the same issues are taken up in Chapter 9 of this volume.

In order to approximate how these relative prices in the Stalinist economy differ from those prevailing in the world economy, let us partition the tradable goods produced and consumed into (1) *finished goods:* largely manufactures and foodstuffs; and (2) *material inputs:* largely energy products and nonfood raw materials. For modeling purposes, assume that all finished goods are import substitutes or imports and are not exported and that material inputs are either exported or used up in the domestic manufacture of finished goods. Reinterpreting the notation and methodology of Tan (1970)[4], denote the gross output of finished-goods industry i by Z_i, where the corresponding production function is

$$(12.7) \qquad Z_i = Z_i (L_1, L_2, \ldots L_n, M_1, M_2, \ldots M_r).$$

The L_i are the primary factors such as labor or land, and the M_i are intermediate material inputs. In considering the production choices facing industry i (Fig. 12.1), however, let us dispense with all but one intermediate input, M, and one domestic factor, L. We can then denote value-added in domestic prices of finished-goods industry i as

$$(12.8) \qquad V_i = P_i Z_i - P_m M,$$

where P_i and P_m are the domestic-currency prices of the finished product and material input, respectively. The value-added by the domestic factor(s) is simply gross value minus the cost of intermediate inputs, and the normal presumption is that value-added at domestic prices is positive.[5] But what determines the relative prices of Z_i and M in domestic commodity markets, and how is that linked to domestic factor costs?

THE COEFFICIENT OF PROTECTION FOR FINISHED GOODS

Consider relative commodity prices first, assuming that one unit of the domestic currency exchanges for one foreign. Because we are dealing with an economy that is a small part of the world economy, foreign currency prices, denoted with asterisks, are fixed. Let t_i represent the implicit tariff protecting

4. Tan was concerned with the structure of differential tariffs in LDCs where finished goods (largely consumer manufactures) received high tariff protection but intermediate inputs entered duty free. For our analysis of the Soviet Union, I treat the taxed export good as the relevant intermediate product. However, for the smaller Eastern European economies where more material inputs are imported, one might want to introduce an untaxed importable as a third commodity in the analytical model, as in McKinnon (1966).

5. In any market economy, positive value-added at domestic prices is a necessary condition (although by no means sufficient to ensure profitability) for the firm to exist. In a socialist economy, in extreme cases one could imagine a degree of public subsidy that enabled an enterprise to keep going even when it was not covering the costs of its material inputs. But I am ruling out this unlikely possibility.

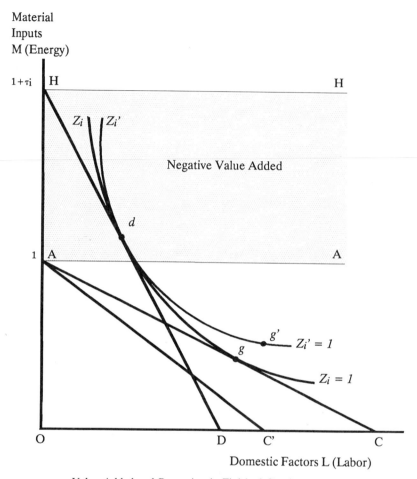

FIGURE 12.1. Value-Added and Protection in Finished Goods

domestic production of the finished product—the gap between the foreign and the quality-adjusted domestic price—such that

(12.9) $$P_i = (1 + t_i)P_i^*,$$

and let t_m represent the similarly calculated implicit export tax on material inputs such that

(12.10) $$P_m(1 + t_m) = P_m^*.$$

In order to see the divergence between domestic relative prices and their foreign counterparts, divide (12.9) by (12.10) and rearrange to get

(12.11) $$P_i/P_m = (1 + t_i)(1 + t_m)(P_i^*/P_m^*).$$

Equation (12.11) captures the dual aspect of the overall protection of the gross output of finished goods: the effect of restricting competing imports *and* of subsidizing the use of material inputs. Indeed, from Lerner's Symmetry Theorem (Lerner 1936), we know that restricting imports and taxing exports have equivalent protective effects in long-run equilibrium (as worked out more fully in the presence of intermediate products by McKinnon [1966]). For industry i, we thus define the overall "coefficient of protection" to be

(12.12) $$1 + \tau_i = (1 + t_i)(1 + t_m).$$

On the vertical scale of Figure 12.1, the coefficient of protection shows the domestic relative price of finished goods in terms of material inputs. To better interpret Figure 12.1, however, let us first consider domestic value-added at world prices:

(12.13) $$V_i^* = P_i^* Z_i - P_m^* M.$$

From equation (12.11), we can rewrite V_i^* in terms of domestic prices to get

(12.14) $$V_i^* = \frac{P_i Z_i - (1 + t_m)(1 + t_i)P_m M}{(1 + t_i)}.$$

Although we presume V_i remains positive, there can be *no presumption that domestic value-added at world prices is positive*. Indeed, if either t_m or t_i is sufficiently high, and if the relatively cheap M is substituted for other factors of production, equation (12.14) tells us that $V_i^* < 0$.

These relationships are depicted in Figure 12.1, which is a modified version of that used by Tan (1970). For a "typical" finished-goods industry i (which is one of many), the unit isoquants Z_i and Z_i' portray alternative possibilities for substituting the tradable material input for the domestic factor of production *in the long run*, that is, not taking transitional adjustment costs into account. The distance OA on the vertical axis represents the material inputs that are equivalent to one unit of finished goods at world prices. For example, at the hypothetical free-trade equilibrium at point g, where the new budget line AC (whose slope now reflects the relatively higher world cost of energy in terms of labor) is tangent to the unit isoquant Z_i, one unit of final output could buy OA in material inputs.

Going one step further, we can scale our measure of output in Figure 12.1 so that one unit of the finished good is worth just one dollar of foreign exchange: the unit isoquants Z_i or Z_i' denote just one dollar's worth of finished good *i*. Similarly, we can scale our measure of material inputs on the vertical axis so the one unit of, say, energy is also worth just one dollar:[6] the distance *OA* in Figure 12.1 is one.

Then, under the preexisting system of implicit protection and using this scaling, equation (12.11) tells us that the *domestic* relative price of the final output in terms of material inputs—the distance *OH* in Figure 12.1—is simply our coefficient of protection $1 + \tau_i$. The higher relative price of finished goods domestically compared to that prevailing on world markets (and compared to the price of material inputs) reflects both the implicit export tax on material inputs and the implicit tariff on competing imports of finished goods. In general equilibrium across many similar industries, the implicit export tax also reduces the price of material inputs relative to domestic wages. Along the unit isoquant in Figure 12.1, therefore, the (protected) industry *i* produces at point *d,* where it uses less labor and more material inputs than under free trade at point *g*.

THE OVERUSE OF MATERIAL INPUTS AND THE SHODDY PRODUCT SYNDROME

Under protected domestic prices, all feasible input combinations (feasible in the sense of domestic value–added being positive in the production of one unit of finished goods) must lie below the horizontal line HH in Figure 12.1. Below HH, the domestic value of finished-goods output exceeds the domestic cost of the material inputs used in their production.

At world relative prices, on the other hand, all feasible input combinations must lie below AA if domestic value-added is to be positive. Indeed, all production points in the shaded area lying above AA in Figure 12.1 show negative value-added at world prices. For example, the point d is profitable under the existing mantle of protection: the budget line HD (whose slope shows relatively cheap energy and expensive labor) is just tangent to the unit isoquant Z_i (or its alternative Z_i'). Nevertheless, d shows negative value-added if the final output had to be sold and material inputs had to be purchased in unrestricted world markets.

Why is this phenomenon of negative value-added at world prices probably commonplace in Soviet (and Eastern European) industry? First, as drawn in Figure 12.1, the relative prices of energy and other material inputs to most sectors of the Soviet economy have been kept very low, causing these material inputs to be used intensively. In addition, the old Stalinist system of rewarding managers when they (over)fulfill gross output targets encourages them to waste material inputs. "According to the calculations of the Soviet Institute of World Economy and International Relations, we use 1.5 times more materials and 2.1 times more energy per unit of national income than the United States. . . .

6. Note that the material equivalent of one unit of domestic output for some given price structure will generally be considerably greater than the amount of material input actually used in its production.

Our agricultural production is 15 percent less than the United States but we use 3.5 times more energy" (Shmelev and Popov 1989, 128).

Second, the Stalinist planning system based on gross output targets tends to produce manufactures and processed goods of uncertain quality. "The quality of Soviet produce appears to have been declining steadily since the 1960s, as a result of permanent excess demand, regardless of technical progress" (Aslund 1989, 76). For example, take a common household product like detergent that is introduced at a certain benchmark standard. The (protected) domestic producer will have continual incentive to degrade product quality if, by so doing, more units can be produced. After complaints roll in, the enterprise might get permission to introduce a new and "improved" benchmark detergent at a higher price and for which it gets more weight in its gross output target.[7] Then the slippage in quality begins all over again. For short, I will call this process the *shoddy product syndrome*.

In Figure 12.1, the shoddy product syndrome affects the position of the unit isoquant because material inputs at world prices—or, equivalently, units of foreign exchange—constitute the numeraire by which final output is measured. The shoddier the product or more uncertain the product quality, the further to the northeast will be the unit isoquant, say at Z'_i rather than Z_i. In the sudden German trade liberalization of 1990, for example, the adverse signaling from simply knowing that a good had been produced in East Germany was sufficient to induce East German consumers to reject it in favor of higher-priced West German goods, thus increasing the distress in East German industry.

NEGATIVE VALUE-ADDED AND THE ADJUSTMENT PROBLEM

In a sudden move to free trade at *any* exchange rate, therefore, a finished-goods industry chosen at random would likely show negative cash flows under the (pre)existing combination of factor inputs and low valuation of the finished product in world markets. A devaluation, coinciding with the (hypothetical) move to free trade, would simply raise material input prices in tandem with the prices of shoddy finished goods. In the short run before input combinations and product quality could be adjusted, negative value-added would persist. Because manufacturing absorbs a much higher proportion of the labor force in the Soviet Union than in the United States (Shmelev and Popov 1989), a wholesale industrial collapse would be intolerable.

Notice that our traditional Ricardian model based on comparable labor productivities and outputs of comparable quality tells a different implicit story about the magnitude of the problem of adjusting to free trade. If the "real" exchange rate was sufficiently devalued, the Ricardian model suggests that a

7. This absence of a market test for valuing final outputs is one important reason why the growth in Soviet gross national product (GNP) may have been significantly overstated in the postwar period. Continual decline in product quality did not reduce measured GNP, and the continual introduction of "new and improved" products was allowed to increase it.

substantial proportion of domestic industry would be viable in the short run and could quickly begin expanding in export markets. In contrast, our substitution model suggests that most domestic industry need not be viable in the short run and that a massive real devaluation would not be all that useful in easing the burden of adjustment to world prices.

In "long-run" free-trade equilibrium, however, could industry i, as depicted in the substitution model of Figure 12.1, be viable? Suppose our putative reformers observe the "protected" starting point d, a combination of output and inputs with negative (or very low) value-added at world market prices. Yet they do not know whether industry i (and similar industries) would be sufficiently productive and capable of ultimately shifting away from its current heavy dependence on material inputs while improving product quality to become profitable under free trade. In the long run, whether industry i was on an "efficient" unit isoquant such as Z_i running through point d or on an "inefficient" unit isoquant such as Z'_i, also running through point d, would be uncertain. In the former case, output at world prices would ultimately be sustainable at point g. In the latter case, the best industry i could manage in the long run after energy became more expensive was a production point like g': the value of gross output at g' remains less than the total cost of production.

Notice that the long-run viability of industry i depends not only on its production efficiency (i.e., whether it is on the unit isoquant Z_i or Z'_j) but also on the prevailing costs of the domestic factors of production after a new free-trade equilibrium is established. Suppose labor is the principal domestic factor of production. Then the budget line AC shows the real wage (in terms of material inputs) to be sufficiently low under free trade that the point g tangent to Z_i is profitable. However, if the equilibrium real wage is higher, so that AC' is now the relevant budget for producing one unit of the finished good, then industry i will *not* be profitable under free trade. AC' lies to the left and below Z_i. The real wage in long-term equilibrium facing any particular industry i will be the outcome of a complex macroeconomic interaction as *all* industries liberalize simultaneously.

Given this fundamental uncertainty about substitution in production, product quality, and equilibrium real factor costs in the long run, could the reformers devise a system of *interim* protection that (1) initially sustains the profitability of most existing production of manufactures and processed goods and, (2) when systematically reduced over the next several years, allows market mechanisms to winnow out the inefficient industries from those that are ultimately viable under free trade?

FROM IMPLICIT TO EXPLICIT TARIFF PROTECTION: THE CASE OF CHILE

The trade liberalization in Chile after 1973 was perhaps the most comprehensive and draconian (before the Polish and East German experiences in 1990) of modern times (see Edwards and Edwards 1987, which places the remarkable empirical details into a solid analytical perspective). With the important caveats noted in Chapter 6, let us presume that Chile got its domestic fiscal and financial policies more or less right. Then, Chile's tariff and foreign exchange policies provide useful clues of what to do, or what not to do, in a similarly comprehensive trade liberalization program in a socialist economy like the Soviet Union's.

On the positive side, from 1974 onward the Chilean government implemented various measures to attain foreign exchange convertibility on current account and to eliminate quotas, tariffs, and exchange controls that restricted foreign trade. By 1976, merchants, farmers, and businesspeople all knew the program that the government, with a high degree of credibility, was following in order to achieve virtually free trade by 1979.

On the negative side, the Chilean government failed to stabilize the real exchange rate. In the late 1970s, excessive capital inflows forced an overvaluation of the currency by 1978–81 that bankrupted much of the newly opened tradable goods sector. Bankruptcies then spread throughout the domestic financial system so that in 1982–83 the commercial banks had to be renationalized (Edwards and Edwards 1987).

Because the Chilean exchange-rate overvaluation was avoidable (for reasons discussed in detail in Ch. 6), let us simply compare the positive aspects of Chile's foreign trade liberalization in the 1970s with what might be done in the Soviet Union in the 1990s.

In 1973, Chile had some very high formal tariffs protecting finished goods, averaging over 90 percent, with some, improbably, going as high as 500 percent (as shown in Table 6.1). However, these numbers conceal the fact that much protection in Chile in 1973 was from *nontariff barriers*. Quota restrictions or absolute prohibitions on imports of finished goods were commonplace, along with restrictions on the export of food and industrial raw materials. In addition, the government refused to allocate foreign exchange for imports that did not suit its immediate social objectives and set multiple exchange rates across different categories of imports and exports so that many tariff rates themselves had become rather meaningless.

Therefore, the first order of business in the Chilean liberalization of foreign trade in 1974 and 1975 was to

1. unify the exchange rate so that all exporters and importers transacted at the same rate and then

2. convert all quota restrictions into some rough tariff equivalent, lumping similar commodities together in the same tariff category, and then

3. move to unrestricted foreign exchange convertibility on current account.

The net effect of these first steps taken in 1974 and 1975 was to convert implicit protection by direct controls into explicit protection by tariffs (albeit still very high tariffs, as Table 6.1 shows). By 1976, this conversion into a system of explicit tariff protection in Chile was virtually complete. Then the government proceeded to phase out the explicit protection slowly over a period of several years by

4. reducing the higher tariffs, in preannounced small steps, to converge to a modest uniform import tariff at a prespecified future date.

In the event, Chile speeded up this process slightly and converged to a uniform 10 percent tariff on all imports (for revenue) by July of 1979 (Table 6.1) with no other significant import restrictions. The uniform tariff was justified on revenue grounds, and from Lerner's Symmetry Theorem, we know such a tariff is equivalent to a 10 percent tax on all exports in long-run equilibrium.

Note that after 1973 Chile also removed all controls and other significant taxes on exports per se. However, in parallel with what should be the case for the natural-resource-based exports of the Soviet Union, the Chilean government continued to tax the profits and other economic rents associated with natural-resource-based industries rather systematically. For example, in Chile's huge copper industry, which dominated Chile's exports much like petroleum now does the Soviet Union's, the government retained ownership and control of a number of major mines; and concessions given to private mining companies—whether international or domestic—were rather carefully taxed. The important point for our purposes, however, is these were "profits" taxes rather than export taxes. Hence, after liberalization, they did not drive a wedge between the price seen by domestic users and by foreign buyers of exportable material inputs—unlike in the Soviet energy industry today.

In summary, in difficult political circumstances, Chile in late 1973 eschewed the "cold turkey" approach to free trade adopted by (forced on?) Poland and East Germany in 1990. Instead, Chilean producers of finished goods had some years in which to adjust; and despite the trauma of the (temporary) exchange rate overvaluation from excessive capital inflows in 1978–82, Chile's trade liberalization itself has been successfully sustained into the 1990s.

A TRANSITION PARABLE FOR SOVIET FOREIGN TRADE

Suppose the spirit of the deliberate Chilean approach to free trade—as summarized in steps (1) to (4) above—can be depicted within the confines of our two-commodity substitution model of the Soviet economy. How might an "idealized" Soviet approach to free trade be worked out?

In Chapter 1, we noted that the Soviets got off to a bad start in 1989 by decentralizing foreign exchange contracting by domestic enterprises before their budget constraints were hardened to allow the decontrol of domestic commodity prices, and before the regime of multiple exchange rates was unified. Indeed, as of 1991, hundreds of individual exchange rates, ranging from the old official rate of 0.64 rubles per dollar to more than 20 rubles per dollar in various black and gray markets, continue to proliferate. Thus, as a practical matter, the Soviet government might have to *recentralize* foreign exchange allocations until the domestic financial controls necessary for supporting a market economy have been established (the monetary overhang is eliminated) as described in Chapter 11 and until the exchange rate is unified as per phase 1 above.

But how should this *single* (unified) nominal exchange rate be set when unrestricted commodity or financial arbitrage with the outside world does not yet exist? We know that the price of exportable material inputs, inclusive of the huge energy sector, must rise sharply relative to domestic factors of production, including labor. Moreover the ruble prices of these fairly homogeneous material inputs can be directly compared with the prices prevailing on world markets, which are typically quoted in dollars. Thus, the exchange rate, in rubles per dollar, can be set according to a limited version of the principle of purchasing-power parity as follows.

Take the prevailing domestic wage level in rubles as a starting point. Then estimate the average increase in the relative price of energy (and other material inputs) against wages that would prevail in long-run equilibrium if the economy were to move toward free trade. Accordingly, adjust the domestic ruble price of energy (and other material inputs) sharply upward—doubling or trebling it in terms of wages at the outset of the trade liberalization process. In Figure 12.2, the *slope* of the budget line BB', running through the old production point d, now represents this higher price of energy relative to labor; whereas HD, also running through d, represents the old budget line when energy was previously underpriced.

Simultaneously, to make the new ruble price level for material inputs effective, set the exchange rate in rubles per dollar to equate (average) domestic prices of material inputs with those prevailing in world markets. This new unified exchange rate would now apply to *all* current-account transacting, on either the import or the export side, for material inputs, finished goods, or services. Once this nominal ruble per dollar exchange rate was established, it would no longer respond to the fluctuations of the average level of world prices for material inputs. At the fixed exchange rate, continual minor reshuffling of the domestic ruble prices of individual material inputs (and other tradables) would keep them aligned with their counterparts on world markets.

What have we accomplished by this exercise in exchange-rate unification? First, the implicit export tax on energy and other material inputs has been eliminated as their ruble prices rise sharply to world levels. (Note, however, that the revenue position of the government would be greatly enhanced if it retained a full claim on the profits or surpluses being generated by natural-resource-based industries at the higher domestic prices.) In the short run, producers in industry i would have immediate incentive to begin economizing on energy and other material inputs.

Second, this nominal exchange rate is now capable of sustaining the real

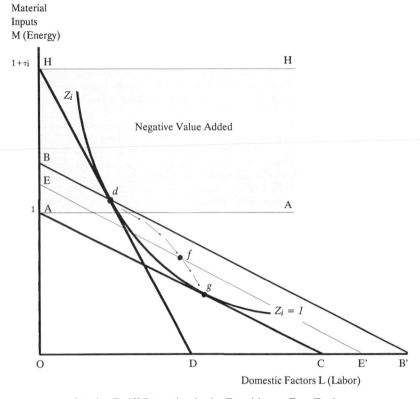

FIGURE 12.2. Interim Tariff Protection in the Transition to Free Trade

purchasing power of domestic money in terms of material inputs—a very broad class of primary commodities produced, traded, and consumed throughout the economy—once full current-account convertibility is achieved.

Third, this potentially stable "real" exchange rate now provides a benchmark for converting the implicit tariff protection associated with quota restrictions and with the existing system of exchange controls into *explicit* tariff equivalents. That is, the authorities can now ensure that the t_i's are sufficient to keep most finished-goods manufacturing in existence after liberalization.

After the prices of material inputs increase to world levels, however, explicit tariff protection from competing imports of finished goods needs to be higher than the old implicit rate if industry i is to survive. Suppose t_i' is the new *explicit* tariff needed to keep finished goods industry i in business once exchange controls were removed and current account convertibility was achieved. Then, to compensate for the increased prices of energy and other inputs of raw materials, $t_i' > t_i$.

In Figure 12.2, the vertical distance AB is the level of this new explicit tariff relative to the (newly increased) price of material inputs. Because the domestic price of material inputs now equals the world level of one dollar, AB also represents the actual ad valorem tariff needed to protect the domestic industry. The domestic price of material inputs has also increased relative to the price of the finished good; thus the distance AB is correspondingly less than AH. At the old combination of domestic factors and material inputs, BB' is the corresponding new budget line just sufficient to sustain production at point d.

However, this is not the end of the parable. At point d, the slope of the new budget line BB' is flatter (reflecting higher energy costs) and now cuts the unit isoquant Z_i rather than being tangent to it. This induces the manager of industry i to raise profits by increasing the demand for domestic factors and reducing energy dependence, that is, to start moving along the new budget line from d in the direction of B' as fast as the reequipment of the enterprise permits. Indeed, this is the great advantage of raising material input prices rather sharply at the outset of the trade liberalization. Firms immediately see the "right" relative factor costs for inducing them to economize on material inputs, exports of which will then slowly increase.

However, our controlled liberalization differs from a strategy of jumping directly to free trade, in which the relative price of material inputs would increase as sharply. Under immediate free trade with no interim protection for domestic finished goods, industry i would face the budget line AC in Figure 12.2, which could *not* support existing production at point d. Because the world market would bid them away from domestic uses, exports of material inputs and energy would jump sharply and so cause the collapse of most domestic manufacturing and goods-processing activities.

That said, our parable based on interim tariff protection should leave no doubt in the minds of domestic industrialists, merchants, and farmers that the economy will eventually move to free trade, as in stage 4 of the Chilean program cited above. Simultaneously with the introduction of explicit tariff protection for finished-goods industries, the Soviet government would announce that the higher tariff rates would be scaled down by small steps each year until, say ten years hence, all rates had converged to some low uniform level. Further reductions in this resulting "revenue tariff" would then depend on the government's fiscal position.

Figure 12.2 nicely illustrates how this declining tariff protection smooths the transition to free trade. Starting with a high explicit tariff equal to the vertical distance AB, the relevant budget line supporting production at point d is BB'. Then, some years later, formal tariff protection for our representative finished good is reduced to AE to support production at point f along the new budget line EE'. Finally, tariff protection for finished-goods industries is phased out altogether; the relevant budget line becomes AC: that prevailing under free trade. (For diagrammatic simplicity, Figure 12.2 does not show the process ending with a low revenue tariff; and I have simply assumed that the initial guess of the authorities in raising the price of material inputs relative to domestic factors turns out to be correct in free-trade equilibrium.)

During this transition, successful in the particular case of industry i shown in Figure 12.2, the combination of factor inputs for producing one unit of the finished good shifts along the locus shown by the arrows from d to f to g. Only at the beginning point d and the end point g are these production combinations actually on the unit isoquant Z_i. That is, the unit isoquant traces out efficient production points in *long-run equilibrium* after the industry has the necessary time to rebuild its capital stock and restructure its labor force when relative prices change. The other points on the locus dfg are above the efficient long-run unit isoquant; and their "excessive" use of material inputs and domestic factors represents the real (social) costs of the transition. These costs are covered by the interim tariff protection and thus are shifted forward to the final user of the finished good in question.

However, the change from implicit quota restrictions and import prohibitions to explicit tariff protection could still benefit users of finished goods. First, even over high tariffs, the new threat of import competition would curb the monopoly power of concentrated domestic manufacturers (Table 12.1). Second, the shoddy product syndrome would be immediately alleviated. The worst domestic products would not survive in the face of even modest competition from abroad. Indeed, the successful transitional production locus in Figure 12.2, the movement from d to f to g, implicitly incorporates improvements in product quality.

A GENERALIZED CASCADING TARIFF?

These advantages from the move to explicit tariff protection presume that the government does not precisely tailor individual tariffs to keep each finished goods producer in business at the outset of the liberalization. Rather, the vertical distance AB in Figure 12.2 is best interpreted as simply a representative initial tariff—a common levy—that applies to imports of all finished goods in a similar category. Following the Chilean experience described earlier and that of other primary-products-producing countries such as Canada, which once had quite high tariffs, one could start off with fairly broad tariff categories: a "cascading" tariff scaled downward according to the distance from the final consumer and degree of manufacturing complexity. Ranked from highest to lowest, a single tariff rate could apply to each of the following or similar categories:

1. Consumer durables: autos, home appliances, and so forth
2. Consumer nondurables: textiles and highly processed foods
3. Capital goods and manufactured intermediate products
4. Industrial materials and basic foods

The highest tariff, category 1, could be over 100 percent depending on how one computed the durables' average survival capability after the prices of material inputs had been raised sharply. The lowest tariff would be the final uniform tariff of, say, 10 percent on imports of material inputs in category 4. As far as possible, the government would set a simple across-the-board "yardstick" tariff in each category. No only would this general approach weed out the most inefficient producers at the outset, but "rent seeking" by individual industries petitioning for protection especially geared to their own needs would be minimized.

Then, over, say, a ten-year interval similar to that used in the recently concluded Canadian-American free-trade agreement, the rates in categories 1, 2, and 3 would be gradually but firmly reduced to those prevailing in category 4—again without accepting special pleading for exceptions. In order to facilitate adjustment in his own mix of inputs and outputs, each producer should know the cumulative tariff reductions[8] at the end of every year until virtual free trade was established.

A cascading tariff schedule, but one that is not adjusted downward, is often used by LDCs to protect "infant" industries for producing finished goods. In our transition parable, by contrast, the purpose is quite different: to make explicit and then phase out already very high levels of implicit protection for domestic manufacturing. Moreover, with the degree of uncertainty involved as to which firms would ultimately survive and which not, it is simply not feasible for those firms that would be viable in the long run to jump immediately to free trade—and to cover their early losses and transition costs by borrowing. Indeed, such massive borrowing by Soviet enterprises would undermine the hard budget constraints, based on limited access to external capital, which are pivotal for achieving domestic financial control, as discussed in Chapter 11. Instead, temporary tariff protection, which increases the internal cash flows of protected manufacturing enterprises, is fully consistent with Chapter 11's emphasis on self-finance as the main financial mode for liberalized enterprises in a transitional socialist economy.

TRANSITIONAL TARIFFS AND THE GATT

Is the introduction of transitional tariffs to protect Eastern European manufacturing consistent with their existing obligations, or new request for membership, to the General Agreement on Tariffs and Trade (GATT)? The answer is important if the socialist countries are to secure most-favored-nation access (the lowest tariffs) on their exports to the Western industrial economies.

The GATT is generally viewed as supplying a procedure for bargaining down tariffs from current levels, and does not say too much specifically about nontariff barriers to trade. However, it presumes, with certain significant exceptions, that contracting parties will move quickly to abolish nontariff

---

8. The authorities do not have to reveal exact dates on which tariffs would be discretely adjusted, which would invite inventory speculation. Continual adjustment by very small amounts to yield a prespecified cumulative change would be much preferred.

barriers altogether when they enter the agreement (Dam 1970, 19). That part is certainly consistent with the rapid move to current-account convertibility with a unified exchange rate, as suggested above for the Eastern European countries. However, if currency convertibility restrictions on current account (implicit protection) are simply replaced with high and approximately equivalent explicit tariffs, this may or may not satisfy the terms of the GATT for *existing* members—say, Hungary.

But the GATT should be able to find a legal device to support the conversion from implicit to explicit protection provided that the latter is temporary and part of the transition to free trade as sketched above. After all, such a transitional package would fit the spirit of the original GATT agreement. If there are unresolved legal uncertainties, however, then *prospective* GATT members such as the Soviet Union might do well to unify their exchange rate and get their cascading tariff in place before their formal membership is finally ratified.

CONCLUDING NOTES ON FOREIGN CAPITAL INFLOWS

Because a properly orchestrated move to free trade presents no inherent problem of foreign exchange shortages for the Soviet Union, our parable of step-by-step trade liberalization, based on the substitution model, did not discuss the role of capital inflows from abroad. Quite the contrary, the country abounds with energy and other material inputs that are overused at home and where the elimination of implicit export taxes should allow exports to increase rather easily. Indeed, flooding the economy with foreign exchange by borrowing abroad could well worsen the adjustment problem because domestic finished-goods industries would have to face additional "subsidized" competition from foreign manufacturers.

Therefore, in the Soviet case at least, the substitution model and the Ricardian model lead to the same conclusion: large net capital inflows (although not the absorption of foreign technology per se) might well make the adjustment problem for socialist economies somewhat more acute. In the context of repressed LDCs back in 1973, I reached the same conclusion in *Money and Capital* before the subsequent huge buildup of LDC indebtedness:

> The absorption of substantial amounts of foreign capital during the liberalization process may be a serious mistake. That is, it may be easier to remove protective tariffs and quotas on foreign trade by *avoiding* extraordinary capital inflows from abroad. Such unconventional wisdom is, of course, in accordance with my optimistic view that most poor countries can secure their own successful development (McKinnon 1973, 4)

Are there circumstances where one might want to mitigate this seemingly harsh judgment against heavy reliance on foreign capital inflows to ease

TABLE 12.2
Trade flows for the CMEA Countries (1988)
(Percentage of Total Exports and Imports)

	Six[a]	U.S.S.R.	Developed Market Economies	LDCs	Rest[b]
			Exports		
Bulgaria	18.1	62.8	6.4	9.1	3.6
Czechoslovakia	29.9	43.1	16.3	4.7	6.0
East Germany	26.1	34.8	29.9	3.6	5.6
Hungary	17.0	27.6	39.5	9.9	6.0
Poland	16.2	24.5	43.3	10.2	5.8
Romania	16.8	24.0	33.7	19.0	6.5
U.S.S.R.	48.9	—	21.9	14.2	15.0
			Imports		
Bulgaria	20.1	53.7	15.5	7.8	2.9
Czechoslovakia	32.3	40.3	18.6	3.5	5.3
East Germany	25.3	36.8	31.8	2.7	3.4
Hungary	18.7	25.0	43.3	7.7	5.3
Poland	17.2	23.4	45.7	7.1	6.6
Romania	24.6	24.0	13.5	18.8	19.1
U.S.S.R.	54.1	—	25.1	8.2	12.6

Source: Finance and Development, September 1990, 29. Based on official statistical yearbooks of the reporting countries and United Nations estimates.

[a]Six: Bulgaria, Czechoslovakia, East Germany, Hungary, Poland, and Romania.

[b]Rest: rest of the world (predominantly Yugoslavia and China).

adjustment to free trade? Unlike the Soviet Union, some of the smaller countries of Eastern Europe are not particularly rich in natural resources that are easily traded internationally. Worse, their extensive manufacturing and agricultural industries have also become addicted to cheap material inputs, particularly energy. Before 1990, at least, the close trade links among the countries of Eastern Europe simply extended the ambit of the old Stalinist industrial system. Through the trading apparatus of the Council for Mutual Economic Assistance (CMEA), the Soviet Union sold relatively cheap energy and other material inputs to smaller Eastern European economies in return for manufactured goods of a lesser quality than those traded in Western markets. In fact, the extensive trade among the CMEA countries (Table 12.2), albeit largely bilateral because of the absence of a freely convertible trading currency, also included the mutual exchange of (shoddy) manufactured goods through direct bargaining by state trading agencies.

The problem of CMEA countries in adjusting to full-scale trade liberalization with the West is obvious. The smaller ones that do not have much in the way of primary products (what we have been calling material inputs) exports would find themselves with an immediate shortage of foreign exchange. First, they stand to lose the subsidies for their Soviet-produced material inputs, that is, the willingness of the Soviet authorities to accept their manufactured products at very favorable terms of trade. Second, the syndrome of negative value-added (at world market prices) means they cannot sell their manufactures without significant improvements in product quality to the West. In effect, they are currently producing at a point like d in Figure 12.1, but where the vertical axis showing material inputs now reflects actual imports, rather than potential exportables as in the Soviet case. Hence, a highly industrialized country like Czechoslovakia, where in 1988 about 80 percent of its exports went to other socialist economies (Table 12.2), faces an immediate foreign exchange shortage if the CMEA trading umbrella collapses.

Converting the CMEA into a full-fledged common market with convertible currencies and a common external tariff (in the mode of Western Europe) seems completely out of the question (Schrenk 1990). This is a much more difficult task than reforming each socialist economy individually. Nevertheless, continuing the bilateral exchange of manufactured products through state trading agencies on an interim basis could be helpful.

In proceeding with the main task of liberalizing its foreign trade with the West, therefore, a smaller Eastern European country might well require carefully crafted bridging finance from some international agency, such as the European Bank for Reconstruction and Development set up in 1990. However, *the conditionality* imposed by this agency for lending the money might well follow our parable sketched above and reflected in Figure 12.2: a discrete increase in the domestic price of energy and other material inputs to world levels coupled with conversion from implicit protection through exchange controls to an interim system of explicit protection through tariffs. At the beginning of such a liberalization, the agency might well provide the foreign exchange necessary for, say, Czechoslovakia, to continue buying material inputs until its manufactured exports become more competitive in world markets.

But accepting official bridging finance based on strict conditionality is *not* tantamount to a general relaxation of controls over private capital movements. Only after the domestic capital market is fully liberalized, with well-defined financial and fiscal constraints on firms and individuals in place so that un-restricted borrowing and lending at equilibrium domestic interest rates becomes feasible, could the domestic currency of any socialist economy be safely made fully convertible into foreign exchange on capital account. Many years hence, individuals and enterprises, including joint ventures with foreign firms, could possibly be allowed to choose freely between domestic and foreign sources of finance. But this is the last, rather than the first, step in the optimum order of liberalization.[9]

9. That the international convertibility of the ruble on capital account comes last rather than first in the optimum order of economic liberalization is well recognized by Academician Abel Aganbegyan (1988).

CHAPTER THIRTEEN

Financial Growth and

Macroeconomic Stability in China,

1978–1992:

Implications for Russia

and Eastern Europe

From 1978 to 1992, China's liberalization was gradual with a fairly stable price level and extraordinarily rapid output growth. Since 1989 in Eastern Europe and the former Soviet Union (FSU), rapid liberalizations attempted in the face of falling real output generated much higher inflation. Yet, both regions' fiscal policies were surprisingly similar. Like its socialist counterparts in Europe, the Chinese government's revenue share in GNP has fallen sharply; in 1991–92, its fiscal deficit approached 10 percent of GNP, as illustrated below. How did China manage to avoid inflation when its government was such a heavy borrower from the state banking system?

There are four ways in which China avoided resorting to the inflation tax. (1) It first liberalized in areas like agriculture where subsequent productivity growth was rapid. (2) It imposed very hard budget constraints on, and gave little bank credit to, the newly liberalized "nonstate" sectors in industry and agriculture. (3) But it did retain intramarginal price controls on, and constrained financial support for, traditional soft-budget state enterprises. (4) It set positive real interest rates on savings deposits. The resulting enormous growth in saving and stocks of financial assets allowed the liberalized sector to finance itself, the Chinese government, and the deficits of the slowly reforming state enterprises.

In this chapter I analyze in statistical detail how the Chinese accomplished this remarkable financial feat. The reader will quickly note similarities with the high financial growth policies followed by Japan in the 1950s and 1960s and Taiwan in the 1960s and 1970s, analyzed in Chapter 3. Yet, there is an important difference: the Chinese government's failure to gain control over public finances at the outset of liberalization (Blejer et al. 1991). Nevertheless, I argue that many important aspects of China's dualistic banking and pricing policies could well be adopted by other transitional socialist economies in Europe and Asia. Indeed, China's dualistic system of financial controls is consistent with, and nicely illustrates, the gradualist approach to the transition advocated for the FSU in Chapter 11.

But China's incredibly high real financial growth is not feasible in Russia and formerly socialist Europe. (Indeed, it may not be sustainable for much longer in China itself.) Thus, to prevent inflation and stem financial decline in the liberalizing European economies, fiscal reforms should come much earlier in their transitions compared to China's. Although China is an important—if temporary—exception on the fiscal side, its interest rate policies and step-by-step foreign trade reforms were fully consonant with the preferred order of economic liberalization outlined in Chapter 1, as we shall see.

I conclude with a brief analysis of the inflationary explosion and sharp output decline in Russia in 1992, which arose out of the Yeltsin-Gaidar government's liberalizing reforms. Did the Russians get the order of economic liberalization wrong, or was this unfortunate event the result of adverse exogenous shocks beyond any government's control?

GRADUAL VERSUS RAPID LIBERALIZATION IN SOCIALIST ECONOMIES

China is often cited as the leading example of a successful gradualist approach to economic liberalization.[1] In 1978, the Chinese began to break up traditional agricultural communes into small farm leases (now 10 to 15 years' duration)—the so-called household responsibility system. From 1979 to 1983, with over three-quarters of the population still in agriculture, farm output surged by 8 to 10 percent per year (D. Gale Johnson 1990). By 1984, the focus of rapid economic growth had shifted to rural light industry, which began to absorb much of the labor force released by productivity improvements in agriculture. Although small-scale private traders flourished, hundreds of thousands of the new manufacturing enterprises (now simply called TVEs) were owned largely by townships and villages. In this so-called nonstate sector, the TVEs were market-driven and outside the web of official price and output controls that still circumscribed activity in the old heavy-industry state sector.

In this traditional sector, the much larger-scale state enterprises (SOEs) remained under the ownership and control of the central government with no attempt at some form of rapid privatization or price decontrol. Step by step, the pricing and financial arrangements facing the old SOEs were also rationalized, but at a more deliberate pace that lasted over a decade. Overall price stability in both the state and the nonstate sectors was surprisingly well maintained, with retail price inflation averaging 6 to 7 percent per year since 1978 (Table 13.1).

The Chinese approach to freeing foreign trade was also gradualist. Instead of a "big bang" that suddenly opened up the whole economy to international competition and world prices, special economic zones somewhat outside the

---

1. Two highly readable overviews of the gradualist Chinese approach are provided by Dwight Perkins (1992) and John McMillan and Barry Naughton (1992).

TABLE 13.1
China's Main Economic Indicators
(Percentage Rate of Growth)

	Real National Income	Real GNP	General Retail Price Index	Urban Cost of Living Index	Free Market Index	Money (M2)	Exports GNP (%)	Foreign Reserves[a] (Billion $)
1975	8.3	—	0.2	0.4	—	—	—	—
1976	−0.3	—	0.3	0.3	4.0	—	—	—
1977	7.8	—	2.0	2.7	−2.4	—	—	—
1978	12.3	—	0.7	0.7	−6.6	—	—	—
1979	7.0	7.6	2.0	1.9	−4.5	9.7	5.31	0.84
1980	6.4	7.9	6.0	7.5	1.9	24.1	6.07	−1.30
1981	4.9	4.4	2.4	2.5	5.8	19.7	7.70	2.71
1982	8.3	8.7	1.9	2.0	3.3	13.1	7.97	6.99
1983	9.8	10.3	1.5	2.0	4.2	19.2	7.55	8.90
1984	13.4	14.6	2.8	2.7	−0.4	42.4	8.34	8.22
1985	13.1	12.7	8.8	11.9	17.2	17.0	9.45	2.64
1986	7.9	8.3	6.0	7.0	8.1	30.2	11.16	2.07
1987	10.2	11.0	7.3	8.8	16.3	25.3	13.01	2.92
1988	11.1	11.0	18.5	20.7	30.3	20.7	12.60	3.37
1989	3.7	4.4	17.8	16.3	10.8	18.7	12.29	5.55
1990	5.1	5.6	2.1	1.3	−5.7	28.9	16.88	11.09
1991	7.9	7.3	2.9	5.1	−0.9	26.7	19.30	21.71
Average 1979–91	8.4	8.8	6.2	6.9	6.5	22.7		
Preliminary 1992		12.8	5.4	8.6		31.0	20.00	

Sources: Wong, Heady, Woo 1993; Qian 1993. M2 data taken from IMF, International Finances Statistics 1992 Yearbook; other data from China Statistical Yearbook 1992, Chinese edition.

[a]Foreign exchange reserves are those held by the central bank (the People's Bank of China). Large reserves held by the foreign trade bank (the Bank of China) are excluded.

control of the traditional state trading monopolies were started in Guangdong in connection with the Hong Kong trade. These then became progressively more numerous and broader in scope. Inside such a zone, exporters could retain all of their foreign exchange earnings while having freer access to imported materials and foreign capital or trading services; they also paid lower taxes on enterprise profits, particularly if they formed joint ventures with foreign companies.

By the end of the 1980s, an export (and import) boom had become China's new engine of economic growth. Exports had risen from less than 8 percent of GNP in the early 1980s to about 20 percent in 1992. Real GNP growth itself averaged almost 9 percent per year from 1979 to 1992 (see Table 13.1). By the early 1990s, however, the distinction between a "Special Economic Zone" and the rest of the economy had eroded. Now, a wide range of SOEs, TVEs, and private enterprises participate with more equal access to foreign trade, and the domestic economy's insulation from world markets has diminished.

Although this great economic transformation has been very rapid, it seems fair to characterize the Chinese government's economic policies as being gradualist—with the possible exception of the "minimum bang"[2] necessary to get the ball rolling in agriculture in 1978–79. In 1985, these early Chinese successes encouraged Mikhail Gorbachev to embark on perestroika, and in 1986 smaller Asian economies like Laos and Vietnam adopted their somewhat gradualist "new economic mechanisms," which have been fairly successful.[3] By 1989, the transition from central planning to more market-based economies had become a political imperative throughout Eastern Europe and the FSU.

But this poses a paradox. If gradualism in China and smaller Asian economies was successful early on, why did the Eastern Europeans in general, and Russians in particular, later attempt more of a big-bang approach to economic liberalization? Why were the Eastern Europeans so enamored with more sweeping transfers of property rights (including elaborate voucher schemes for transferring state property) and sudden full-scale price and output decontrol in traditional enterprises? This big-bang approach was often coupled with the intention—not always carried out in practice—swiftly to open the whole economy to unrestricted foreign trade with the hard-currency industrial economies.

At least in the initial stages of these rapid liberalizations, abrupt policy changes in Eastern Europe were associated with economic disorganization, sharp falls in output, and, in some cases, inflationary explosions (Aslund 1992). For the much briefer time series on the transition processes in Bulgaria, Czechoslovakia (before its dissolution), Hungary,[4] Poland, Romania, and the Soviet Union (before its dissolution), Tables 13.2 and 13.3 depict the sharp decreases in output experienced by virtually all these economies from 1989 to 1992. This falling output has been accompanied by high, sometimes explosive, inflation—nowhere more evident than in Russia and the Ukraine in 1992–93. In contrast, Chinese output rose sharply after 1978, and throughout the early 1980s, price inflation remained very low (see Table 13.1).

WERE CIRCUMSTANCES IN EASTERN EUROPE (INCLUDING THE FSU) ESSENTIALLY DIFFERENT?

To explain the output decline in Eastern Europe, there were exogenous political and economic circumstances that differed from those prevailing in China (and

2. Terminology used by John Williamson (1991).

3. See recent studies done for the Asian Development Bank by Fforde and Vylder (1993) on Vietnam and by Vokes and Fabella (1993) on Laos.

4. Because Hungary has gradually been liberalizing for some time, one could plausibly argue that Hungary does not belong in this group of rapidly liberalizing transitional economies.

TABLE 13.2
Gross Domestic Product (GDP) Growth Rates, 1989–1992

	Percentage Change in Real GDP			
	1989	1990	1991	1992[a]
Bulgaria	−0.5	−10.6	−23.0	−3.0
Czechoslovakia	0.7	−0.4	−15.9	−5.0
Hungary	−0.2	−4.3	−10.2	−5.0
Poland	0.2	−11.6	−7.2	−1.0
Romania	−5.8	−7.4	−13.7	−10.0
Soviet Union	3.0	−2.3	−17.0	N.A.

Sources: Aslund 1992; International Monetary Fund, "Financial Sector Reforms and Exchange Rate Arrangements in Eastern Europe," Occasional Paper no. 102, February 1993.
[a]Preliminary Estimates.

TABLE 13.3
Inflation, Unemployment, and Budget Balance, 1990, 1991, and 1992

	Inflation (% Change)			Unemployment (% in December)		General Government Balance (% of GDP)		
	1990	1991	1992[a]	1990	1991	1990	1991	1992[a]
Bulgaria	26	460	49	1.6	10.5	−8.5	−3.7	−3.5
Czechoslovakia	11	59	10	1.0	6.6	0.1	−2.2	−4.4
Hungary	33	32	22	1.7	8.5	0.4	−3.3	−10.6
Poland	586	70	46	6.5	11.4	3.5	−5.6	−7.2
Romania	50	161	203	N.A.	4.3	−0.5	−2.6	−1.9
Soviet Union	6	152	N.A.	0.0	0.0	−8.0	−26.0	N.A.

Sources: Aslund, 1992; International Monetary Fund, "Financial Sector Reforms and Exchange Rate Arrangements in Eastern Europe," Occasional Paper no. 102, February 1993.

in similarly agrarian economics like Vietnam and Laos) and that were largely beyond the economic control of individual reform governments:

1. Eastern Europe was more industrialized and overly specialized in heavy industry. Because agrarian populations were proportionally smaller than in the Asian socialist economies, the possibility of, and the immediate gains from, returning to small-holder agriculture were more limited.

2. The collapse of the Council for Mutual Economic Assistance (CMEA) disrupted trade within the former Soviet bloc, and then trade among the republics of the former Soviet Union was disrupted.

3. The precipitous decline in the power of the Communist party in most of Eastern Europe and the FSU was coupled with the weakening of centralized political control over the economy at large and the weakening of decentralized party monitoring of state-owned enterprises.

In contrast to China, (1) denies typical Eastern European economies a substantial margin on which to liberalize to get immediate increase in output. So pervasive has been this pattern of falling output that many observers suggest that the transition from socialism must naturally have to follow a J-curve:

output must fall before a long-term growth path more characteristic of a liberal economy can be established (e.g., Gomulka 1991; Murrell 1990). On this J-curve view, liberalization must first largely destroy the old order before economic resources can be efficiently redeployed.

Countering this view, many argue that the trade shocks under (2) were so enormous that some decline in output was inevitable in any event, given the high degree of specialization in the old CMEA trading regime (e.g., Brada and King 1991). And in the 1980s, CMEA trade was about half the total foreign trade of Eastern Europe and the FSU. Then, in 1991, CMEA trade imploded, with 60 to 70 percent of member countries' trade with each other suddenly drying up (Borenstein and Masson 1993). Because this CMEA shock was so enormous, one could argue that a more rapid opening of trade with advanced industrial economies was imperative in Eastern Europe, unlike the situation in the early stages of China's liberalization.

Under (3), ability of the typical European reform government to establish central control of resources was so limited that rapid privatization and price decontrol in the industrial sector were more essential in socialist Europe than in socialist Asia. More crudely, ripoffs of the assets of the state-owned enterprises (SOEs) had previously had been prevented by the monitoring and oversight of the Communist party. With the decline in the party's power, Jeffrey Sachs (1992) has vehemently argued that more rapid privatization of both industrial and financial enterprises is needed to stem the tide.

Without denying the great importance of (1), (2), and (3) for what happened in Eastern Europe in general and Russia in particular, I hypothesize that China's longer-running experience with the transition from a planned to a market economy still contains valuable lessons for Eastern Europeans. But rather than trying to cover the whole liberalization landscape at the microeconomic level, I focus on the problem of macroeconomic control. Using China as a benchmark, what are the fiscal and monetary problems that a reform socialist government will typically face, and how can these be best resolved in ways that encourage output growth while maintaining price-level stability in the liberalizing economy?

A CHINESE PUZZLE: PRICE-LEVEL STABILITY IN THE FACE OF FISCAL DECLINE

In the early 1980s, how stable was the "true" Chinese price level in an environment when most prices were still controlled? Figure 13.1—courtesy of Gelb, Jefferson, and Singh (1993)—shows that, as late as 1981, only about 10 percent of retail sales were free of price controls. By the early 1990s, more than 70 percent of retail prices and 85 percent of the output prices of the collectively owned enterprises (COEs) had become market determined. (Even the output and input prices of SOEs were 70 percent decontrolled by 1991.) Consequently, three different consumer prices are presented in Table

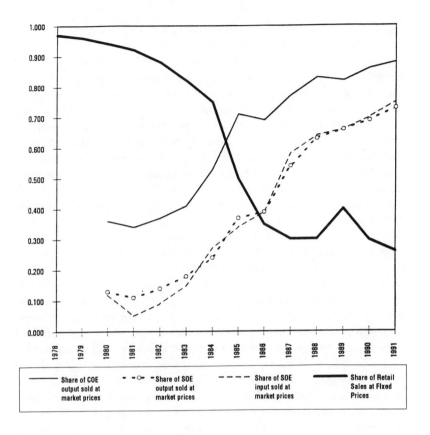

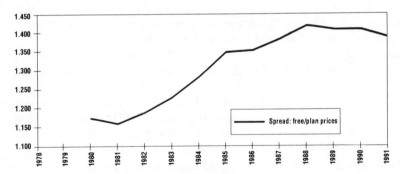

FIGURE 13.1. Price and Market Reform. (*Sources*: *Top*: Share of COE and SOE at market prices are estimated by Zou [1992] from a sample of 253 enterprises. Share of retail sales at fixed prices from Schmidt-Hebbel 1992. *Bottom*: Spread of free/plan prices estimated by Zou [1992] from a sample of 253 enterprises; also Gelb, Jefferson, and Singh 1993.)

13.1. From 1979 to 1991, an urban employee's cost of living index rose the most, averaging 6.9 percent per year, while the more general retail price index averaged 6.2 percent and the "free market" index, made up only of commodities whose prices were decontrolled, rose by 6.5 percent.

Because of this relatively modest growth in the free market and other price indexes, it appears that China began its liberalization in 1979–81 without significantly repressed inflation. At the outset, no major macroeconomic adjustment was needed to work off a monetary overhang by a one-time inflation, as planned in Poland in 1990 or in Russia in 1992 or possibly by a currency reform where outstanding cash balances were canceled, as in West Germany in June 1948. Thus, for many years after 1978, official price controls in trade among the old state enterprises could be effectively enforced with centrally determined deliveries at those prices.

But price liberalization occurred at the margin. The SOEs could sell their surplus output beyond what the state contracted for in the newly burgeoning "nonstate" sector at market prices. Figure 13.1's lower panel shows the 20 to 40 percent premium in prices charged in this free market. Fortunately, the absence of a monetary overhang limited this price gap and thus limited (but did not eliminate) the tendency for supply diversion—illicit transfers of scarce goods from the state sector to higher-price nonstate uses.[5] As general liberalization proceeded by rapid industrial growth in the nonstate sector, the number of price-controlled goods in the state sector was continually reduced. But even these pegged prices were rationalized as raw materials prices were increased in stages, and finished goods prices were sometimes scaled down.

China does not calculate a general producer price index (PPI). Because a PPI excludes services, it would show lower rates of price inflation, once the effects of price decontrol are removed, than do Table 13.1's retail price indices. Measured productivity growth in services is typically much less than in agricultural and industrial goods, particularly in a rapidly growing economy like China's. The upshot is that, since 1979, China had had a very stable price level in comparison to the often explosive price inflation in Eastern Europe.

Even without a monetary overhang at the outset, how was macroeconomic control in China subsequently sustained through 1992? One cannot look to Chinese fiscal policy for an answer. On the contrary, like all communist countries, China depended on price controls and ownership of state enterprises for generating and then collecting huge surpluses from the industrial sector. By world standards, the domestic prices of industrial raw materials and agricultural wage goods were kept down compared to the prices of finished industrial

---

5. This problem of supply diversion bedeviled the old Soviet economy in 1990–91, when price controls were in the state sector with very high price premiums in the marginal free or "black" economy (Murphy, Shleifer, and Vishny 1992).

TABLE 13.4
China's Fiscal Situation in the Reform Period
(Percentage of GNP)

	Revenue		Expenditure		Budget Deficit		
	Chinese Definition	*"Standard" Definition*	*Chinese Definition*	*"Standard" Definition*	*Chinese Definition*	*Government Borrowing Requirement Definition*	*Stock Definition*
1978	31.24	34.77	30.96	34.49	−0.28	−0.28	−0.28
1979	27.66	31.69	31.94	36.86	4.28	5.16	5.16
1980	24.28	29.10	27.13	32.91	2.85	3.82	3.28
1981	22.83	27.28	23.36	29.35	0.53	2.06	1.17
1982	21.64	27.14	22.21	29.32	0.56	2.18	1.41
1983	21.50	27.66	22.25	29.78	0.75	2.11	1.64
1984	21.57	26.47	22.21	28.22	0.64	1.75	1.51
1985	21.81	26.84	21.56	27.64	0.25	0.80	0.50
1986	23.31	25.23	24.04	27.39	0.73	2.15	1.85
1987	20.96	22.79	21.67	25.00	0.70	2.20	1.75
1988	18.68	19.93	19.24	22.41	0.56	2.48	2.16
1989	18.43	20.41	19.01	22.75	0.58	2.35	2.09
1990	18.50	19.63	19.28	22.51	0.78	2.88	2.15
1991	18.13	18.52	19.30	21.88	1.17	3.36	N.A.

Source: Wong, Heady, and Woo 1993.
Note: "Standard" definition for revenue means subtracting borrowing from Chinese definition, and adding in the subsidies that were counted as negative revenue. "Standard" definition for expenditure means adding to the Chinese definition subsidies that were considered negative revenue. Government Borrowing Requirement (GBR) definition deficit is "Standard" Expenditure minus "Standard" Revenue. Stock definition of deficit is GBR definition minus principal repayments.

goods. The resulting financial surpluses in most SOEs were then deposited in the state bank in blocked accounts as de facto government revenue.

But, in all socialist countries, this implicit revenue system begins to unravel naturally as liberalization begins, as described in Chapter 11 and McKinnon (1991). First, the government-owned share of industrial assets begins to fall. Second, price decontrol and industrial competition from both domestic and foreign sources tend to shrink the profit margins in all industrial enterprises, whether owned by the government or not. Indeed, many once (artificially) profitable SOEs become loss makers. This tendency toward fiscal deterioration was qualitatively the same in China as in Eastern Europe or the FSU.

Table 13.4 shows the very sharp decline in the revenue of the Chinese (consolidated) government from about 34.8 percent of GNP in 1978 to only 18.5 percent in 1991. To be sure, the government also sharply curbed expenditures, but the ambiguous financial position of loss-making SOEs makes the net deficit hard to calculate. By including "policy loans"—that is, "forced" lending to the SOEs by the People's Bank of China, Christine Wong, Christopher Heady, and W. T. Woo (1993) calculate that the true consolidated fiscal deficit may have reached 10 percent of China's GNP in 1991, as shown in Table 13.5.

TABLE 13.5
Consolidated Deficit of Chinese Government and State-owned Enterprises, 1988–91
(Percentage of GNP)

	Open Deficit[a]	Hidden Deficit[b]	Consolidated Deficit (1) + (2)	A Conservative Re-estimate on Assumption That Hidden Deficit Is 70 Percent of Column (2) Deficit
	(1)	(2)	(3)	(4)
1988	2.48	5.14	7.62	6.08
1989	2.35	5.22	7.57	6.01
1990	2.88	7.55	10.43	8.17
1991	3.36	6.76	10.12	8.09

Source:Wong, Heady, and Woo 1993.
[a]Public Sector Borrowing Requirement as in Table 13.4.
[b]Central Bank financing for the deficits of the state-owned enterprises.

TABLE 13.6
China: Household Bank Savings Deposits (Billion Yuan), 1978–1991

	Total Household Deposits	Increase over Previous Year (%)	Urban Household Deposits[a]	Increase over Previous Year (%)	Rural Household Deposits[b]	Increase over Previous Year (%)	Total Household Deposits/GNP (%)
1978	21.06		15.49		5.57		5.87
1979	28.10	33.43	20.26	30.79	7.84	40.75	7.05
1980	39.95	42.17	28.25	39.44	11.70	49.23	8.94
1981	52.37	31.09	35.41	25.35	16.96	44.96	10.97
1982	67.54	28.97	44.73	26.32	22.81	34.49	13.01
1983	89.25	32.14	57.26	28.01	31.99	40.25	15.36
1984	121.47	36.10	77.66	35.62	43.81	36.95	17.45
1985	162.26	33.56	105.78	36.21	56.48	28.92	18.96
1986	223.76	37.90	147.15	39.11	76.61	35.64	23.08
1987	307.33	37.35	206.76	40.51	100.57	31.28	27.19
1988	380.15	23.69	265.92	28.61	114.23	13.58	27.12
1989	514.69	35.39	373.48	40.45	141.21	23.62	32.34
1990	703.42	36.67	519.26	39.03	184.16	30.42	39.66
1991	911.03	29.51	679.09	30.78	231.94	25.94	45.88

Sources: Statistical Yearbook of China 1992; Qian 1993.
[a]Deposits held by households in the state banking system.
[b]Deposits held by households in rural credit cooperative only.

In summary, there was ongoing fiscal deterioration in China from 1978 into the early 1990s. Increasing open and hidden deficits have largely been covered by borrowing from the state banking system. And broad money growth in China has been very high—averaging about 23 percent per year for more than a decade. Whence our puzzle: how did China succeed in containing this inflationary pressure better than the socialist countries in Eastern Europe, which faced similar revenue declines? To be sure, China suffered significant price increases in 1985 and again in 1988–89, but successfully recovered by disinflating.

SELF-FINANCE AND HARD-BUDGET CONSTRAINTS FOR CHINESE FARMERS

After 1978, China swiftly moved to dissolve the communes in favor of small-holder agriculture—a change in incentive structures that immediately raised farm productivity. Equally important but less well appreciated, state marketing agencies sharply raised—toward world-market levels—procurement prices paid farmers for compulsory quotas of grains and other foodstuffs (Wong 1992). The remaining surpluses could then be freely sold in private markets. Together with the increase in output, this big improvement in the newly independent farmers' terms of trade greatly increased their cash flows. In the early 1980s, this improved cash position meant that farmers could self-finance their on-farm investments, including residential construction, *without* borrowing significantly from the state banking system or from officially controlled rural credit cooperatives. In effect, very hard budget constraints, but improved terms of trade, were imposed on farmers as they entered the market economy.

As long as the price level remained relatively stable, as it did in the early 1980s (see Table 13.1), the newly independent farmers viewed themselves as being undermonetized for purposes of financing on-farm investments. In part because farmers did not have access to bank credit, their desired *stock* of liquid assets was too small relative to their current income *flow*. They began building up their cash and savings deposits relative to their rising incomes. More by accident than by design, farmers, who were over three-quarters of the population in the early 1980s, became big net lenders to the government through the state banking system.

To show this, farmers' financial position cannot easily be separated from that of the rest of the population. Table 13.6 shows that compared to "urban" household deposits, "rural" household savings deposits—that is, those accruing in rural credit co-ops—initially grew proportionately faster, rising from about 1.5 percent of GNP in 1978 to 6.3 percent in 1984. Nevertheless, the most important part of farm financial assets in the undermonetized state was probably hand-to-hand currency. Table 13.7 shows currency holdings also sharply rising in the early 1980s from about 6 to 11 percent of GNP, and one suspects that currency is more heavily utilized than savings deposits in agricultural pursuits. (A currency buildup amounts to lending to the government through the central bank.) Finally, in Table 13.6, some unknown fraction of the urban household savings deposits—that is, those held in regular banks rather than rural credit co-ops—is undoubtedly owned by farm households and smaller-scale rural enterprises. The rapid rate of growth of rural income, combined with the buildup of farmers' financial assets relative to their income, greatly augmented the lending resources of the state banking system.

But also critically important for China's macroeconomic stability at this early stage was the relative absence of direct lending to the newly independent farmers. Table 13.8, courtesy of Yingyi Qian (1993), shows that the total

TABLE 13.7
China: Monetary Aggregates As Share of GNP

	Savings Household Deposits/GNP (%)	Currency/GNP (%)	M1/GNP	M2/GNP (%)
1978	5.87	5.91		28.0[a]
1979	7.05	—	—	—
1980	8.94	—	—	—
1981	10.97	—	—	—
1982	13.01	—	—	—
1983	15.36	—	—	—
1984	17.45	—	—	—
1985	18.96	11.5	39.0	60.8
1986	23.08	12.6	43.6	69.3
1987	27.19	12.9	43.8	73.7
1988	27.12	15.2	42.5	71.8
1989	32.34	14.7	39.9	74.7
1990	39.77	14.9	43.0	86.4
1991	45.88	16.0	47.5	97.0

Source: Almanac of China's Finance and Banking 1990.

Note: M1 = currency + enterprise and institution demand deposits. M2 = M1 + household savings deposits (demand and time) + enterprise and institution time deposits.

In China, household demand deposits are not checkable, but enterprise and institution demand deposits are checkable.

[a]Preliminary estimate.

TABLE 13.8
China: Rural Credit Cooperative Activities (Billion Yuan)

	Total Deposits	Loans to Household	Loans to TVEs	Loans to Collective Agriculture	Total Loans/ Total Deposits (%)
1979	21.59	1.09	1.42	2.24	22.0
1980	27.23	1.60	3.11	3.45	30.0
1981	31.96	2.52	3.55	3.57	30.2
1982	38.99	4.41	4.23	3.48	31.1
1983	48.74	7.54	6.01	2.82	33.6
1984	62.49	18.11	13.5	3.84	56.7
1985	72.49	19.42	16.44	4.14	55.2
1986	96.23	25.80	26.59	4.46	59.1
1987	122.52	34.76	35.93	6.45	63.0
1988	139.98	37.24	45.61	8.01	64.9
1989	166.95	41.57	57.19	10.73	65.6
1990	214.49	51.82	76.07	13.41	65.9
1991	270.93	63.14	100.73	16.99	66.8

Source: Qian 1993. Data taken from Statistical Yearbook of China 1992.

loans of the rural credit co-ops to farm households, to TVEs, and to collective agriculture remained about a third to half of total deposits from 1979 to 1984. (Even by 1991, these loans were still only two-thirds of total deposits.) And farm households borrowed less than half of this reduced total of loans outstanding from the rural credit co-ops. What was not lent out was kept on

TABLE 13.9
China: Bank Lending to the Nonstate Sector as
Proportion Total Outstanding Bank Loans

	Urban Collectives (%)	Urban Individuals (%)	TVEs (%)	Agriculture (%)	Total Nonstate Loans (%)
1985	4.95	0.17	5.63	6.85	17.60
1986	5.11	0.13	6.82	6.68	18.94
1987	5.47	0.16	7.25	7.28	20.16
1988	5.58	0.17	7.59	7.19	20.53
1989	5.15	0.11	7.39	7.12	19.97
1990	4.93	0.09	7.42	7.17	19.61
1991	4.74	0.08	7.63	7.39	19.84

Sources: Almanac of China's Finance and Banking 1990; Qian 1993.

deposit as an informal reserve requirement with the Agricultural Bank of China (ABC). Because the ABC was a division of the state banking system, these funds were lent back to the government or its designees—an example of an "optimum" reserve tax, described in Chapter 5. Also taking their unrequited currency buildup into account, farmers were big *net* lenders to the rest of the economy at the critically important outset of liberalization between 1979 and 1984.

FINANCIAL DEEPENING AND MACROECONOMIC BALANCE: THE IMPORTANCE OF POSITIVE REAL INTEREST RATES

From the mid-1980s through 1992, this dramatic and voluntary buildup of savings by rural households was replicated throughout the rest of the economy as industry succeeded agriculture as China's leading growth sector. Table 13.7 shows the enormous increase in broad money holdings (M2) from about 28 percent of GNP in 1978 to about 97 percent in 1991. Because of the central government's continued ownership and control of the state banking system, it could offset its deteriorating fiscal position by borrowing back these rapidly rising financial surpluses of urban and rural households, or of the nonstate sector generally.

This government borrowing was not inflationary only because the relatively liberalized nonstate sector, including the TVEs, was itself not a major claimant on the state banking system. In Table 13.9 Qian (1993) shows that in the late 1980s loans to this nonstate sector—whether urban or rural—were generally only about 20 percent of the total outstanding loans of consolidated banking-type financial intermediaries. (And this 20 percent "limit" appears to be holding into the 1990s as industrial output in the nonstate sector now exceeds that of the traditional SOEs.) Without the government's having to resort to a substantial inflation tax, the remaining 80 percent was sufficient to cover the financing

TABLE 13.10
China: Selected Interest Rates, 1980–1991
(Percent per Year)

	National Retail Price Index (% Change)	Nominal Interest Rates				Real Interest Rates	
		Household 1-year Time Deposit	Household 3-year Time Deposit	Loan to Industry	Loan to Township- Village Enterprise	Household 1-year Time Deposit	Household 3-year Time Deposit
1980	6.0	5.40	6.12	2.52	2.16	−0.60	0.12
1981	2.4	5.40	6.12	2.52	2.16	3.00	3.72
1982	1.9	5.76	6.84	3.60	4.32	3.86	4.94
1983	1.5	5.76	6.84	7.20	4.32	4.26	5.34
1984	2.8	5.76	6.84	7.20	7.92	2.96	4.04
1985	8.8	7.20	8.28	7.92	10.08	−1.60	−0.52
1986	6.0	7.70	8.28	7.92	10.08	1.70	2.28
1987	7.3	7.20	8.28	7.92	10.08	−0.10	−0.98
1988	18.5	8.64	9.72[a]	9.00	10.08	−9.86	−8.78[a]
1989	17.8	11.34	13.14[a]	11.34	11.34	−6.46	−4.66[a]
1990	2.1	8.64	10.08	9.36	9.36	6.54	7.98
1991	2.9	7.56	8.28	8.64	8.46	4.66	5.38

Sources: Statistical Yearbook of China 1992; Almanac of China's Finance and Banking, 1990, 1992; Qian 1993.

Note: Year-end figures. Loan to industry is for circulation capital (one year). Loan to township-village enterprises is for equipment.

[a] Cost of living adjustment allowance not included. See Table 13.11.

needs of the old SOEs and the central government. This noninflationary mobilization of large-scale finance to cover the government's fiscal deficits, both open and hidden, was the precarious keystone of macroeconomic stability in China in the 1980s—and remains so today (1993) in the absence of major revenue-raising tax reforms.

But why was the Chinese propensity to save in financial form so remarkably high? Price stability in China was, and still is, not perfect. Table 13.1 shows inflationary episodes in 1985 and 1988–89, and 1993 itself could be a year of a substantial cyclical upturn in the inflation rate. So China's interest rate policy—particularly on savings deposits—remains very important in preserving the incentives of households and enterprises to build up their financial asset positions. Table 13.10 shows that the authorities have done a pretty good job of keeping savings deposit rates positive in real terms, if we use annual inflation rates in the national retail price index as the benchmark. (As discussed above, these real rates might look even higher if one used a decontrolled producer price index as the deflator.) A major problem arose in 1988–89 when inflation soared to 17 to 18 percent per year. This turned the standard fixed interest rates on deposits and loans sharply negative (Table 13.10). But the government responded by fully indexing some interest rates. Nominal rates on three-year household time deposits were increased into the range of 20 to 26 percent in 1988–89 (Table 13.11) and so remained strongly positive in real terms. Once inflation fell back to a very low level in 1990–91, however, indexing was discontinued.

TABLE 13.11
China: Deposit Interest Rates with Cost of Living Adjustment Allowance,
1988:IV–1991:IV

	Household 3-year Time Deposit (Nominal) (%)	Annual Rate of Cost of Living Adjustment Allowance (%)	Effective Household 3-year Time Deposit (Nominal) (%)
1988:IV	9.72	7.28	17.00
1989:I	13.14	12.71	25.85
1989:II	13.14	12.59	25.73
1989:III	13.14	13.64	26.78
1989:IV	13.14	8.36	21.50
1990:1	13.14	0.89	14.03
1990:2	13.14	1.46	14.60
1990:3	13.14	0.0	13.14
1990:4	13.14	1.42	14.56
1990:5	13.14	1.38	14.52
1990:6	13.14	0.0	13.14
1990:III	10.08	0.0	10.08
1990:IV	10.08	0.0	10.08

Sources: Almanac of China's Finance and Banking, 1990; Qian 1993.

Thus did China preserve the incentives for the nonstate sector in general, and households in particular, to accumulate monetary assets—including, in more recent years, government and industrial bonds. Because potentially excess household purchasing power was soaked up, the supply and demand of "hard" money in the nonstate sector remained more or less in balance.

What about productivity growth in the nonstate sector? Although new industry in the nonstate sector did not get much in the way of bank loans, financial deepening through higher deposit rates could still contribute to the nonstate sector's high productivity growth observed by Gelb, Jefferson, and Singh (1993). In line with the arguments and evidence put forward in Chapter 2, having access to attractive liquid financial assets inhibits bad physical investments with low or negative yields; at the same time, such access encourages intertemporal arbitrage for making good investments (McKinnon 1973; Burkett and Vogel 1991). In effect, attractive financial assets and productive physical capital are complementary.[6]

INDUSTRIAL AND FINANCIAL DUALISM IN CHINA: THE MACROECONOMIC ROLE OF PRICE CONTROLS IN THE STATE SECTOR

If there was no hard money overhang in Chinese households in 1978–79, why, then, did the Chinese government retain (or only slowly remove) price

6. In the early 1990s, important new empirical research for the World Bank over a huge 80-country, 30-year (1960–89) sample pooled in cross-section and time series provides further strong empirical support for the link between financial depth and high productivity growth. See particularly Levine (1992) and King and Levine (1993).

controls in the old state sector after 1978? Unlike Eastern Europe, China did not attempt any sudden big-bang liberalization or privatization of state-owned industry, which had been built up with distorted prices under the umbrella of central planning. Traditional heavy industry—whether in manufacturing, public utilities, or natural resources—remained firmly the responsibility of the central government.

The Chinese government recognized that parts of the old heavy industrial sector would inevitably become unprofitable as prices were decontrolled or "rationalized." State enterprises that became unprofitable with, typically, thousands of workers could not be allowed to collapse just because of a change in economic regime. The social consequences were too dire, and the economic costs would be too great. While slowly raising the prices of raw materials relative to finished manufactured goods into a better alignment with world-market prices, the central government continued to prop up much of state-owned industry with low-cost bank loans and other subsidies. Because this perpetuated the syndrome of the "soft" budget constraint, state enterprises remained on a tight financial leash.

For example, at the outset of the liberalization in the early 1980s, the SOEs were not permitted to bid freely with one another for scarce domestic resources, or to bid unrestrictedly in an open market for foreign exchange. Producer prices in transactions among state-owned enterprises remained under central-ized control and were only gradually phased out as the decade progressed. However, the government allowed a two-part pricing system to develop. Once state enterprises had satisfied their delivery commitments to one another at centrally controlled prices, they could sell at the margin any excess production to rapidly growing nonstate enterprises at market-determined—and usually somewhat higher—prices, as we have already seen in Figure 13.1. Similarly, the central government initially allocated all foreign exchange at the official exchange rate, and then gradually allowed an interenterprise swap market to develop at a variable but modest premium over the official rate—to be dis-cussed in Chapter 14, below. Only by the early 1990s did this open swap market become dominant for allocating foreign exchange among enterprises.

Contrast this cautious approach with the big-bang price decontrol followed by Russia on January 1, 1992. Suddenly state-owned enterprises (with very soft budget constraints) could bid, and negotiate prices freely, for all goods and services or foreign exchange purchased from one another. Russian households, however, remained somewhat wage and cash constrained. The result in 1992 was a price explosion at the producer level, as shown in Figure 13.2. This explosion was led by a tremendous increase in the ruble price of foreign exchange, from about 5 rubles to the dollar at the beginning of the year to about 500 rubles at the end. (Because of multiple rates in 1991, the "true" ruble/dollar rate beginning 1992 is ambiguous.)

Unlike in Russia, the Chinese authorities correctly recognized that price

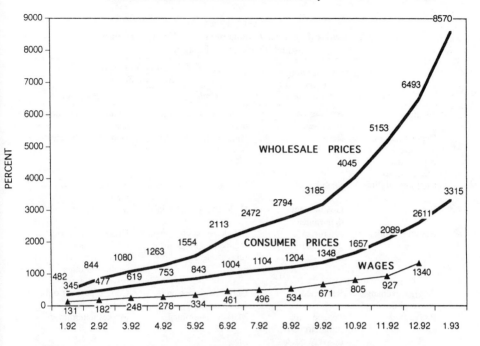

FIGURE 13.2. Wage and Wholesale and Consumer Price Indexes, in Percent (December 1991 = 100%), Russia, January 1992–January 1993. Collated by Mikhail Bernstam, Hoover Institution, Stanford University. (*Sources:* Russian State Committee on Statistics data requested by the Office of Deputy Prime Minister G. S. Khizha. Russian State Committee on Statistics data in *Ekonomika I Zhizn*, no. 51 [December 1992]: 1; Ministry of Labor data in *Izvestiia*, February 9, 1993, 2; Institute of Economic Policy (Gaidar's) data in *Moscow Business News* no. 10 [March 1993]: 11.)

controls are necessary to anchor the producer price level when (1) enterprise budget constraints are still very soft, and (2) there wasn't yet sufficient competition in the provision of individual raw materials or more complex producer goods from a hard-budget nonstate sector. Even if the government succeeded in controlling both wages in SOEs and the stock of "hard" household cash in circulation among households and the nonstate sector, this by itself would be insufficient to peg the producer price level. Although the Chinese authorities slowly adjusted *relative* producer prices, they still anchored the producers' price *level* by pegging most of the nominal prices of goods and services traded among state enterprises in the early years of their liberalization.

(In positing an optimal order of economic liberalization, I earlier argued, in Chapter 11, that a dualistic set of financial, fiscal, and price controls should apply differentially to the traditional and the liberalized sectors in the early years of the transition, as briefly summarized in Table 11.5. This industrial and financial dualism corresponds loosely to China's distinction between

TABLE 13.12
Alternative Financial Arrangements for Enterprises in a
Model Transitional Economy

	Traditional[a] Enterprises (State Sector)	Liberalized Enterprises (Nonstate Sector)	
		Collective[b]	Private
Taxation	Expropriation of surpluses[c]	Uniform value-added tax	Uniform value-added tax
Deposit money: domestic commodity convertibility	Restricted	Unrestricted interest-bearing	Unrestricted interest-bearing
Credit eligibility	State bank	Nonbank capital market	Nonbank capital market
Wages	Government determined	Collectively determined	Market determined
Residual profits	Accrue to government	Dividends to collective: retained earnings for reinvestment	Dividends to owners:[e] retained earnings for reinvestment or lending to other private enterprises
Foreign exchange convertibility	Restricted	Current account only (swap market)	Current account only (swap market)
Producer prices	Pegged with intramarginal delivery quotas[f]	Market determined	Market determined

[a]"Traditional" enterprises are those whose output and pricing decisions are still largely determined by a central government authority or planning bureau with centrally allocated inputs and credits from the state bank to cover possible negative cash flows. In China, traditional enterprises would be in the so-called state sector, while new entities outside these traditional controls would be in the nonstate sector.

[b]"Collective" can refer to any level of government ownership or sponsorship as with Chinese TVEs—township and village enterprises. For example, the VAT administered by the central government would apply equally to liberalized enterprises owned or registered in different local jurisdictions.

[c]Although residual profits revert to the state, they could include a "shadow" VAT levy in order better to understand the "true" profitability of traditional enterprises.

[d]"Commodity convertibility" here means the freedom to spend for domestic goods and services or to buy and hold domestic coin and currency, but need not imply convertibility into foreign exchange.

[e]Dividends would be subject to the personal income tax when paid out to private owners, but retained earnings would not be taxed.

[f]After satisfying delivery commitments to other traditional enterprises, marginal output can be sold at free-market prices.

its state and nonstate sectors. A more elaborated "model" dualistic control mechanism—taking the Chinese experience through 1992 recounted in this chapter into account—is displayed in Table 13.12.)

However, once the cash-constrained nonstate sector becomes big enough to compete vigorously with the old state sector in product markets, the government can relax price controls in the state sector. Together, the TVEs and private industries in the nonstate sector, broadly defined, now rival in size the aggregate industrial output of the old state sector. In 1978, collective or private industry in China was officially tabulated to be 22 percent of total output; but, mainly because of the growth of the TVEs, by 1991 this had risen to 53.7 percent (Perkins 1992). Because these new enterprises operating with hard budget constraints now compete vigorously with the old state sector, in the early 1990s price controls within the latter could be almost entirely eliminated without upsetting the producer price level—providing the amount of hard cash in circulation in the nonstate sector remains under control. Even into the 1990s, however, the old SOEs still need to be financially constrained from bidding for scarce resources like foreign exchange, insofar as they are also recipients of soft loans from the state banking system.

TAX REFORM AND THE OPTIMAL PACE OF FINANCIAL LIBERALIZATION: CHINA AND EASTERN EUROPE COMPARED

To be soundly financed and for the state banking system to stay profitable, the reform government's high interest rate strategy for household deposits requires even higher average interest rates on loans. China did not always manage this. Occasionally, an inversion made some loan rates lower than the equivalent deposit rates, particularly during the 1988–89 period, when nominal deposit rates were indexed. Such an inversion adds to the banking system's and the government's "hidden" deficit, beyond simply the deficit associated with the nonrepayment of bad loans to the SOEs.

Even without this inversion, this high-interest noninflationary finance implies that the Chinese central government's open and hidden debt, through the state banking system to the nonbank public, is building up fast. But measuring the size of this official debt is complicated and cannot be undertaken here.

Moreover, as long as the government is leaning on the state banking system as a crutch to cover its own fiscal deficits, the scope for liberalizing—let alone privatizing—the banks is limited. At this stage, the government cannot afford a parallel system of independent banks, with unrestricted deposit and lending privileges, to serve the TVEs or the private sector. They would compete away the deposit-taking capabilities of the state banking system. (This may be already happening. To escape the direct credit controls imposed by the People's Bank of China, the state banks themselves may be transferring some of their activities to less highly regulated and taxed finance and trust companies [Qian 1993].) If the Chinese government threw away its financial crutch—by, say, permitting unrestricted wildcat banking in the mode of the FSU as described in Chapter 11—an inflationary explosion would ensue.

Like Eastern European governments, the Chinese central government failed to set up an effective internal revenue service for collecting revenue in a decentralized market economy. Unlike Eastern Europe, however, the Chinese resorted more effectively to various "second-best" schemes for revenue collection. After 1978, by retaining control over traditionally profitable industrial enterprises, the central government could continue collecting revenue—turn-

taxes and residual profits—directly for itself. Then, by the mid-1980s, revenue from state-owned enterprises fell, the central government began elaborate system of tax contracting with local governments to remit revenue to the center (Wong, Heady, and Woo 1993).

Still, this left the Chinese central government with a serious revenue shortfall for financing infrastructure investments, subsidizing loss-making old-line industrial enterprises, providing higher agricultural procurement prices, and so on. The salaries of high-level civil servants and educators have declined sharply relative to those paid in the nonstate sector. This decline in the fiscal position of the central government is clearly neither sustainable nor in the best long-run interests of Chinese economic development; among other problems, officials become more easily corrupted when their salaries are low.

The Chinese government cannot rely indefinitely on such heavy borrowing because households are no longer "undermonetized," and the M2/GNP ratio will not rise to infinity. When the ratio of household liquid assets to income peaks out, or even before, there could be a financial crisis if state-sector borrowing continues. The great economic accomplishments of the last 13 years would then be at risk, and an Eastern European-style inflation cannot be ruled out.

The solution is obvious economically but difficult politically. The Chinese central government must quickly institute an internal revenue service capable of directly taxing all industries—central government, local government, and private—as well as the agricultural sector. Domestic and foreign trade should be covered uniformly so that the rate of business taxation can be kept moderate, as with a uniform value added tax. At a somewhat later stage, households could systematically be brought under a personal income tax, but that is only feasible as people get wealthier. Aspects of how to implement this new tax regime are analyzed in Chapter 11, in McKinnon (1993), and in Wong et al. (1993).

In the transition in Eastern Europe and the FSU, by contrast, the need for fiscal reform is more immediate than was the case in China. The initial decreases in output (see Table 13.2) and unfavorable inflationary expectations (see Table 13.3) make it much more difficult for these governments to obtain noninflationary finance by borrowing from their banking systems in the Chinese mode. The growth in the real size of their financial systems is too small, and could even be negative. Thus, if further inflationary explosions are to be avoided, effective fiscal reforms must come much earlier in their transitions.

RUSSIA'S ECONOMIC DILEMMA BEFORE THE BIG BANG, JANUARY 1992: PARTIAL PRICE LIBERALIZATION AND SUPPLY DIVERSION

It was a major mistake for the Russian Federation, in January 1992, to suddenly decontrol virtually all prices within the state sector and to stop trying to enforce normal patterns of delivery within that sector. As we have seen, this big-bang approach was very different from Chinese gradualism. On the other hand, some conditions in Russia in 1992 were very different from those prevailing in China in 1979. Moreover, the Yeltsin-Gaider reform government in Moscow was acting in good faith and seemed to be following the advice of international agencies like the IMF and the World Bank as well as most Western economists. So a careful review of some of the arguments that were presented, prior to that fateful January, in favor of the big-bang approach seems worthwhile.

Two related arguments in favor of sudden liberalization in Russia can be adduced. The first was mainly macro and, following the Polish precedent of January 1990, was directed toward eliminating a monetary overhang at previously controlled prices by a one-time inflation. In the last section of this chapter, I take up this influential monetary-overhang argument.

The second argument was more micro in nature and was concerned with the sievelike character of the previous system of price controls. In 1990–91, a substantial fringe of unregulated activities had developed in Russia's nonstate sector, where prices were free and hard money(ies) circulated. Unlike China, there was more small-scale trade, both legal and illegal, and relatively little production in this nonstate sector, if only because Russia had made little progress in liberalizing agriculture. Black-market activities were rampant. This second influential argument emphasizes "supply diversion."

A recent article, "The Transition to a Market Economy: Pitfalls of Partial Reform" (Murphy, Shleifer, and Vishny 1992), argues that partial reform, where prices are decontrolled in the nonstate sector but not in the state sector, is a mistake. (The authors had been to Russia and had written their paper before January 1992.) If controlled prices in the state sector are set below those in the free market dominated by the nonstate sector, scarce inputs could be diverted from high-value to low-value uses, including diversion into foreign trade. Such massive supply diversion from partial price liberalization, they argued, provoked the fall in output in 1990–91 in the FSU in general, and Russia in particular.

These authors illustrate their important and influential argument with several examples, one of which is worth repeating. Suppose an important industrial input, say timber, can be used for the production of railway boxcars in the state sector or for the production of family homes in the nonstate sector. The demand for timber to be used for boxcars is relatively inelastic, reflecting a high producer surplus within the railway industry for providing general transportation. In contrast, the demand for timber in the housing industry is relatively elastic, with consumer surplus being relatively low. Like most raw materials in socialist economies, timber traditionally has been underpriced in terms of finished manufactures. Suppose such price controls are retained in the state sector: users of boxcars cannot bid beyond a set price, say P*, for timber.

In a partial liberalization, suppose now that a nonstate housing industry can bid for timber from forestry enterprises in the state sector at free-market prices. By bidding slightly above P*, the nonstate housing industry could expand very rapidly at the margin. Unrestricted entry by small construction firms could rapidly absorb this key raw material and cause a collapse of the output of vital railway cars in the transportation network. (The same output collapse of railway cars could also happen if the nonstate sector bid away timber products for export.) When output fell in Russia in 1990–91, there were price controls on what state firms could pay for various inputs in terms of quasiblocked enterprise money, while nonstate firms in the "cash" economy sometimes had a much freer hand in the bidding process—including bidding with more attractive household money.

This provocative article does not refer to the different financial circumstances, including different monetary circuits, of state and nonstate enterprises. It focuses only on the anomalies of the two-part pricing system. In this narrower context, the authors identify two solutions to this problem of supply diversion:

1. Keep the two-part pricing system in place but strengthen the old system of state orders for enforcing minimal deliveries of price-controlled inputs in critical industries within the old state sector; or

2. Abandon two-part pricing within the state sector, and thus eliminate both price controls and bidding restraints on state firms competing with nonstate firms for scarce inputs.

In assessing (1), the authors note that the Chinese government started off its liberalization with an extensive two-part pricing system in the traditional state sector. However, Christine Wong (1992) notes that relative prices within the state sector were also realigned to push them closer to those prevailing internationally.

> During the first period in 1979–84, in agriculture state procurement prices were raised substantially across the board. . . . In industry, the prices of 29 producers' goods were raised during 1979–81, including those for coal, pig iron, coking coal, cement, plate glass, and some steel products. Other prices were reduced: those for machinery, instruments, and tools. The prices of many consumer goods were also reduced from their initially very high levels, including wrist watches, televisions, tape recorders, radios, synthetic fabrics, etc.
>
> At the same time more prices were freed to market determination through two devices. The first was to reduce the scope of planned allocation. In agriculture, the number of products was reduced from 46 to 22 in 1982, and further to 12 in 1984. In industry, the number of producers' goods under plan allocation was reduced from 256 in 1979 to 30 in 1984. By 1984, virtually all "minor" consumer prices had been freed.
>
> The second device was to allow some of the goods in the key sectors that remained under state control to enter into market channels, a development that gave rise to the "dual" price system that emerged in the mid-1980s . . . whereby the proportion

of output under state plans would continue to be traded at plan prices, while extra-plan output would be traded at (higher) "extra-plan" prices . . . to provide better (profit) incentives at the margin. (Wong 1992, 72)

However, for the Russian case, Murphy, Schleifer, and Vishny reject the Chinese solution of partial liberalization with dual pricing. They claim that the different political circumstances in China, where the Communist party retains centralized power, could force state firms to deliver their assigned quotas at below market prices, so that private buyers could only buy surplus production at the higher prices. Because of the decline of the Communist party in Russia, however, the authors claim that delivery quotas for state enterprises have already been relaxed, and it would now be impossible to enforce such delivery quotas even if the Russian government wanted to. Therefore, they conclude that the gradualist approach based on partial price reform—(1) above—should be scrapped in favor of full price liberalization—(2) above. "The most natural implication of the analysis in this paper is that price reform should take the form of a big bang, with all prices being freed at once. . . . Fortunately, the Russian government moved to an almost complete price liberalization in 1992" (Murphy, Shleifer, and Vishny 1992, 906).

Unfortunately, unrestrained bidding for scarce inputs by Russian state enterprises from January 1992 onwards led to an even bigger inflationary explosion and sharper fall in real output than under the partial price reforms of 1990–91.

The Russian economic depression deepened dramatically in 1992 with GDP falling 19% and NMP (net material product) produced down 20%. Since reaching a peak in 1989, the level of NMP produced has fallen by nearly 32%, with GDP falling slightly less. The major change in 1992 compared to 1990–91 is that consumption had to bear the brunt of the decline in aggregate output—it fell by 15–16% compared to less than 3% drop in 1991. The level of net investment . . . in 1992 fell to less than one third (!) of its peak 1988 level. . . .

Russia made no headway in controlling inflation last year. The end-December level of consumer prices was up by a factor of 26.3 relative to December 1991 while the industrial wholesale price index was up a staggering 62.2 times for the same period. These figures imply average monthly inflation rates of 31.3% and 41.1% respectively. (*PlanEcon Report*, March 1993, 1)

What went wrong? Was there some major flaw in the three authors' persuasive argument for a big-bang price reform jointly encompassing both the state and nonstate (household) sectors? Or, did Russian reformers again simply not go far enough—a line of thought to which many influential outsiders[7] still adhere?

7. See the commentary "If He Goes" in *The Economist*, March 13, 1993, 17–18, which argues for even more sweeping price decontrol in Russia.

INDETERMINACY IN THE PRODUCER PRICE LEVEL WITH UNCONSTRAINED
BIDDING BY STATE ENTERPRISES

The big-bang argument for total price decontrol is flawed if some of the important actors bidding for scarce resources have soft budget constraints. If Russia's state enterprises are not financially constrained, no meaningful equilibrium in producer prices exists. Until their budget constraints are hardened, unconstrained bidding by state enterprises will cause the producer (wholesale) price level to increase indefinitely—and thus also increase relative to retail prices facing cash-constrained households. After presenting some evidence on this point, I then discuss the underlying financial mechanisms.

Taking December 1991 as the base month just prior to the massive price increases of January 1992 and using data from the Russian Ministry of the Economy, Mikhail Bernstam of Stanford University's Hoover Institution plotted Figure 13.2: the course of Russian wholesale and consumer prices and wages on a monthly basis from January 1992 through January 1993. The key point to notice is the explosive growth in wholesale prices relative to consumer prices or wages in the initial months after price decontrol. All the increases are astronomical, but, by October 1992, wholesale prices had risen almost 2.5 times as much as consumer prices. And from the fragmentary data, by the end of the year consumer prices had risen twice as much as wages—so that wholesale or producer prices had actually risen five times as much as wages.

However, in such a financially volatile context, data sources are hard to reconcile. Because of the more or less complete decontrol of prices (but not wages) in January 1992, rates of growth in monthly time series data in 1992 are particularly difficult to interpret. For example, in December 1991, the general retail price index stood at 282.6 (1990 being 100) and then jumped to 941.0 in January 1992, an increase of 230 percent in just one month. But this one-shot outburst of extraordinary inflation was designed to work off the large cash overhang that had been rapidly building in 1991 when retail prices were still partially controlled. (Although difficult to measure, the overhang component of household cash holding might have been as high as 50 percent of total wage and salary income in 1991.) But nominal wages remained controlled and rose only about 31 percent in January 1992. So real wages fell very sharply in January 1992, a fall not recouped by subsequent substantial, but controlled, increases in nominal wages relative to retail prices.

Because the Russian government's power to tax the household sector directly is very limited, these imperfect wage controls are the principal means by which the Russian government could restrict the supply of new money—including savings deposits—in the household monetary circuit. And indeed, household saving deposits as a share of retail sales turnover fell dramatically, from 60 percent in 1991 to about 25 percent in mid-1992, and virtually vanished by year's end. Similarly in this world of imperfect statistics, the (ruble) currency to GNP ratio was about 10 percent at the beginning of 1992 and had fallen to about 3 percent by the end of the year. This is one reflection of the 1992 "cash shortage" in Russia and other former Soviet republics.

(In great contrast to the financial deepening in China, with M2/GNP near 100 percent by the end of 1992, the purchasing power of money (in rubles) held by the nonbank public in Russia had become very small—probably on the order of 3 percent of GNP, with the household deposit base of the banking system wiped out.)

Another data source showing the extraordinary pattern of price changes in the Russian economy in early 1992 is in various parts of the *PlanEcon Report* that are collated and rearranged in Table 13.13. Focus initially on just the price movements in the right-hand column. From December 1991 through June 1992, ruble wages increased about 4 times, retail prices between 6 and 7 times, wholesale prices between 18 and 19 times, and the ruble price of dollars about 33 times.

To help interpret this incredible increase in the price of foreign exchange, the *PlanEcon Report* (September 1992) estimated that the purchasing power parity (PPP) exchange rate (using CPI comparisons) was 6 rubles/dollar when the "commercial" rate was pegged at 55 rubles/dollar in June 1992. Subsequently, this commercial rate was further freed to be determined by "market" forces in the Moscow interbank currency exchange (opened in 1991) and rose to 143 rubles to the dollar in July 1992 and to 241 on September 22, 1992.

"At the end of trading, [the ruble] had sunk to 241 against the dollar—a loss of 35.5 rubles on last week's level of Rbs 205.5 to the dollar. The volume of dollars traded was also a record, at $68.8m—*a sign of the willingness of Russian enterprises to use Rbs15bn to buy the US currency as a hedge against inflation*" (*Financial Times*, September 23, 1992, 4; italics added).

What is going on here? As in the classical centrally planned socialist economy, Russian enterprises were still on a soft money circuit—deposits with, and credits from, the state banks. In contrast, households and the emerging nonstate commercial sector were on the relatively hard money or cash circuit. This softness of financial constraints on the old state enterprises has two related aspects.

First, central government enterprises have traditionally had access to low (nominal) interest-rate credits from the state banking system and from other state enterprises. In the face of rapid price inflation, which resulted in almost complete debt forgiveness in real terms as in 1992, these bank credits become a massive subsidy. In addition, by simply not repaying their trade credits, state enterprises have also borrowed heavily from one another. Although ostensibly commercial in nature, this credit is not subject to ordinary commercial restraints and became a prime cause of softness in enterprise budget constraints in 1992.

TABLE 13.13
Key Russian Inflation Indicators, 1985–June 1992
(Annual Change in Percent)

	1985	1986	1987	1988	1989	1990	1991	Jan-June 1992/ Jan-June 1991	June 1992/ Dec. 1991
Wholesale industrial prices	—	—	—	—	1.2	3.9	138.1	1360	1850
Consolidated retail prices	0.6	2.2	1.7	0.3	2.5	5.6	95.0	730	620
Food (excluding alcohol)	0.1	0.6	2.1	0.4	0.7	4.9	118.7	780	600
Alcoholic beverages	6.2	24.7	15.4	0.0	0.0	1.9	26.6		
Nonfood products	−0.9	0.9	−1.1	0.0	3.1	6.5	100.7		
Prices for paid services						—	70.6	480	510
Retail prices in:									
State and cooperative trade	0.5	2.2	1.6	0.2	2.4	5.2	89.5	790	660
Cooperative trade	1.2	3.4	2.4	0.6	0.5	14.1	111.7	—	—
Collective farms	5.2	1.1	3.7	2.5	7.4	132.1	132.1	—	—
Nominal wages									397
Commercial exchange rate							71.6		3290

Source: Russian Goskomstate and PlanEcon Report, September 3, 1992.

Second, enterprises had no hard deposit money or interest-bearing assets denominated in rubles which they could hold either for short-term liquidity or as a longer-term store of value. Indeed, in the traditional Soviet monetary system, enterprises were, and still are, enjoined from holding household cash balances, and have had to hold noninterest (or trivially low-interest) deposits with the state bank in several categories of quasiblocked accounts. Not only are these ruble accounts not liquid, but in the past they have been subject to arbitrary seizure and confiscation by the government as an informal method of tax collection. (Residual profits of state enterprises traditionally accrue to the central government anyway.) From the existing explosive inflation, the low nominal rates of interest, and the threat of confiscation, enterprises see very negative real deposit rates on any ruble monetary assets they cannot avoid accumulating.

In these circumstances, if state enterprises are given the option of bidding (with their soft money) for foreign exchange assets in virtually any form, they will grossly overbid, as discussed in Chapters 9 and 11. Although imported producer and consumer goods are in heavy demand, enterprises are even more desperate to find a nondepreciating liquid financial asset which they can legally hold through time. Apart from excess physical inventories of inputs and outputs, foreign bank accounts or other foreign exchange assets are very attractive inflation hedges at this unfortunate juncture in Russia's financial affairs. Thus, in a market for foreign exchange dominated by state enterprises, the ruble price of dollars is bid up beyond any conceivable level warranted by purchasing power parity.

THE ROLE OF PRICE CONTROLS ON STATE-SECTOR ENTERPRISES IN THE TRANSITION

Before liberalization, price-wage controls in a typical socialist economy have a dual economic function.

1. Government revenue depends implicitly on the structure of *relative prices*. The government "distorts" relative prices in order to generate surplus profits within the state-owned industrial sector (Chapter 11; McKinnon 1993). In comparison to world markets, domestic prices of primary products, industrial materials, and money wages are deliberately kept low relative to the domestic prices of finished manufactures. As described above, the resulting surpluses in enterprise cash flows are then deposited in blocked accounts with the state bank: the government's operative tax revenue.

2. Price controls are also necessary to peg the *absolute producer price level*—that is, to provide a nominal anchor for prices charged in trade among state enterprises with soft budget constraints. Otherwise, if any open bidding were allowed, producer prices would be indeterminate, as with the 1992 Russian price explosion. (If excess money issue and price inflation

existed at the consumer level, continual movement—or indexing—of wholesale prices to ever higher official pegs would become necessary.)

In an optimal order of liberalization for the economy as a whole, both (1) and (2) constrain the pace at which prices in the state sector can be safely decontrolled. When liberalization begins, the government's revenue position is undermined if competitive pressure undermines monopoly profits in the industrial sector: finished goods prices fall relative to material inputs and wages. This fall in tax revenue could result in excessive hard money creation in the household sector and inflationary pressure, first manifest at the consumer level.

Consequently, without a satisfactory internal revenue service for collecting income and commodity taxes on a general basis, liberalizing socialist governments must retain wage controls as a second-best way of taxing personal income. These wage controls maintain the profit position of the state enterprises, on the one hand, and prevent too much soft enterprise money from being converted into hard household cash—hand-to-hand currency and savings deposits—on the other. For example, to maintain the government's revenue position and a modicum of monetary control, Poland's otherwise big-bang price liberalization at the beginning of 1990 was accompanied by stringent wage controls. Initially, money wages in Poland rose more slowly than the final output prices which consumers had to pay. Similarly, in Russia's big-band liberalization at the beginning of 1992, wage controls led to a sharp fall in real wages as inflation accelerated.

This draconian, albeit informal, system of personal income taxation may initially succeed in curbing inflation at the retail-household level. Hard cash in circulation may be effectively limited, as was initially true in Russia in 1992. But by themselves, wage controls are not enough to prevent an inflationary explosion in prices prevailing in trade among state enterprises, including the price of foreign exchange. Whence the dramatically unbalanced inflation process observed in Russia in 1992.

Consequently, price and credit controls may have to be retained in the old state sector, even after a proper system of general taxation is put in place and the revenue position of the central government appears to be balanced. As long as the money and credit position of the old state enterprises remains soft, direct price controls in this sector will remain necessary until a cash-constrained nonstate sector becomes large enough to be an effective competitor.

CHOOSING THE RIGHT MODEL OF INFLATION IN ORDER TO DISINFLATE EFFICIENTLY: A SIMPLE TAXONOMY

In designing an efficient program for ending price inflation in any economy, it is important to choose the right model of the inflationary process itself. Consider three possibilities.

1. Open Inflation in Market Economies. The traditional textbook analysis of open inflation starts with a unified monetary system and market-determined prices. Excessive lending by the central bank to the government or its designees causes cash or "high-powered" money in circulation to rise sharply. With a lag, prices then begin moving upward and eventually catch up with the increased amount of nominal money outstanding. But the money supply is the proximate causal variable for the increase in prices, as in most Latin American inflations.

2. Repressed Inflation with a Cash Overhang. In the now standard analysis of repressed inflation with general price-wage controls, economists (see Barro and Grossman [1976] generally, or Lipton and Sachs [1990] for Poland in particular) envisaged a single well-defined monetary overhang interchangeably owned by households and enterprises in an essentially unified monetary system. If the economy is to begin functioning properly, however, the overhang must be eliminated by canceling much of the outstanding nominal money in circulation, as in West Germany in 1948, or by open inflation. By removing price controls and devaluing the currency in the foreign exchanges in January 1990, the Polish government planned to inflate away the purchasing power of its monetary overhang, and was fairly successful in doing so. In principle, by limiting new sources of cash injections into the economy, inflation should come to a halt after a once-and-for-all increase in the price level. (Because Poland's fiscal policy remains weak, however, the Poles may not fully succeed in reasserting monetary control.)

These two highly simplified models of either open or repressed inflation assume a unified monetary system where households and enterprises are on essentially the same monetary circuit, and both have fairly hard budget constraints. Was this a reasonable assumption for Poland on January 1, 1990? In the 1980s, Poland had a history of attempted financial liberalizations and banking reforms—with a lot of missteps—which tended to obliterate the sharp distinction between household cash and savings accounts and the deposit or credit money owned by firms. Both could traffic with cash and were subject to restraint in bidding for scarce resources by their cash positions, if the government limited new credits or other subsidies. Then, if the Polish government could get control over the cash base within this unified monetary system, that would be sufficient for bringing inflation under control.

3. Producer Price Inflation in Enterprises with Soft Budget Constraints. Russia's financial-monetary system—and that of other CIS republics—in 1991–93 would seem to be qualitatively different from Poland's at the beginning of 1990. Russia had essentially retained the old socialist distinction between enterprises, which were not cash constrained in their ability to bid for scarce resources, and cash-constrained households. Even so, Russia went ahead and suddenly decontrolled all producer prices with disastrous consequences. Although this Russian model of inflation is not yet in any textbook, it soon will be.

How does Russia get the inflation genie back into the bottle? In the short run, successful macroeconomic stabilization requires a major recentralization of the government's control over money and credit and a reassertion of the primacy of the state-controlled banking system with the elimination of independent "wildcat" banks. Because of the special characteristics of socialist industry, price setting at the producer level, including the exchange rate, may also have to be recentralized as part of the stabilization package. So we have an unfortunate policy dilemma: to secure macroeconomic stabilization in the near term, important banking and commodity pricing policies may have to move counter to what most of us would like to see for the long-run liberalization of the Russian economy.

But this dilemma between short and long run is less acute for fiscal policy. A drastic improvement in the Russian government's ability to collect tax revenue is necessary for macro stabilization, on the one hand, and for sustaining the longer term market-oriented and institutional reforms, on the other.

CHAPTER FOURTEEN

Gradual versus Rapid Liberalization

in Socialist Foreign Trade:

Concluding Notes on

Alternative Models

In transitional socialist economies, the pace of liberalizing foreign trade must be carefully geared to the pace of price decontrol, existing tax mechanisms, and the degree of financial liberalization in domestic commerce. These initial conditions are important in determining whether a move to current-account convertibility between domestic and foreign monies should be rapid, as in Chile after 1973 or Poland after 1989, or more gradual, as in China and Vietnam in the 1980s. Otherwise, a debacle like the ill-fated Russian liberalization of 1992 (discussed in Ch. 13) cannot be ruled out.

In this chapter I consider two highly stylized but logically consistent approaches to liberalizing foreign trade. The first, on the *Chilean model,* is rapid; it presumes that domestic market and price decontrol are virtually complete when the trade reforms begin. Individuals and enterprises have commercial contacts with foreigners and some familiarity with international markets. Chile's move to freer trade and full currency convertibility on current account, after the fall of the socialist Allende regime in 1973, is briefly laid out in an idealized format, consolidating and summarizing the previous analyses of Chile in Chapters 6 and 12.[1]

The second approach, on the *Chinese model,* is more gradual liberalization; it presumes that domestic market and price decontrol are still incomplete. At the outset of the trade reforms, a dualistic system of financial and price controls treats the state and nonstate sectors differently, as summarized in Table 13.12, above. This financial dualism is important for maintaining the economy's monetary equilibrium and generating revenue for the government (Ch. 13). Then any rapid move to full current-account currency convertibility must be ruled out. Yet other measures for encouraging foreign trade—special economic zones, broader exporter retentions, and delimited interenterprise swap markets in foreign exchange—can still be very effective in gradually opening the

---

1. From Chapter 6, we know that Chile made major mistakes in financial policy leading to exchange rate overvaluation and a financial crash in 1982–83. But trade policy per se was sound, and it is an appropriate model for others to follow with similar initial conditions.

economy. To illustrate this more gradual approach, this chapter draws on the Chinese experience after 1978—again in an idealized format, which omits many details and missteps.

Which of these two paradigms of trade liberalization is more appropriate depends on the initial economic conditions facing a new reform government.

THE CHILEAN MODEL OF RAPID TRADE LIBERALIZATION

First, let us briefly review the chaotic situation that the new Chilean government faced in 1974. From 1970 to 1973, the previous populist government had intervened to reduce prices relative to wages. Most enterprises were thus forced to operate with severe losses, which were covered by borrowing from the nationalized banking system. Together with huge central government fiscal deficits also covered by the banks, this enterprise borrowing caused the Chilean money supply to spiral out of control with price inflation that was only partly suppressed. As shops were emptied of goods at the controlled prices, a cash overhang developed. But the underlying monetary system was still unified: Chile's experience with socialism was too short for the government to develop dual monetary circuits where "soft" enterprise deposit money was separated from "hard" household cash. Thus, to get control over the unified money supply, rapid price decontrol was a feasible method of eliminating enterprises' current deficits, on the one hand, with the subsequent one-time high inflation eliminating the excess stocks of cash balances, on the other. Similar to Poland in 1990 but unlike China in 1978, immediate price decontrol, where prices rose relative to wages, was necessary for establishing monetary and fiscal balance. (Using the VAT as the centerpiece of its revenue-raising effort, Chile also successfully restructured public finances in parallel with freeing domestic prices.)

From 1970 to 1973, interventions in foreign trade paralleled those in domestic trade. Multiple exchange rates had proliferated, with the peso cost of foreign exchange being ten or more times as high in some categories as in others, with widespread foreign exchange rationing. Similarly, tariffs were extremely high in some categories with the import of many goods prohibited; yet, a few favored importers received blanket exemption from these trade restrictions.

Parallel with the decontrol of domestic prices, the new government completely unified the exchange rate system by 1975 and rationalized commercial policy with full current account convertibility by 1976. All previous quantitative restrictions on imports and exports were replaced by "equivalent" ad valorem tariffs, which cascaded from relatively high rates on finished consumer goods to moderate rates on finished producer goods and to a basic 10 percent rate on industrial raw materials. From the government's perspective, this immediately increased revenue. Then, in 1977 it was announced that the highest tariffs in the cascade would be reduced step by step to a uniform 10 percent level by the end of 1979, as described in Chapter 12. Provided that the real exchange rate was not allowed to become overvalued (unlike what actually happened in Chile in 1980–81, as discussed in Ch. 6), this relatively rapid liberalization of foreign trade was intended to remove the bias against exporting from the old regime's heavy protection for import-substituting industries. This intention was eventually realized in the late 1980s and early 1990s when a major export boom developed. Protectionism had been eliminated, and import tariffs were confined to a low uniform level of 10 to 15 percent for purposes of raising revenue. (But into the early 1990s, Chile has had to retain various exchange controls on capital account—mainly on capital inflows—to prevent the exchange rate from once more becoming overvalued.)

In summary, the initial economic conditions in Chile favored rapid commodity price decontrol and currency convertibility on current account as a means of securing domestic financial equilibrium. Because an appropriate system of commodity and income taxation had been relatively quickly reestablished, both measures tended to improve the government's revenue position. The rapid privatization of nationalized industries—accomplished in part by simply returning them to their original owners—virtually eliminated the syndrome of the soft budget constraint affecting the core of Chilean industry. Because budget constraints on enterprises were hardened,[2] Chile could move quickly to full current-account convertibility. Enterprises that wished to import could bid freely for foreign exchange at a unified exchange rate. But even Chile did not move to complete free trade at the outset. Quantitative restrictions on imports were converted into temporarily cascaded tariffs in order to give domestic producers a few years to adjust before being fully exposed to world relative prices.

THE CHINESE MODEL OF GRADUAL LIBERALIZATION

Detailed descriptions of the evolution of Chinese foreign trade practices before and after liberalization began in 1978 are now available (Cheng 1991; Lardy 1992; Wong 1992; Panagariya 1993). Here, I shall take a different tack. First, let us identify the Chinese trade and payments regime's key facets that supported classical central planning prior to 1978. To maintain domestic monetary and fiscal balance under centralized price controls and output allocations, financial insulation from the rest of the world was necessary. Second,

2. In practice, the budget constraints facing the recently privatized firms were not hard enough. The failure of the Chilean monetary authorities adequately to supervise the lending practices of the newly liberalized commercial banks from 1974 to 1980 led to excessive lending to insider business groups that controlled both banks and enterprises (Ch. 3). I am simply treating this unfortunate event as being outside the Chilean paradigm of trade liberalization.

with domestic liberalization after 1978 taking the form of industrial and financial dualism, as described in Chapter 13, what evolutionary path of relaxing restraints on foreign trade was consistent with maintaining macroeconomic balance while the economy became progressively more open? (Unlike Chile or Poland, China had no monetary overhang or other serious macroeconomic disequilibria in 1978 at the outset of its liberalization.)

CENTRAL PLANNING AND COMMODITY INCONVERTIBILITY

Within the industrial sector of a centrally planned economy, the current output of producer goods and services is centrally allocated by administrative fiat. Instead of being determined by the market, prices serve only a passive role in accounting for cash flows when goods pass from one enterprise to another. Nominal prices often remain unchanged for years. However, in order to generate cash surpluses in state-owned manufacturing enterprises, the prices of raw materials and intermediate inputs are generally kept low relative to the prices of finished (consumer) goods. Relative to world market prices, the prices of agricultural goods are kept similarly low in order also to set nominal wages low and further increase the cash surpluses in enterprises (Chs. 11 and 12).

Because these controlled prices do not reflect relative scarcity either domestically or internationally, any attempt to open a market, with free bidding for goods at these prices, could well lead to a perverse allocation of resources. But this potential problem is suppressed by having goods allocated by central planning and by blocking the cash balance holdings of the enterprises so they cannot bid freely for scarce inputs. In effect, the money of domestic enterprises is not freely convertible into domestic commodities; that is, there is *commodity inconvertibility*.

Because prices are not used to allocate goods domestically, it is inconceivable that foreigners be permitted to do what domestic enterprises cannot do, that is, freely exercise domestic monetary claims to buy whatever goods seem attractive at prevailing prices. Not only would centrally administered materials be upset, but low price tags on some potentially exportable goods—like industrial raw materials—may well conceal the fact that they are very costly in real resources or are in actual shortage. Formal accounting prices need bear no systematic relationship to their value in use as seen by the planners. Thus, commodity inconvertibility also prevents nonresident foreign enterprises from freely purchasing domestic goods or services should they be unlucky enough to build up domestic deposits with the state bank.

Nor are foreign-owned domestic balances freely convertible into foreign exchange. Commodity and foreign exchange inconvertibility go hand in hand.

A natural concomitant of commodity convertibility, therefore, is the concentration of all import and export activity in a state trading agency or agencies for purchasing foreign goods to be sold domestically, or domestic goods which are to be sold abroad. Centralized state trading agencies act as necessary buffers between foreign and domestic relative prices. At the official exchange rate(s), they ignore any profits or losses from selling or buying domestic goods abroad—all of which are mandated by the central plan. These purchases and sales are insensitive to how the official exchange rate is set.

For China, we have Christine Wong's description:

> The preform trade system was characterized by centralized planning and management under the Ministry of Foreign Trade (MFT). All foreign trade was dictated from the center, which specified the products and quantities to be imported and exported. Trading was undertaken by 12 Foreign Trade Corporations (FTCs) under MFT, each specializing in a different product line. The FTCs had headquarters in Beijing and branch offices in the provinces. The system was highly centralized— only the FTC head offices had the right to sign contracts for exports and imports, although fulfillment of the contracts was often assigned to provincial bureaus and branches.
>
> All procurement for export was done by the FTCs and assigned to enterprises as part of their production and delivery plans. With the procurement conducted at domestic prices, enterprises were indifferent between selling on the domestic or export markets. On the import side, FTCs were given an allocation of foreign exchange to fulfill their import plans for sale at domestic prices. In this way, the FTCs acted as sole contact points for external trade, completely insulating Chinese enterprises from the world market and its prices—a role that has been described as "air lock." Since Chinese prices for manufactures were higher than world prices, FTCs engaged in importing were generally profitable, and their profits subsidized the losses of the exporting FTCs (except those in raw material products, which were also profitable). (Wong 1992, 50)

This air lock system was strongly biased against foreign trade. Domestic enterprises did not become familiar with foreign selling or buying opportunities, and had no economic incentive to exploit them should they appear. In particular, exporting was not at all commercialized. Because the central planning authorities first determined import needs by domestic demand and supply conditions—or, more accurately, unanticipated gaps between planned supplies and planned usage—a list of exports would be more or less arbitrarily identified in order to generate the needed foreign exchange. However inefficient it might have been in an allocative sense, the air lock system preserved the government's ability to collect revenue domestically by rigging the domestic relative prices to generate "monopoly" profits in state-owned manufacturing enterprises. The 1970s were generally a period in which the Chinese central government's revenues rose quite strongly as a share of GNP (Wong 1992), undergirding the price stability of that period by avoiding the buildup of a monetary overhang.

After 1978, the philosophy governing China's foreign trade policies shifted dramatically from repression to expansion, although the policies themselves did not change all at once. Starting from a situation of highly repressed foreign trade and a very small foreign trade sector of a little over 5 percent of GNP in 1979, in a rapidly growing economy exports had risen even more rapidly, reaching 20 percent of GNP by 1992 (see Table 13.1, above).[3]

To accomplish this great feat, China first had to end the commercial isolation of its domestic manufacturing industries from world markets and to improve the allocative efficiency of exporting and importing. Second, this liberalization had to be accomplished at the margin so as not to quickly undermine the commercial viability of the old state-owned enterprises (SOEs)—many of which would have exhibited negative or very low value added at world market prices (Ch. 12)—or to undermine the government's ability to collect revenue from these SOEs even faster than it declined in practice (see Tables 13.4 and 13.5, above). Third, in the more liberalized setting, the Chinese could not afford to let the foreign exchange regime itself become an engine of inflation by, say, engineering a deep discrete devaluation when the economy became more open, as did Poland in January 1990, or simply by losing control of the foreign exchange market altogether with an even deeper ongoing devaluation cum inflation, as did Russia in 1992. Without any access to foreign aid or financial support from abroad in the late 1970s and early 1980s, China depended heavily on the willingness of domestic households and nonstate enterprises voluntarily to build up financial claims on the state banking system (denominated in the domestic currency) in order to finance the government and the SOEs (as described in Ch. 13). Thus, an inflationary policy of loosening foreign exchange constraints too rapidly so as to allow domestic nationals to switch into foreign monies (see Ch. 9), or precipitately opening the whole economy to free importing and exporting while simultaneously protecting domestic tradable goods industries by a deep devaluation, would have undermined the incentives for high real financial growth, that is, for domestic financial deepening.[4]

Gradual trade liberalization in China had complementary foreign exchange and commercial policy aspects after 1978. But both were geared to giving

3. One has to be careful with exchange rate valuations because the renminbi may well have become undervalued in the latter part of the period, thus exaggerating export growth in the GNP accounts. By any alternative standard, however, real export growth was enormous from 1978 to 1992.

4. Indeed, undue credit expansion in China in early 1993, coupled with undue depreciation of the renminbi in the interenterprise swap market for foreign exchange, seems to be resulting in higher domestic inflation, which is violating these historical guidelines.

potential exporters of manufactured goods strong incentives to begin breaking out of the air lock imposed on them by the FTCs. Instead of import needs arbitrarily determining exports as in the old regime, the idea was to develop new exports on a commercial basis, that is, where exporters could begin to see more or less correct relative prices in world market terms. Although imports would remain restricted by the FTCs themselves or by new licensing procedures, the scope for importing would gradually be liberalized more or less in line with any increase in export earnings. (And China has, from 1978 through 1992, achieved a rough balance between cumulative export earnings and cumulative expenditures for imports; net foreign debt remains very small for the size of the economy.) So what were the principal measures for promoting exports at the liberalizing margins of the economy?

Special Economic Zones (SEZs). As is well known, in order to begin a more open-door policy outside the ambit of domestic relative prices, the policy of creating SEZs was begun in 1978, first with Guangdong and Fujian, and then by many others. In these quasi-free trade zones, exporters were allowed to keep 100 percent of foreign exchange earnings for purposes of importing needed inputs of raw materials or capital goods into the zone. Joint ventures with foreigners were given preferentially low tax rates on profits or gross output in these zones. Within these SEZs, the relative prices facing exporters more closely reflected those prevailing in world markets; and the low taxes were a kind of subsidy toward developing normal commercial contacts, which had been unnaturally repressed, with the outside world. Using Hong Kong as a commercial contact point and entrepot, this strategy was enormously successful in promoting explosive growth in manufactured exports from these areas.

Decentralization of the FTCs. Less known is that much decision making in the FTCs themselves was transferred to provincial and local governments, which resulted in a tremendous proliferation in their number, from 12 in 1978 to 1,000 in 1984 to 5,000 in 1990 (Wong 1992). These trading agencies were still constrained in a general sense: import and export licensing was introduced in 1984 to replace direct centralized controls. Concomitantly, the number of products whose quantities of imports or exports were centrally planned fell from about 3,000 on the eve of reform in 1978 to about 130 by 1988 (Lardy 1992). Export licenses had to be retained on those raw materials and agricultural goods still kept below world prices.

Export retentions and foreign exchange contracting. Instead of confining the export retentions to the SEZs, in 1979 the government further increased incentives for export promotion by allowing local governments—perhaps represented by their own FTCs—to retain a portion of their foreign exchange earnings, typically 25 percent. By the late 1980s, this culminated in an export contracting system whereby exporters retained a fixed proportion of their basic quota earnings for the year, but could then retain a much higher proportion of export earnings, typically 80 percent, for exports beyond the negotiated basis. Again, this was a very substantial incentive for increasing exports at the margin throughout China, whether in an SEZ or not.

Swap markets for foreign exchange. However, to prevent exporting enterprises from holding foreign exchange outright (a form of capital outflow), the "retained" foreign exchange had to be deposited with the People's Bank of China and only drawn on when the enterprise wanted to make approved imports. Initially these entitlements were not transferable, and the holder would bear substantial exchange risk should the renminbi be officially devalued before the right to import was exercised. Moreover, the holder might have no need to import in the immediate future. To break this logjam,

> The first swap market for foreign exchange opened in 1985 in Shenzhen, followed by a second in Shanghai in 1986. By 1988, there were 39 centers, and by 1989 over 90. Total volume reached $6.3 billion in 1988, and $8.57 billion in 1989. To date, participation in the markets has been limited to organizations and enterprises which have foreign exchange earnings. Individuals and enterprises without other access to foreign exchange cannot participate. The main form of trading is bilateral: enterprises have to find buyers/sellers on their own, and then use the swap market to actualize the exchange. (Wong 1992, 49)

The development of foreign exchange swap markets, albeit limited and very imperfectly arbitraged geographically, was a major step forward in liberalization. It increased the incentives for exporting because exporters could immediately get cash for their quota rights, on the one hand, and it increased allocative efficiency, on the other. A wider range of enterprises and organizations could bid for foreign exchange at the free swap rate. Nevertheless, the government still retained substantial control over who could participate in the market on current account, and over international capital flows.

The foreign exchange rate and the swap rate. Although China began with an apparently overvalued exchange rate of 1.49 yuan per U.S. dollar in 1979, that hardly made any difference because most trade had to be filtered through the FTCs. But as decision making became more decentralized down to the enterprise level, getting the foreign exchange rate right became progressively more important. The official exchange rate has been devalued several times so that in 1992 it was 5.8 yuan per U.S. dollar, with the swap rate varying between 7.0 and 9.0 yuan to the dollar. In 1993, the concern may well be that the renminbi is undervalued; that is, the price of foreign exchange is above the level that would yield purchasing power parity with the outside world.

PROJECTING THE CHINESE EXPERIENCE

Because the overall economy is now much more open, and the foreign trade sector is now large, this undervaluation seems to have been a factor in generating too much inflationary pressure in the economy in 1993. Subsequently, the exchange rate should be set with more of an eye to controlling domestic price inflation rather than simply stimulating exports.

China's step-by-step liberalization of its foreign exchange and foreign trade regime has been very successful in building up a manufactured export base that has incorporated best practice technologies from the rest of the world. Up to 1993, at least, no major mishaps in the foreign exchanges upset the domestic economy's macroeconomic equilibrium. Foreign trade truly has been a major engine of growth in the remarkable increase in per capita GNP in China since 1978.

However, the use of special economic zones has caused this development to be seriously unbalanced. Coastal provinces are getting very rich, while those in the interior tend to languish by comparison. To some extent, the Chinese government is recognizing this. In 1991, export retentions, whether in an SEZ or not, were made more uniform throughout the country.

In the long run, tax concessions to SEZs and foreign joint ventures tend to undermine further the government's revenue position as well as to worsen regional imbalances. For raising revenue, China's foreign trade may now be undertaxed relative to the rest of the economy. Given the pre-1978 policy of severe repression of foreign trade, providing tax relief for a substantial learning period can hardly be faulted, particularly when the foreign trade sector is still small. But once the infant becomes very large and the air lock is effectively dismantled, taxing foreign trade in line with the rest of the economy becomes more urgent. Having a uniform VAT, administered by a centralized internal revenue service (see Ch. 11), fits in quite naturally because the tax is most easily collected at border crossings.

At this point, the Chinese model begins to dovetail with Chilean one. Much earlier in its liberalization process, Chile managed to impose a uniform VAT and dismantle all trade restrictions except for a low, uniform revenue tariff. And Chile never had to resort to the establishment of special economic zones whose privileges would later have to be rescinded.

REFERENCES

Aganbegyan, Abel. 1988. *The New Stage of Perestroika.* Washington, D.C.: Institute for East-West Security Studies.

Aghevli, Bijan, and Jorge Marquez Ruarte. 1985. "A Case of Successful Adjustment: Korea's Experience during 1980–84." International Monetary Fund Occasional Paper, no. 39. Washington, D.C.: IMF.

Angell, Wayne. 1989. "Monetary Policy in a Centrally Planned Economy: Restructuring toward a Market-Oriented Socialist System." The Institute of the U.S.A. and Canada Working Paper. Moscow. September 4.

Arndt, H. W., and P. J. Drake. 1985. "Bank Loans or Bonds: Some Lessons of Historical Experience." *Banca Nazionale del Lavoro Quarterly Review* 155 (December): 373–92.

Aslund, Anders. 1989. *Gorbachev's Struggle for Economic Reform.* Ithaca, N.Y.: Cornell University Press.

Babicheva, Yulia, et al. 1990. "Commercial Banks: A Game without Rules." *Business in the USSR,* July–August, 36–40.

Balassa, Bela. 1978. "Export Incentives and Export Performance in Developing Countries: A Comparative Analysis." *Weltwirtschaftliches Archiv* 114:24–61.

Belkin, V., A. Kazmin, and A. Tsimailo. 1990. "The Program of Transition to Rouble Convertibility." Unpublished.

Bhagwati, Jagdish. 1965. "On the Equivalence of Tariffs and Quotas." In R. Baldwin et al., eds., *Trade, Growth and the Balance of Payments: Essays in Honor of Gottfried Harberler,* 53–67. Chicago: Rand McNally.

———. 1968. "The Theory and Practice of Commercial Policy: Departures from Unified Exchanges Rates." Princeton Special Papers in International Economics, no. 8.

———. 1971. "The Generalized Theory of Distortions and Welfare." In J. Bhagwati et al., *Trade, Balance of Payments and Growth: Papers in Honor of Charles P. Kindleberger,* 69–90. Amsterdam: North-Holland.

———. 1978. *Anatomy and Consequences of Exchange Control Regimes.* Foreign Trade Regimes and Economic Development, vol. 11. Cambridge, Mass.: Ballinger, for the National Bureau of Economic Research.

Blejer, Mario, and K. Y. Chu, eds. 1988. "Measurement of Fiscal Impact: Methodological Issues." International Monetary Fund Occasional Paper, no. 59. Washington, D.C.: IMF.

Blejer, Mario, and Gyorgy Szapary. 1989. "The Evolving Role of Fiscal Policy in Centrally Planned Economies under Reform: The Case of China." International Monetary Fund Working Paper, no. 0407. Washington, D.C.: IMF.

Brock, Philip L. 1982. "Government Deficits and the Composition of Inflationary

Finance." Center for Research in Economic Growth, Stanford University, memo no. 254. Stanford, Calif.: Stanford University.

————. 1983. "Optimal Monetary Control during an Economic Liberalization: Theory and Evidence from the Chilean Financial Reforms." Ph.D. dissertation, Stanford University.

————. 1984. "Inflationary Finance in an Open Economy." *Journal of Monetary Economics,* July, 37–54.

Burkett, Paul, and Robert Vogel. 1991. "Financial Assets, Inflation Hedges, and Capital Utilization in Developing Countries: An Extension of McKinnon's Complementarity Hypothesis." *The Quarterly Journal of Economics* (forthcoming).

Cheng, Hang-Sheng. 1986. "Financial Policy and Reform in Taiwan, China." In H.-S. Cheng, ed., *Financial Policy and Reform in Pacific Basin Countries,* 143–60. Lexington, Mass.: Lexington Books.

Cho, Yoon Je. 1985. "Status of Financial Liberalisation." Unpublished. World Bank. December.

————. 1986. "Inefficiencies from Financial Liberalization in the Absence of Well Functioning Equities Markets." *Journal of Money, Credit and Banking* 18 (May): 191–99.

Corbo, Vittorio. 1985. "Reforms with Macroeconomic Adjustment in Chile during 1974–84." *World Development* 13:893–916.

————. 1986. "The Role of the Real Exchange Rate in Macroeconomic Adjustment: The Case of Chile, 1973–82." Paper presented at the Central Bank of Ecuador Conference on Trade Liberalization, Quito, January 24.

Corbo, Vittorio, and Jaime de Melo, eds. 1985. "Liberalization with Stabilization in the Southern Cone of Latin America." *World Development* 13:863–66.

Dam, Kenneth. 1970. *The GATT: Law and International Economic Organization.* Chicago: University of Chicago Press.

Deaton, Angus. 1990. "Saving in Developing Countries: Theory and Review." *Proceedings of the World Bank Annual Conference on Developing Economies 1989,* 61–96. Washington, D.C.

Díaz-Alejandro, Carlos. 1985. "Good-Bye Financial Repression, Hello Financial Crash." *Journal of Development Economics* 19 (September–October): 1–24.

Donald, Gordon. 1976. *Credit for Small Farmers in Developing Countries.* Boulder, Colo.: Westview Press.

Dornbusch, Rudiger, 1985. "Inflation Exchange Rates and Stabilization." National Bureau of Economic Research Working Paper, no. 1739, pp. 823–39.

Dornbusch, R., S. Fischer, and P. A. Samuelson. 1977. "Comparative Advantage, Trade, and Payments in Ricardian Model with a Continuum of Goods." *American Economic Review* 67:823–39.

Edwards, Sebastian. 1984. "The Order of Liberalization of the External Sector." Princeton Essays on International Finance, no. 156.

————. 1985. "Stabilization with Liberalization: An Evaluation of Ten Years of Chile's Free Market Policies, 1973–83." *Economic Development and Cultural Change* 33 (January): 223–54.

————. 1988. "Implications of Alternative International Exchange Rate Arrangements for the Developing Countries." In H. G. Vosgerau, ed. *New Institutional Arrangements for the World Economy,* 34–84. Berlin: Springer-Verlag.

————. 1989. *Real Exchange Rates, Devaluation, and Adjustment: Exchange Rate Policy in Developing Countries.* Cambridge, Mass.: MIT Press.

Edwards, Sebastian, and Alejandra Cox Edwards. 1987. *Monetarism and Liberalization: The Chilean Experiment.* Cambridge, Mass.: Ballinger.

Feder, G., L. Lau, J. Lin, and L. Xianpeng. 1989. "Agricultural Credit and Farm Performance in China." *Journal of Comparative Economics* 13:508–26.

Friedman, Milton. 1971. "Government Revenue from Inflation." *Journal of Political Economy* 79 (July/August): 846–56.

Fry, Maxwell J. 1978. "Money and Capital or Financial Deepening in Economic Development." *Journal of Money, Credit and Banking* 10 (November): 464–75.

————. 1981. "Government Revenue from Monopoly Supply of Currency and Deposits." *Journal of Monetary Economics* 8 (September): 261–70.

————. 1982. "Models of Financially Repressed Developing Economies." *World Development* 10:731–50.

————. 1988. *Money, Interest, and Banking in Economic Development.* Baltimore: John Hopkins University Press.

————. 1989. "Financial Development: Theories and Recent Experience." *Oxford Review of Economic Policy* 5:13–28.

Gelb, Alan H. 1989. "Financial Policies, Growth and Efficiency." World Bank Working Paper, Country Economics Department, no. WPS 202.

Gonzales Arrieta, G. M. 1988. "Interest Rates, Savings and Growth in LDCs: An Assessment of Recent Empirical Research." *World Development* 16:589–605.

Grossman, Gregory. 1989. "Monetary and Financial Aspects of Gorbachev's Reform." In C. Kessides et al., eds. *Financial Innovations in Socialist Economies.* Washington, D.C.: World Bank.

————. 1990. "Problems of Monetary Reform." Paper presented at Hoover-Rand Symposium, Santa Monica, Calif., March.

Hanson, James A., and C. R. Neal. 1987. "The Demand for Liquid Assets." World Bank, Industry Department, January 3.

Harberger, Arnold C. 1985. "Lessons for Debtor Country Managers and Policy Makers." In G. W. Smith and John Cuddington, eds. *International Debt and the Developing Countries,* 236–57. Washington, D.C.: World Bank.

Heilbroner, Robert. 1989. "The Triumph of Capitalism." *New Yorker,* January 23, 98–109.

Hewett, Edward A. 1988. *Reforming the Soviet Economy.* Washington, D.C.: Brookings Institution.

Hinds, Manuel, 1990. "Issues in the Introduction of Market Forces in Eastern European Socialist Economies." World Bank, Internal Discussion Paper. April.

Horiuchi, Akiyoshi. 1984. "The 'Low Interest Rate Policy' and Economic Growth in Postwar Japan." *Developing Economies* 22 (December): 476–80.

International Monetary Fund. 1983. "Interest Rate Policies in Developing Economies." IMF Occasional Paper, no. 22. Washington, D.C.: IMF.

Johnson, Harry. 1965. "Optimal Trade Intervention in the Presence of Domestic Distortions." In R. Baldwin et al., eds., *Trade, Growth and the Balance of Payments: Essays in Honor of Gottfried Harberler,* 3–34. Chicago: Rand McNally.

Kane, Edward J. 1985. *The Gathering Crisis in Federal Deposit Insurance.* Cambridge, Mass.: MIT Press.

Kapur, Basant. 1976. "Alternative Stabilisation Policies for Less Developed Economies." *Journal of Political Economy* 84, no. 4, pt. 1:777–95.

———. 1986. *Studies in Inflationary Dynamics: Repression and Financial Liberalization in Less Developed Countries*. Singapore: Singapore University Press.

Kohsaka, Akira. 1987. "Financial Liberalization in Asian NICs: A Comparative Study of Korea and Taiwan in the 1980s." *Developing Economies* 25 (December): 419–52.

Kornai, János. 1986a. *Contradictions and Dilemmas: Studies on the Socialist Economy and Society*. Cambridge, Mass.: MIT Press.

———. 1986b. "The Hungarian Reform Process: Visions, Hopes, and Reality." *Journal of Economic Literature* 24:1687–1737.

———. 1990. *The Road to a Free Economy*. New York: W. W. Norton.

Krueger, Anne O. 1978a. "Alternative Trade Strategies and Employment in LDCs." *American Economic Review* 68 (May): 270–74.

———. 1978b. *Liberalization Attempts and Consequences*. Foreign Trade Regimes and Economic Development, vol. 10. Cambridge, Mass.: Ballinger, for the National Bureau of Economic Research.

Krugman, Paul, and Lance Taylor. 1978. "Contradictory Effects of a Devaluation." *Journal of International Economics* 8, no. 3:445–56.

Leff, Nathaniel, and Kazuo Sato. 1980. "Macroeconomic Adjustment in Developing Countries: Instability, Short-Run Growth, and External Dependency." *Review of Economics and Statistics* 62 (May): 170–79.

Lerner, A. P. 1936. "The Symmetry between Import and Export Taxes." *Economica* 111 (August): 308–13.

Lipton, David, and Jeffrey Sachs. 1990a. "Creating a Market Economy in Eastern Europe: The Case of Poland." *Brookings Papers on Economic Activity* 1:75–133.

———. 1990b. "Privatization in Eastern Europe: The Case of Poland." *Brookings Papers on Economic Activity* 2:293–342.

Litwack, John. 1991. "Discretionary Behavior and Soviet Economic Reform." *Journal of Soviet Studies* (forthcoming).

Luders, Rolf. 1985. "Lessons from Two Financial Liberalization Episodes: Argentina and Chile." Unpublished. November.

McKinnon, Ronald I. 1966. "Intermediate Products and Differential Tariffs: A Generalization of Lerner's Symmetry Theorem." *Quarterly Journal of Economics* 80 (November): 584–615.

———. 1973. *Money and Capital in Economic Development*. Washington, D.C.: Brookings Institution.

———. 1977. "La Intermediacion Financiera y el Control Monetario en Chile." *Cuadernos de Economia* 43 (December).

———. 1979a. "Foreign Trade Regimes and Economic Development: A Review Article." *Journal of International Economics* 9 (August): 429–52.

———. 1979b. *Money in International Exchange: The Convertible Currency System*. New York: Oxford University Press.

———. 1981a. "Financial Repression and the Liberalisation Problem within Less Developed Countries." In S. Grassman and E. Lundberg, eds., *The Past and Prospects for the World Economic Order*, 365–86. London: Macmillan.

———. 1981b. "Monetary Controls and the Crawling Peg." In John Williamson, ed.,

Exchange Rate Rules: The Theory, Performance and Prospects of the Crawling Peg, 38–49. New York: Macmillan.

———. 1982. "The Order of Economic Liberalisation: Lessons from Chile and Argentina." *Carnegie-Rochester Conference Series on Public Policy* 17:159–86.

———. 1984a. "Financial Repression and Economic Development." Chung-Hua Series of Lectures by Invited Eminent Economists, no. 8. Institute of Economics, Academia Sinica, Nankang, Taiwan.

———. 1984b. "The International Capital Market and Economic Liberalization in LDCs." *Developing Economies* 22 (December): 476–81.

———. 1988a. "Financial Liberalization and Economic Development." International Center for Economic Growth Occasional Paper, no. 6. Panama City.

———. 1988b. "Financial Liberalization in Retrospect: Interest Rate Policies in LDCs." In G. Ranis and T. R. Schultz, eds., *The State of Development Economics,* 386–415. New York: Basil Blackwell.

———. 1989a. "Macroeconomic Instability and Moral Hazard in Banking in a Liberalizing Economy." In P. Brock et al., eds., *Latin American Debt Adjustment,* 99–111. New York: Praeger.

———. 1989b. "The Order of Liberalization for Opening the Soviet Economy." Paper prepared for the International Task Force on Foreign Economic Relations. New York. April.

———. 1990. "Stabilizing the Ruble." *Communist Economies* 2 (June): 131–42.

———. 1991. "Monetary Stabilization in LDCs and the International Capital Market." In Lawrence Krause and Kihwan Kim, eds., *The Liberalization Process in Economic Development: Essays in Honor of Kim Jae-Ik.* Forthcoming.

McKinnon, Ronald I., and Donald Mathieson. 1981. "How to Manage a Repressed Economy." Princeton Essays in International Finance, no. 145.

Mathieson, Donald J. 1978. "Financial Reform and Stabilization Policy in a Developing Economy." Unpublished. Research Department, Internation Monetary Fund. March.

———. 1979. "Financial Reform and Capital Flows in a Developing Economy." *IMF Staff Papers,* September 26, 450–89.

Nichols, Donald A. 1974. "Some Principles of Inflationary Finance." *Journal of Political Economy* 82 (March/April): 423–30.

Nove, Alec. 1969. *An Economic History of the USSR.* London: Penguin Press.

Parker, Karen. 1989. "Internal Debt in Latin America and the Philippines." Unpublished. Bankers Trust. October.

Patrick, Hugh T. 1966. "Financial Development and Economic Growth in Underdeveloped Countires." *Economic Development and Cultural Change* 14:174–89.

Remolona, Eli, 1982. "Inflation, Debt and the Reserve Tax in a Theory of Optimal Deficit Finance." Ph.D. dissertation, Stanford University.

Richter, R., ed. 1979. "Currency and Economic Reform in West Germany after World War II." *Zeitschrift für die Gesamte Staatswissenschaft* 19 (September): 297–30.

Rowen, Henry S., and Charles Wolf, eds. 1990. *The Impoverished Superpower: Perestroika and the Soviet Military Burden.* San Francisco: ICS Press.

Salter, W. E. 1959. "Internal and External Balance: The Role of Price and Expenditure Effects." *Economic Record* 35 (August): 226–38.

Schrenk, Martin. 1990. "Whither Comecon?" *Finance and Development* 27 (September): 28–31.

Shaw, Edward S. 1973. *Financing Deepening in Economic Development*. New York: Oxford University Press.

Shelton, Judy. 1989. *The Coming Soviet Crash: Gorbachev's Desperate Pursuit of Credit in Western Markets*. New York: Free Press.

Shmelev, Nikolai, and Vladimir Popov. 1989. *The Turning Point: Revitalizing the Soviet Economy*. New York: Doubleday.

Soros, George, Ed Hewett, Wassily Leontief, and Jan Mladek. 1988. Paper prepared for the International Task Force on Foreign Economic Relations. Moscow. October.

Spigelman, David. F. 1987. "Macroeconomic Instability of the Less Developed Country Economy When Bank Credit Is Rationed." Center for Research in Economic Growth, memo no. 272. Stanford, Calif.: Stanford University.

Stiglitz, J., and A. Weiss. 1981. "Credit Rationing in Markets with Imperfect Information." *American Economic Review* 71 (June): 394–410.

Suzuki, Yoshio. 1980. *Money and Banking in Contemporary Japan: The Theoretical Setting and Its Applications*. New Haven: Yale University Press.

Tan, Augustine. 1970. "Differential Tariffs, Negative Value-Added and the Theory of Effective Protection." *American Economic Review* 60 (March): 107–16.

Thornton, John, and Sri Lam Poudyal. 1990. "Money and Capital in Economic Development: A Test of the McKinnon Hypothesis for Nepal." *Journal of Money, Credit, and Banking* 22 (August): 395–399.

Tsiang, S. C. 1980. "Exchange Rate, Interest Rate, and Economic Development." In L. Klein, M. Nerlove, and S. C. Tsiang, eds., *Quantitative Economics and Development: Essays in Honor of T. C. Liu*, 309–46. New York: Academic Press.

Tybout, James. 1986. "A Firm Level Chronicle of Financial Crises in the Southern Cone." *Journal of Development Economics* 24 (December): 371–400.

Vancus, Jan, ed. 1990. *Plan Econ Report*, February 21, vol. 6.

Wanniski, Jude. 1989. "Gold-Based Ruble." *Barron's*, September 25, 9.

Williamson, John H. 1965. "The Crawling Peg." Princeton Essays in International Finance, no. 50.

REFERENCES TO CHAPTER 13

Aslund, Anders. 1992. *Post Communist Revolutions: How Big a Bang?* Washington, D.C.: CSIS.

Barro, Robert, and Herschel Grossman. 1976. *Money, Employment, and Inflation*. Cambridge: Cambridge University Press.

Blejer, Mario, David Burton, Steven Dunaway, and Gyorgy Szapary. 1991. "China: Economic Reform and Macroeconomic Management." International Monetary Fund Occasional Paper, no. 76. Washington, D.C.: IMF.

Borenstein, Eduardo, and Paul R. Masson. 1993. "Exchange Rate Arrangements of Previously Centrally Planned Economies." International Monetary Fund. Occasional Paper, no. 102. Washington, D.C.: IMF.

Brada, Josef, and Arthur King. 1992. "Is There a J-Curve in the Economic Transition from Socialism to Capitalism?" *Economics of Planning* 25, no. 1: 37–54.

Burkett, Paul, and Robert Vogel. 1991. "Financial Assets, Inflation Hedges, and Capital Utilization in Developing Countries: An Extension of McKinnon's Complementarity Hypothesis." *Quarterly Journal of Economics* (August).

Gelb, Alan, Gary Jefferson, and Inderjit Singh. 1993. "Can Communist Countries Transform Incrementally? The Experience of China." World Bank Working Paper. February.

Gomulka, Stanilslaw. 1991. "The Causes of Recession following Stabilization." *Comparative Economic Studies* 33, no. 2: 71–89.

Fforde, Adam, and Stefan de Vylder. 1993. *The Socialist Republic of Vietnam*. Report to the Asian Development Bank, Manila.

Johnson, D. Gale. *The People's Republic of China, 1978–90*. 1990. San Francisco: International Center for Economic Growth, ICS Press.

King, Robert, and Ross Levine. 1993. "Finance, Entrepreneurship, and Growth." Paper presented at the World Bank conference, *How Do National Policies Affect Long-Run Growth?* Washington, D.C., February 8–9.

Levine, Ross. 1992. "Financial Intermediary Services and Growth." *Journal of the Japanese and International Economies* 6, no. 4 (December): 383–405.

Lipton, David, and Jeffrey D. Sachs. 1990. "Creating a Market Economy in Eastern Europe: The Case of Poland." *Brookings Papers on Economic Activity* 1: 75–147.

McKinnon, Ronald I. 1973. *Money and Capital in Economic Development*. Washington, D.C.: Brookings Institution.

———. 1991. "Financial Control in the Transition from Classical Socialism to a Market Economy." *Journal of Economic Perspectives* 5, no. 4 (Fall): 107–22.

———. 1993. "Macroeconomic Stabilization in Liberalizing Socialist Economies: Asian and European Parallels." In Alberto Giovannini, ed., *Finance and Development: Issues and Experience*. Cambridge: CEPR, Cambridge University Press.

McMillan, John, and Barry Naughton. 1992. "How to Reform a Planned Economy: Lessons from China." *Oxford Review of Economic Policy* 8, no. 1 (Spring): 130–33.

Murphy, Kevin, Andrei Shleifer, and Robert Vishny. 1992. "The Transition to a Market Economy: Pitfalls of Partial Reform." *Quarterly Journal of Economics* 57, no. 3 (August): 889–906.

Murrell, Peter. 1990. "Big Bang versus Evolution: Eastern European Reforms in the Light of Recent Economic History." *PlanEcon Report* (June 29).

Perkins, Dwight. 1992. "China's Gradual Approach to Market Reforms." Paper presented at a conference, *Comparative Experiences of Economic Reform and Post-Socialist Transformation*. El Escorial, Spain. July.

PlanEcon Report. 1992. "The Russian Economy during the First Half of 1992" (September 3).

PlanEcon Report. 1993. "Russian Economic Monitor" (March 10).

Qian, Yingyi. 1993. "Lessons and Relevance of the Japanese Main Bank System for Financial Reform in China." Center for Economic Policy Research, Stanford University. March.

Sachs, Jeffrey. 1992. "Privatization in Russia: Some Lessons from Eastern Europe." *American Economic Review* (May): 43–48.

Vokes, Richard, and Armand Fabella. 1992. *Economic Reform in the Lao People's Democratic Republic*. Asian Development Bank, Manila.

Williamson, John. 1991. "The Opening of Eastern Europe." Policy Analysis 31. Washington, D.C.: Institute for International Economics. May.

Wong, Christine. 1992. *Economic Reform in China*. Asian Development Bank, Manila.
Wong, Christine, Christopher Heady, and W. T. Woo. 1993. *Economic Reform and Fiscal and Fiscal Management in China*. Asian Development Bank, Manila.

REFERENCES TO CHAPTER 14

Cheng, H. S. 1991. "China's Foreign Trade Reform, 1979–90." Working Paper PB92-01, Federal Reserve Bank of San Francisco. February.
Lardy, Nicholas R. 1992. *Foreign Trade and Economic Reform in China, 1978–1990,* Cambridge: Cambridge University Press. 1992.
Panagariya, Arvind. 1993. "Unravelling the Mysteries of China's Foreign Trade Regime." *World Economy,* 16, no. 1: 51–68.
Wong, Christine. 1992. *Economic Reform in China,* Asian Development Bank, Manila.

Index

Adverse risk selection: and immature capital markets, 13; and inflationary expectations, 80; and interest rates, 41, 51–52, 69, 85; and macroeconomic instability, 88–89; and macroeconomic stability, 86–88; and orthodox tight money policy, 81

Africa: economic malaise, 2; fiscal credibility, 5; quality of investments in, 26; trade protection, 99

Aganbegyan, Abel, 132, 187

Aghevli, Bijan, 80

Agricultural Bank of China, 141

Agricultural distortions, 46–47

Albalkin, Leonid, 128

Allende, Salvador, 69

Angell, Wayne, 155

Argentina: capital inflow controls, 105; deposit insurance, 40; domestic debt, 6; efforts to end inflation, 3; failure of financial decontrol, 38; instability and moral hazard, 89; overborrowing, 113

Arndt, H. W., 118

Asia: economic malaise, 2; interest policy, 16; quality of investments in, 26–27; taxation in socialist economies, 121; trade liberalization, 93; trade protection, 99

Aslund, Anders, 127–28, 175

Austral plan, 3

Babicheva, Yulia, 147

Banking system: in Chile, 38, 71; in Colombia, 43–45; deregulation prior to financial deepening, 38; role in providing government revenue, 59–60; small business lending in LDCs, 25; socialist, 6–7; transition to competitive, 53; wildcat, in the Soviet Union, 144–48

Bank of Chile, 67

Bank of Japan, 32, 34–35

Bank of Korea, 78, 81

Bank panics, 2–3

Banks: establishing independent commercial, 6–7; lack of success in creation in China and Poland, 105; minimizing the probability of panics, 6; monitoring in Chile, 40; profit maximization, 86; and removal of directed credits, 53; savings and loan crisis in U.S., 6; zero-profit condition, 49

Base money, demand for, 61

Bhagwati, Jagdish, 8, 92–102

Black market, 52, 127, 156–57, 164

Blejer, Mario, 5, 57, 123

Brady plan, 77n

Brazil: domestic debt, 6; exchange rate stabilization, 106; failure to secure financial equilibrium, 3; government freeze of outstanding liabilities, 6; trade, 92–93, 96

Bretton Woods, 13, 18, 28

Brock, Philip L., 56–57, 64n, 104

Budget constraint, lack of an effective, 125

Burkett, Paul, 23

Canada, 182

Capital, scarcity price of, 12

Capital absorption: and economic liberalization, 116–17; during transition to free trade, 169

Capital account transacting, 8

Capital controls: in Chile, 69; in Japan, 33; in market economies, 138, 157, 159–60; premature elimination of, 10; recommended restrictions, 156–57; in South Korea, 78

Capital flight, 10, 71, 77, 94

Capital gains, taxation of, 137

Capital inflow, 184–87; in Chile, 70, 73; and financial repression, 12; in Germany, 167–70; and inflation tax, 104; in the Southern Cone, 76–77; unsustainable levels, 115–16

Index

Designed by Christopher Harris/Summer Hill Books
Weathersfield, Vermont.
Composed by WorldComp in Times Roman text
and Helvetica display.
Printed on 50-lb. BookText Natural by BookCrafters.